Adobe® Audition® CS6

# CLASSROOM IN A BOOK®

The official training workbook from Adobe Systems

Adobe

# WHAT'S ON THE DISC

**Here is an overview of the contents of the Classroom in a Book disc**

The *Adobe Audition CS6 Classroom in a Book* disc includes the lesson files that you'll need to complete the exercises in this book, as well as other content to help you learn more about Adobe Audition CS6 and use it with greater efficiency and ease. The diagram below represents the contents of the disc, which should help you locate the files you need.

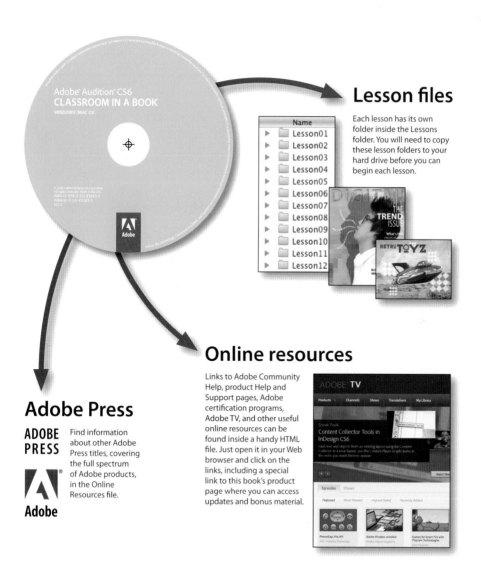

## Lesson files

Each lesson has its own folder inside the Lessons folder. You will need to copy these lesson folders to your hard drive before you can begin each lesson.

## Online resources

Links to Adobe Community Help, product Help and Support pages, Adobe certification programs, Adobe TV, and other useful online resources can be found inside a handy HTML file. Just open it in your Web browser and click on the links, including a special link to this book's product page where you can access updates and bonus material.

## Adobe Press

Find information about other Adobe Press titles, covering the full spectrum of Adobe products, in the Online Resources file.

# CONTENTS

# GETTING STARTED

Adobe Audition is a professional audio application that combines advanced digital audio editing and multitrack recording in the same program. This unique approach integrates the two elements so that, for example, audio used in a multitrack project can be edited with great detail in the digital audio editor, then transferred back to the multitrack session. Mixdowns (mono, stereo, or surround) exported from the multitrack session are available automatically within the digital audio editor, where a variety of mastering tools are available to polish and "sweeten" the mix. The final mix can then be burned to a recordable CD, which is created according to the standard Red Book specification, or converted into "web-friendly," data-compressed formats like MP3 and FLAC. Furthermore, the Multitrack Editor has a video window that enables recording soundtracks and narration in Audition while previewing video.

Audition is cross-platform and runs equally well with Macintosh or Windows computers. Thanks to combining two programs within a single, integrated application, Audition has multiple uses—restoring audio, multitrack recording for musicians, mastering, sound design, broadcast, video game sound, narration and voiceovers, file format conversion, small-scale CD production, and even forensics. Fortunately, all of this is available from a clean, easy-to-use, straightforward interface whose workflow has benefited from over a decade of continuous development and refinement.

The latest version, Audition CS6, deepens the level of integration with Premiere Pro and After Effects for easy exchange of files and even complete sequences. This greatly simplifies the process of creating a soundtrack that reflects changes in the video due to editing. There are also significant editing enhancements, such as envelope keyframe editing, clip grouping, multiple clipboards, real-time clip stretching, and more. Other new features include Automatic Speech Alignment to greatly simplify ADR, a media browser for quickly locating and previewing files, control surface support for multiple protocols, pitch correction, side-chaining, improved batch processing, and the ability to import and export more file formats than ever before. These are just the highlights; long-time Audition users will appreciate the many little extras that enhance workflow and audio quality, whereas those new to Audition will welcome its depth and flexibility.

# About Classroom in a Book

*Adobe Audition CS6 Classroom in a Book* is part of the official training series for Adobe graphics, audio, and publishing software developed by experts in association with Adobe Systems. The lessons are designed to let you learn at your own pace. If you're new to Adobe Audition, you'll learn the fundamental concepts and features needed to start mastering the program. And, if you've been using Adobe Audition for a while, you'll find that Classroom in a Book teaches basic to intermediate features, including tips and techniques for using the latest version of the application for a wide variety of projects.

Although each lesson concentrates on providing step-by-step instructions to reach specific goals, there's room for exploration and experimentation. You can follow the book from start to finish, or do only the lessons that match your interests and needs. Each lesson has an introduction that explains what you can expect to learn from a chapter, and concludes with a review section summarizing what you've covered.

# What's in this book

This edition covers many new features in Adobe Audition CS6, and how to apply them optimally in real-world situations. It addresses audio and music professionals who depend on Audition's tools to accomplish a variety of tasks, as well as videographers who want to become more involved in the process of creating, editing, and sweetening audio intended for video productions.

The book is organized in three separate parts. The introduction starts with how to get audio in and out of Audition on both Mac and Windows platforms, then progresses to an overview of the Audition Workspace—a collection of modules, each dedicated to specific tasks, that you can open, close, and rearrange, depending on the nature of the project, to optimize workflow and efficiency. The second part concentrates on digital audio editing in the Waveform Editor, and covers such topics as editing, signal processing and effects, audio restoration, mastering, and sound design. To segue into the final third, it also covers recording, and integration with the Multitrack Editor.

The final section covers the Multitrack Editor in detail, including editing, automation, creating music with sound libraries, in-depth coverage of mixing, and creating soundtracks for video. Throughout the book, examples using digital audio clips created specifically for this book give practical, hands-on experience that brings to life the theory presented in these pages. Even non-musicians will learn how to create music using sound libraries and loops in conjunction with Audition's extensive toolset for sound creation and editing. You'll even learn how to do rough testing of your room acoustics prior to mixing, using tools within Audition.

As you progress through the lessons, you'll also discover many time-saving features Audition offers such as file conversion, automation, Multitrack and Waveform Editor integration, clip automation, time-stretching, and more. All of these can help you meet deadlines more easily than ever before—and that alone is a good reason to become familiar with Audition's workflow, capabilities, and user interface.

## Prerequisites

Before you begin to use *Adobe Audition CS6 Classroom in a Book*, you should have a working knowledge of your computer and its operating system. Make sure that you know how to use the mouse and standard menus and commands, and also how to open, save, and close files. If you need to review these techniques, see the documentation included with your Microsoft Windows or Macintosh system. It's also highly recommended that you read over the introduction to the Audition manual that covers digital audio basics.

You'll also need the ability to get audio in and out of your computer. Virtually all computers include on-board audio capabilities (audio input for recording, and internal speakers or a headphone jack for monitoring), but be aware that these use consumer-grade components and while adequate, will not showcase what Audition can do to the fullest extent. Professional and "prosumer" audio interfaces are available at very reasonable costs, and are recommended not just for doing the lessons in this book, but also for any future audio work involving computers.

## Installing Adobe Audition

Before you begin using *Adobe Audition CS6 Classroom in a Book,* make sure that your computer is set up correctly and that it meets the necessary system requirements for software and hardware. You'll need a copy of Adobe Audition CS6, of course, but it's not included with this book. If you haven't purchased a copy, you can download a 30-day trial version from www.adobe.com/downloads. For system requirements and complete instructions on installing the software, see the Adobe Audition CS6 Read Me file on the application DVD or on the Web at www.adobe. com/products/audition.html.

Note that Audition is a very efficient program, and one of its attributes is that it will run reasonably well even on older computers. However, as with most audio and video programs, having sufficient RAM is essential for a smooth computing experience. Although Audition will run with 1GB of RAM, for multitrack recording 2GB is better, and 4GB is preferable; this is also the maximum amount of RAM usable with 32-bit versions of Windows. Current versions of Mac OS X and 64-bit

Windows 7 have no practical limitation on how much RAM they can address, so 8GB of RAM or more is highly recommended.

Make sure that your serial number is accessible before installing the application. You need to install Audition from its application DVD, or the online trial version you downloaded, onto your hard disk; you cannot run the program from the DVD. Follow the onscreen instructions for a successful installation.

## Starting Adobe Audition

You start Audition just as you do most software applications.

**To start Adobe Audition in Windows XP or Windows 7 (32- or 64-bit):**

Choose Start > All Programs > Adobe Audition CS6.

**To start Adobe Audition in Mac OS X:**

Open the Applications/Adobe Audition CS6 folder, and then double-click the Adobe Audition CS6 application icon.

## Copying the Classroom in a Book files

The *Adobe Audition CS6 Classroom in a Book* CD-ROM includes folders containing all the electronic files for the lessons in the book. Each lesson has its own folder; you must copy the folders to your hard disk to complete the lessons. To save room on your disk, you can install only the folder necessary for each lesson as you need it, and remove it when you're done.

To install the lesson files, do the following:

1   Insert the Adobe Audition CS6 Classroom in a Book CD into your CD-ROM drive.

2   Browse the contents and locate the Lessons folder.

3   Do one of the following:

  • To copy all the lesson files, drag the Lessons folder from the CD onto your hard disk.

  • To copy only individual lesson files, first create a new folder on your hard disk and name it **Lessons**. Then, open the Lessons folder on the CD and drag the lesson folder or folders that you want to copy from the CD into the Lessons folder on your hard disk.

# Additional resources

*Adobe Audition CS6 Classroom in a Book* is not meant to replace documentation that comes with the program or to be a comprehensive reference for every feature. Only the commands and options used in the lessons are explained in this book. For comprehensive information about program features and tutorials, please refer to these resources:

- **Adobe Community Help:** Community Help brings together active Adobe product users, Adobe product team members, authors, and experts to give you the most useful, relevant, and up-to-date information about Adobe products.

- **To access Community Help:** To invoke Help, press F1 or choose Help > Audition Help.

- Adobe content is updated based on community feedback and contributions. You can add comments to content or forums—including links to web content, publish your own content using Community Publishing, or contribute Cookbook Recipes. Find out how to contribute at www.adobe.com/community/publishing/download.html

- See community.adobe.com/help/profile/faq.html for answers to frequently asked questions about Community Help.

- **Adobe Audition Help and Support:** www.adobe.com/support/audition is where you can find and browse Help and Support content on adobe.com. Adobe Audition Help and Adobe Audition Support Center are accessible from Audition's Help menu.

- **Adobe Forums:** forums.adobe.com lets you tap into peer-to-peer discussions, questions, and answers on Adobe products. The Audition forum is accessible from Audition's Help menu.

- **Adobe TV:** tv.adobe.com is an online video resource for expert instruction and inspiration about Adobe products, including a How To channel to get you started with your product.

- **Adobe Design Center:** www.adobe.com/designcenter offers thoughtful articles on design and design issues, a gallery showcasing the work of top-notch designers, tutorials, and more.

- **Adobe Developer Connection:** www.adobe.com/devnet/audition.html is your source for technical articles, code samples, and how-to videos that cover Adobe Audition, as well as the Audition SDK.

- **Resources for educators:** www.adobe.com/education offers a treasure trove of information for instructors who teach classes on Adobe software. Find solutions for education at all levels, including free curricula that use an integrated approach to teaching Adobe software and can be used to prepare for the Adobe Certified Associate exams.

Also check out these useful links:

- **Adobe Marketplace & Exchange:** www.adobe.com/cfusion/exchange/ is a central resource for finding tools, services, extensions, code samples, and more to supplement and extend your Adobe products.

- **Adobe Audition CS6 product home page:** www.adobe.com/products/audition

- **Adobe Labs:** labs.adobe.com gives you access to early builds of cutting-edge technology, as well as forums where you can interact with both the Adobe development teams building that technology and other like-minded members of the community.

- **Free audio content:** Your purchase of Audition CS6 includes free libraries containing thousands of royalty-free loops, sound effects, music beds, and more. You can access them by choosing Help > Download Sound Effects and More, and then following the onscreen directions to download the content.

Also check out this useful site:

- Inside Sound (blogs.adobe.com/insidesound/): The Adobe Audio blog

## Audition and social media

For the latest news and Audition-related events, follow Adobe Audition on Twitter: twitter.com/#!/Audition. The Twitter feed is also accessible from Audition's Help menu.

You can also find Adobe Audition on Facebook: www.facebook.com/AdobeAudition. This Facebook page is also accessible from Audition's Help menu.

## Checking for updates

Adobe periodically provides updates to software. You can easily obtain these updates through Adobe Updater, as long as you have an active Internet connection and are a registered user.

1  In Audition, choose Help > Updates. Adobe Updater automatically checks for updates available for your Adobe software.

2  In the Adobe Updater dialog box, select the updates you want to install, then click Download and Install Updates to install them.

# Adobe certification

The Adobe training and certification programs are designed to help Adobe customers improve and promote their product-proficiency skills. There are four levels of certification:

- Adobe Certified Associate (ACA)
- Adobe Certified Expert (ACE)
- Adobe Certified Instructor (ACI)
- Adobe Authorized Training Center (AATC)

The Adobe Certified Associate (ACA) credential certifies that individuals have the entry-level skills to plan, design, build, and maintain effective communications using different forms of digital media.

The Adobe Certified Expert program is a way for expert users to upgrade their credentials. You can use Adobe certification as a catalyst for getting a raise, finding a job, or promoting your expertise.

If you are an ACE-level instructor, the Adobe Certified Instructor program takes your skills to the next level and gives you access to a wide range of Adobe resources.

Adobe Authorized Training Centers offer instructor-led courses and training on Adobe products, employing only Adobe Certified Instructors. A directory of AATCs is available at http://partners.adobe.com.

For information on the Adobe Certified programs, visit www.adobe.com/support/certification/main.html.

# 1 AUDIO INTERFACING

## Lesson overview

In this lesson, you'll learn how to do the following:

- Configure a Macintosh computer's on-board audio for use with Audition

- Choose the appropriate sample rate for a project

- Set up the on-board audio in Windows computers for use with Audition

- Set up Windows audio interfacing regardless of whether you're running XP (with Service Pack 3) or Windows 7 (Service Pack 1, 32-bit, or 64-bit)

- Configure Audition to work with Macintosh or Windows computers

- Test your configurations to make sure all connections are correct

 This lesson will take about 45 minutes to complete. There are no audio lesson files because you'll be recording your own files to test the interface connections.

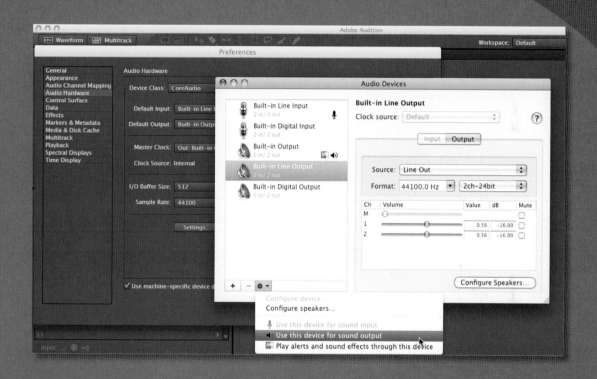

Before you can use Audition, you need to configure your computer and audio system to work with the program. This lesson covers audio interfacing for both Mac and Windows computers.

# Audio interface basics

Recording audio into a computer requires converting audio signals into digital data that your computer and Audition can recognize. Similarly, playback requires converting that digital data back to analog audio so you can hear it. The device that performs these conversions is usually called a *sound card* when built into the computer or *audio interface* if it's an external piece of hardware. Both include analog-to-digital (A/D) and digital-to-analog (D/A) converters. In addition, software *drivers* handle communications between your computer and audio hardware.

This lesson concentrates on a computer's on-board audio capabilities, because the same concepts translate to more sophisticated (and higher performance) audio interfaces. Note that there are many brands and models of audio interfaces, making universally applicable lessons impossible. As a result, multiple sidebars in this lesson explain audio interface characteristics to provide important background information.

Several lessons are divided into versions for Macintosh and Windows computers. You won't need to read the Windows-specific lessons if you use a Mac, and vice versa. However, all users should read the sidebars, because they cover information that's applicable to both platforms.

To make the best use of these lessons, you'll need the following:

- An audio source, such as an MP3 or CD player with a 1/8-inch minijack output (or other device with a suitable adapter to give a 1/8-inch minijack output). Laptops may also have an internal microphone you can use; however, using a line-level device is recommended, and the lessons will reference that type of input. You can also use USB microphones that plug directly into a computer's USB port; however, note that they may introduce significant latency, as described later in this lesson, when used as class-compliant devices with Windows computers.

- Patch cable with male-to-male 1/8-inch plug to connect the audio source to your computer's audio input jack.

- Your computer's internal speakers for monitoring or earbuds/headphones with a 1/8-inch stereo plug suitable for plugging into your computer's stereo output. You can also patch the output to a monitoring system if you have suitable cables.

# Common audio interface connectors

The following are the most common input and output connectors found in computers and audio interfaces:

- **XLR jack.** This is compatible with microphones and other balanced-line signals. Balanced lines use three conductors, which can be designed to minimize hum and noise pickup when carrying low-level signals.

- **1/4-inch phone jack.** This is common with musical instruments and much pro audio gear. The jack can handle balanced or unbalanced lines; balanced line inputs can handle unbalanced lines as well. Headphone jacks also use 1/4-inch phone jacks.

- **Combo jacks.** A fairly recent introduction, a combo jack can accept either an XLR or 1/4-inch phone plug.

- **RCA phono jack.** A mainstay of consumer gear, RCA jacks are also found in some DJ audio interfaces and video equipment.

- **1/8-inch minijack.** This is common for on-board computer audio, but rare for external interfaces except when included to interface with MP3 players and similar consumer devices. The 1/8-inch minijacks sometimes provide headphone outputs as well.

- **S/PDIF (Sony/Philips Digital Interconnect Format).** This consumer digital interface typically uses RCA phono jacks but can also use an optical connector and (very rarely) XLR.

- **AES/EBU (Audio Engineering Society/European Broadcast Union).** This is a professional-level digital interface that uses XLR connectors.

- **ADAT (Alesis Digital Audio Tape) optical.** This optical connector carries eight channels of digital audio. It's used most commonly with interfaces for expanding the interface's inputs; for example, if you have an interface that lacks sufficient mic inputs but has an ADAT input, eight-channel mic preamps are available that send their outputs to an ADAT connector. This allows for easily adding eight mic inputs to an existing interface.

# Mac OS X audio setup

This lesson describes how to configure Audition to work with the Macintosh's inputs and outputs. Apple standardized on Core Audio drivers for Macintosh-series computers starting with OS X; Macs running earlier operating systems are not compatible with Audition.

1 Connect the audio source to the Mac's 1/8-inch line input jack via the 1/8-inch patch cord. If you're not using internal speakers, plug the earbuds/headphones or monitoring system input to the Mac's line-level output or headphones jack.

2 Open Audition and choose Audition > Preferences > Audio Hardware.

3 Don't change the Device Class or Master Clock preferences, because they will default correctly. The Default Input drop-down menu lists all available audio inputs. Choose Built-In Line Input.

4 The Default Output drop-down menu lists all available audio outputs. If you're using the built-in speaker, choose Built-In Output; for the line-level output, choose Built-In Line Output.

**Note:** Compared to the Mac's Sound setup under System Preferences, the Audio/MIDI Setup accessed from Audition's Settings button (Preferences > Audio Hardware) offers additional level controls, the option to mute inputs, and the ability to click on any input or output and examine its characteristics.

5 I/O Buffer Size determines the system latency. (See the sidebar "About latency [computer-based delay]" for more information.) Low values result in less delay through the system, whereas higher values increase stability. A value of 512 samples is a good compromise.

6 The Sample Rate drop-down menu lists all available sample rates. For most Macs, the choices are 44100, 48000, 88200, and 96000kHz; choose 44100, which is the standard for CDs. (In theory, higher sample rates improve fidelity, but the difference is subtle at best.) Windows computers and external audio interfaces generally offer a wider choice of sample rates.

7 Click Settings to open the Mac OS Audio/MIDI Setup dialog box, and then click Built-In Line Input.

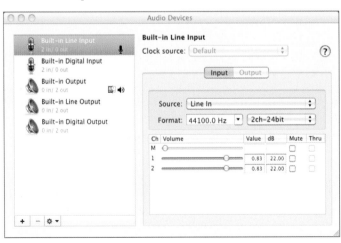

The settings will mimic what you set in Preferences (e.g., if you selected a 44.1kHz sample rate, this will be shown as the sample rate under Format).

**8** The other format field specifies Bit Resolution; choose 2-channel, 24-bit.

**9** All Mac OS X audio-related parameters are now set. Close the Audio Devices dialog box, and click OK in Audition's Preferences dialog box.

**10** Choose Audition > Preferences > Audio Channel Mapping. This correlates Audition's channels to the hardware inputs and outputs. For example, Audition's 1(L) channel will be mapped to Built-in Output 1. Click OK to close this dialog box.

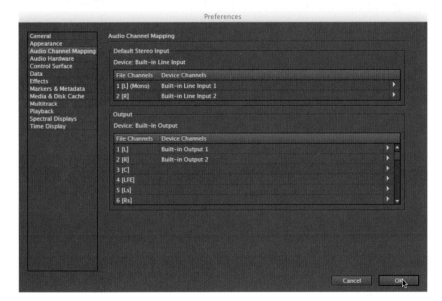

**Note:** The mapped defaults seldom need to be changed; however, you can remap if (for example) you were given a file where the right and left channels were accidentally reversed: Map Audition's 1(L) channel to the Built-in Output 2, which connects to the physical right output.

Proceed to the section "Testing inputs and outputs with Audition (Mac or Windows)."

## About latency (computer-based delay)

Latency occurs in the conversion process from analog to digital and digital to analog, as well as in the computer—even the most powerful processor can only do so many millions of calculations per second, and sometimes can't keep up. As a result, the computer stores some of the incoming audio in a *buffer*, which is like a savings account for your audio input signal. When the computer is so busy elsewhere that it misses handling some incoming audio, it makes a "withdrawal" from the buffer instead.

The larger the buffer (measured in samples or milliseconds), the less likely the computer will run out of audio data when it's needed. But a large buffer also means that the input signal is being diverted for a longer period of time before being processed by the computer. As a result, if you listen to the audio coming out of the computer, it will be delayed compared to the input. For example, if you're monitoring your vocals, what you hear in your headphones will be delayed compared to what you're singing, and this can be distracting. Reducing the Sample Buffer value minimizes delay at the expense of system stability (you may hear clicking or popping at low latencies).

# Bit resolution

Bit resolution expresses the accuracy with which the analog-to-digital converter measures the input signal. A good analogy is pixels and images: The more pixels in images of the same size, the more detail you'll see in the picture.

CDs use 16-bit resolution, which means that audio voltages are defined with an accuracy of approximately 1 part in 65,536. A resolution of 20- or 24-bit provides a higher level of accuracy, but as with higher sample rates, higher bit resolution requires more storage: A 24-bit file is 50 percent larger than a 16-bit file if both are at the same sample rate. Unlike higher sample rates, few dispute that 24-bit recording sounds better than 16-bit recording.

Recording at 44.1kHz with 24-bit resolution is a common trade-off among storage space, ease of use, and fidelity.

# Windows setup

Unlike newer Macs, Windows systems typically have several drivers: legacy drivers (primarily MME and DirectSound) for backward compatibility and higher-performance drivers (WDM/KS, which is different from yet another driver type called WDM). However, for Windows music applications, the most popular high-performance audio driver is ASIO (Advanced Stream Input/Output), created by software developer Steinberg. Virtually all professional audio interfaces include ASIO drivers, and many include WDM/KS drivers.

Unfortunately, ASIO is not part of the Windows operating system, so for these lessons you'll use the MME (Multimedia Extensions) protocol. It has relatively high latency but is stable and predictable. Experienced computer users can download the general-purpose ASIO driver ASIO4ALL, which is available free of charge from www.asio4all.com. It is the de facto ASIO driver for laptop owners who want to use ASIO with internal sound chips. Although you'll use MME for now, with a professional audio interface, use the ASIO or WDM/KS drivers provided with it, or as an alternative, ASIO4ALL.

> **Tip:** If there's a microphone input and you're not using it, make sure it's not selected (or its fader is down) to prevent it from contributing any noise.

1  Windows motherboards typically have both mic and line 1/8-inch inputs. Connect the audio source to the computer's 1/8-inch line input jack via the 1/8-inch patch cord.

2  If you're not using internal speakers, plug the earbuds/headphones or monitoring system input to the computer's line-level output.

3  Proceed to the section describing the operating system you're using.

# Audition on the Mac vs. Windows

Using Audition on the Mac versus using it on Windows was once a hot topic, but over time, the operating systems and associated hardware have become more alike. Once you open Audition, for all practical purposes, it operates identically on both platforms.

Each platform has strengths and limitations. The Mac handles audio transparently, avoiding the multiple drivers found with Windows. However, independent benchmarks show that all other factors being equal, Windows 7 can apply more power to audio projects than OS X. Realistically, though, with today's computers the situation is analogous to saying that a car capable of going 270 mph is more powerful than a car that tops out at 250 mph—yet you probably won't drive over 90 mph anyway.

Ultimately, if there are Mac-only or Windows-only programs that are essential for what you do, that will tend to dictate which platform is best. The reality is that both platforms have pretty much reached parity, and either will run Audition equally well.

## Windows 7 (32- or 64-bit) assignments

This lesson describes how to configure Audition to work with a typical Windows 7 machine's inputs and outputs.

1   In Windows, choose Start > Control Panel, and then in the Control panel double-click the Sound icon.

2   Click the Playback tab. Click either Speakers or Headphones, depending on what you have plugged into the computer's output jack. After clicking the appropriate choice, click the Set Default button to make this your default audio output.

► **Tip:** Click the Sound Playback dialog box's Properties to bring up a dialog box where you can click the Levels tab and adjust the volume and balance, and also mute the output.

3   Click the Sound dialog box's Recording tab.

**Tip:** Click the Sound Recording dialog box's Properties to bring up a dialog box where you can click the Levels tab and adjust the volume and balance, and also mute the input.

4   Click Line In, and then click Set Default. Click the Sounds tab, and for Sound Scheme, choose No Sounds—it's distracting to hear system sounds while you're working with audio. Click OK.

## Windows XP assignments

This lesson describes how to configure Audition to work with a typical Windows XP machine's inputs and outputs. Note that Windows XP is no longer recommended for most modern music programs, because several improvements have been made in Windows 7 with respect to handling audio, memory management, and hard disks.

1   In Windows, choose Start > Control Panel, and then in the Control panel double-click the Sound and Audio Devices icon.

2   Click the Audio tab. Choose the desired input and output devices from the Sound Playback Default device and Sound Recording Default device drop-down menus, respectively.

**3** To adjust the input volume, click the Volume button in the Sound Recording section. A small mixer appears; select the Stereo Mix Select check box, and use the associated fader to adjust the input levels.

**4** To adjust the output volume, click the Volume tab. A master fader lets you adjust the volume; select the "Place volume icon in the taskbar" check box to be able to adjust the output volume without having to open any windows or dialog boxes.

**5** Click the Sound dialog box's Recording tab.

**6** Click the desired input (for a laptop, this will often show Stereo Mix), and then click Set Default. Click the Sounds tab, and for Sound Scheme, choose No Sounds—it's distracting to hear system sounds while you're working with audio. Click OK.

▶ **Tip:** If there's a microphone input and you're not using it, make sure it's not selected, or its fader is down, to prevent it from contributing any noise.

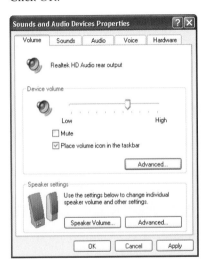

## Audition settings for Windows audio

Now that the computer has been configured properly for the audio inputs and outputs, you need to configure settings in Audition as well.

**1** Open Audition, and choose Edit > Preferences > Audio Hardware.

**2** From the Device Class drop-down menu, choose MME.

3 From the Default Input drop-down menu, choose the default input device (Line In) you specified previously; from the Default Output drop-down menu, choose the default output device (Speaker or Headphones) you specified previously. Do not change the Master Clock preference.

4 Latency determines the delay through the computer. Low values result in less delay through the system, whereas high values increase stability. A value of 200ms is "safe" for most computers.

5 The Sample Rate drop-down menu lists all available sample rates. Most Windows internal audio chips offer a wide variety of sample rates, often from 6000Hz to 192000Hz. Choose 44100 (in theory, higher sample rates improve fidelity, although few people can hear a difference). External audio interfaces typically offer fewer options that are intended for professional audio and video projects. After selecting the Sample Rate, click OK.

6 Choose Edit > Preferences > Audio Channel Mapping. This correlates Audition's channels to the hardware inputs and outputs. For example, Audition's 1(L) channel will be mapped to Line 1. Click OK to close this dialog box.

## Common sample rates

**Note:** The mapped defaults for channel mapping seldom need to be changed. However, you can remap if (for example) you were given a file where the right and left channels were accidentally reversed: Map Audition's 1(L) channel to the Built-in Output 2, which connects to the physical right output.

Different sample rates are typically used for different applications. This list covers the most common sample rates used for pro audio:

- **32,000 (32kHz).** Typically used for digital broadcast and satellite transmissions.

- **44,100 (44.1kHz).** The sample rate for CDs and most consumer digital audio.

- **48,000 (48kHz).** The most common sample rate used in broadcast video.

- **88,200 (88.2kHz).** Some engineers claim this sounds better than 44.1kHz but is rarely used.

- **96,000 (96kHz).** Sometimes used in DVDs and other high-end audio recording processes.

- **176,400 and 192,000 (176.4 and 192kHz).** These ultra-high sample rates generate much larger files and stress your computer more, yet offer no significant audio advantage.

# Testing inputs and outputs with Audition (Mac or Windows)

Because you already specified default inputs and outputs in the previous lessons, Audition will default to using these for recording and playback. Now you'll test these connections to ensure that the inputs and outputs are set up properly.

1   Choose File > New > Audio File to create a new file in the Waveform Editor. A dialog box opens.

2   Name the file. The sample rate should default to the value you selected in Preferences.

3   Choose the number of channels. Their inputs will default to what you specified in Preferences. If you choose Mono, only the first channel of the input channel pair will be recorded.

4   The bit depth represents the project's internal bit depth, not the bit resolution of your interface's converters. This resolution will be used to calculate changes in volume, effects, and the like, so choose the highest resolution, which is 32 (float).

5   Click OK to close the dialog box.

6   Click the Transport Record button, and then start playback from your audio source. If all connections are defined and all levels set properly, you'll see a waveform being drawn in the Waveform Editor window. Record several seconds of audio.

7   Click the Move Playhead to Previous button in the Transport, or drag the playhead (also called the current time indicator [CTI]) back to the beginning of the file. Click Play, and you should hear what you recorded in your chosen output device (internal speakers, earbuds, headphones, or monitoring system). Click the Transport Stop button to end playback.

**8** Now test recording and playback in the Multitrack Editor. Choose File > New > Multitrack session. A dialog box opens.

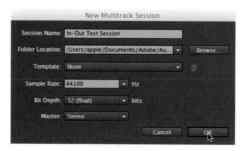

**9** Name the file. For Template, choose None. The sample rate should default to the value you selected in Preferences.

**10** As with the Waveform Editor, choose the highest resolution of 32 (float), and then choose the number of output channels (Stereo) for the Master Track.

**11** Click OK to close the dialog box.

**12** Arm a track by clicking the R (Record) button. Start playing your audio source; the channel's meter should indicate signal. Note that the input will connect automatically to the default input; however, if you click the input field's right arrow, you can choose just one input for mono tracks or you can open the hardware section under Preferences if you have a multi-input audio interface and want to choose an input other than the default.

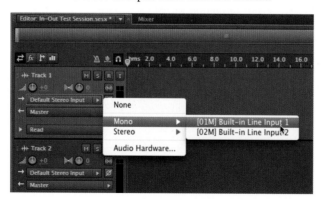

**13** Click the Transport Record button. If all connections are defined and all levels set properly, you'll see a waveform being drawn in the Multitrack Editor window. Record several seconds of audio.

**14** Click the Transport Move Playhead to Previous button, or drag the playhead (CTI) back to the beginning of the file. Click Play, and you should hear what you recorded in your chosen output device (internal speakers, earbuds, headphones, or monitoring system). Click the Transport Stop button to end playback.

# Using external interfaces

It's not possible to present an exercise in this lesson, because there is no way to know what interface you're using. However, keep the following in mind when you're using external interfaces:

- Professional interfaces usually have capabilities beyond those offered by internal audio and therefore have their own control panels for routing signals, controlling levels, and the like.

- Interfaces often have more than one set of stereo inputs and outputs. When you're choosing default inputs and outputs, you'll have a much wider selection compared to using a computer's internal sound capabilities.

- With interfaces that provide USB 2.0 *and* FireWire connections, try both on extended sessions to determine if one option works better than the other.

- Windows USB interfaces can be *class-compliant,* meaning they don't need custom drivers. However, always use the custom ASIO or WDM drivers provided with an interface for maximum functionality and minimum latency.

- With Windows computers, never use a driver called "emulated," such as "ASIO (emulated)." These result in the worst performance of all possible drivers.

- Some interfaces include a feature called zero-latency monitoring. This means the input can be mixed directly to the output, and the mixing is typically controlled by using an applet that shows up onscreen to bypass any latency caused by going through the computer.

- With ASIO interfaces, Audition will default to monopolizing any sound capabilities. To access the ASIO interface in other applications that are running, select the "Release ASIO driver in background" check box in Audition's Preferences > Audio Hardware dialog box. Giving the other application the focus will allow it use the ASIO interface, unless Audition is recording.

# Audio interface/computer connections

There are several ways external audio interfaces communicate with a computer:

- **USB.** USB 2.0 can stream up to dozens of audio channels over a single cable that connects between the interface and a computer's USB port. USB 1.1 interfaces are also available for less-demanding applications and can typically stream six channels of audio, making them suitable for surround. Class-compliant interfaces are plug-and-play, but most professional interfaces use specialized drivers to improve speed and efficiency.

- **FireWire.** Like USB, this also connects the interface to your computer with a cable, although the connector configuration is different than USB. Although still common, FireWire has been eclipsed somewhat by USB for several reasons: Many laptops no longer include FireWire ports, most audio interfaces require specific FireWire chip sets, and the performance advantage FireWire once offered was more relevant when computers weren't as powerful. Some audio interfaces include both FireWire and USB 2.0.

- **PCIe card.** This plugs directly into a computer's motherboard, so it provides the most direct pathway to a computer. However, this option is less common because USB and FireWire offer more convenience—you don't need to physically open the computer to install the card—with virtually no performance decrease.

- **ExpressCard.** This is suitable for plugging into laptops that have ExpressCard slots, but again, is ceding its role to USB or FireWire interfaces.

- **Thunderbolt.** This interface protocol, which carries data over a cable, is just starting to appear in computers; few Thunderbolt-compatible interfaces are available as of this writing. However, Thunderbolt promises PCIe-type performance and compatibility with existing audio interfaces, as well as dedicated Thunderbolt interfaces.

# Review questions

1 What are the most popular driver protocols for Mac and Windows?

2 What is an unavoidable, negative by-product of working with computer-based audio?

3 How can you minimize latency?

4 What are the advantages and disadvantages of high sample rates and high bit resolutions?

5 Although many external audio interfaces include ASIO drivers, the Windows operating system does not. How can you use ASIO with laptop sound chips?

# Review answers

1 Core Audio for the Mac and ASIO for Windows are the most popular driver protocols for pro audio.

2 System latency causes a time delay between the output and what's being recorded at the input.

3 Change the number of sample buffers to alter latency. Using the smallest number possible, consistent with the audio not producing clicks or pops, provides minimum latency.

4 High sample rates and bit resolutions have the potential to deliver better audio quality but create larger audio files and stress the computer more than lower rates and resolutions.

5 Free driver software, ASIO4ALL, provides ASIO drivers for sound hardware that was not designed for ASIO compatibility.

# 2 THE AUDITION ENVIRONMENT

## Lesson overview

In this lesson, you'll learn how to do the following:

- Create custom workspaces for particular workflows

- Arrange panels and frames for optimum workflow

- Use the Media Browser to find files in your computer

- Listen to files before loading them using the Media Browser's Playback Preview function

- Create shortcuts to frequently used folders

- Navigate to specific sections of a file in the Waveform Editor or a Session in the Multitrack Editor

- Use markers to create points you can jump to immediately in the Waveform Editor or a Session in the Multitrack Editor

- Use zooming to focus in on particular sections in the Waveform or Multitrack Editor

This lesson takes about 60 minutes to complete. This assumes you've copied the Lesson02 folder that contains the project examples into the Lessons folder that you created on your hard drive for these projects. Remember that you needn't be concerned about modifying these files, because you can always return to the original versions by copying them from the *Adobe Audition CS6 Classroom in a Book* CD-ROM.

You can create custom workspaces with particular selections of windows and window arrangements, as well as choose various ways to navigate through Audition's Waveform Editor and Multitrack Editor.

# Audition's dual personality

A unique aspect of Audition is that it combines the functionality of two programs within a single piece of software:

- A Waveform Editor that can perform highly detailed and sophisticated editing

- A Multitrack Editor for creating multitrack music productions

In addition, the two sections are interrelated in that audio can move freely between the two environments. Audio in the Multitrack Editor can be transferred to the Waveform Editor for detailed editing and then transferred back. Files brought into the Waveform Editor can be tweaked prior to making them the basis of a multi-track project.

Both editors have highly customizable workspaces that you can optimize for any of Audition's uses—not just editing or multitrack productions but also audio for video, sound library development, audio restoration, sound effects creation, and even forensics. This lesson concentrates on the Waveform Editor, but operations in the Multitrack Editor are similar, and in many cases, identical.

## The editing/multitracking connection

Traditionally, multitrack recording programs and digital audio editing programs were separate and optimized for their specific tasks (in fact, Audition started as a digital audio editor with no multitracking capabilities). Inherently, both types of programs are quite different: Multitrack recorders can have dozens of tracks, or even over a hundred, and therefore require effects that minimize CPU power consumption (because so many tracks will incorporate effects), and both mixing and automation are extremely important. Digital audio editors deal with a limited number of tracks—usually just stereo audio—don't require mixing, and tend to have "mastering quality" effects that use a lot of CPU power.

What's interesting about Audition is that it doesn't just stick two isolated programs together but instead integrates them. There are often occasions when working with a multitrack recording where you need to do detailed editing on a track. This would normally require exporting the file, opening it in a second program, editing it, and then reimporting it back into the multitrack recording software. With Audition, you just click on the Waveform Editor, and all the tracks in the Multitrack Editor are already loaded and available. When you export a mixdown of a Multitrack Session, it also loads automatically into the Waveform Editor so you can master it, save it as an MP3 file (or other Internet-friendly format), or even burn it to an audio CD.

This fluid movement between the two environments improves workflow. And another advantage is that the two sections have similar user interfaces, so you don't have to learn two separate programs.

# The Audition Workspace

Audition's Workspace, which is consistent with other Adobe video and graphics applications so you needn't learn multiple user interfaces, consists of multiple windows. You choose which windows make up a workspace, and you can add or remove them at any time. For example, you don't need a video window if you're not doing an audio-for-video project, but you'll need it if you're creating a soundtrack. Or, when you're creating a multitrack project, you may need the Media Browser open to locate files you want to use, but when mixing, you can close the Media Browser to create space for inserting other windows. You can also save a particular window setup as a workspace.

Once windows are brought into a workspace, they are arranged as frames and panels.

## Frames and panels

Frames and panels are the main elements in a workspace, and you can rearrange them to suit your particular needs.

1  With Audition open, navigate to the Lesson02 folder, and open the file WaveformWorkspace.aif.

2  Choose Window > Workspace > Classic.

3  To make sure the workspace uses the stored version, choose Window > Workspace > Reset Classic.

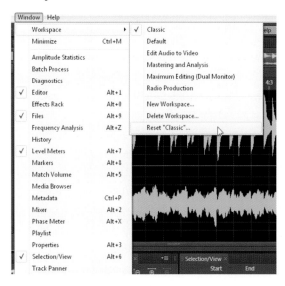

**Note:** When you open Audition, it opens to the last workspace you were using. You can modify a workspace as much as you want, but always revert to the original version you created (as described later) by choosing Window > Workspace > Reset [name of workspace].

**4** A dialog box asks if you want to reset Classic to its original layout. Click Yes.

**5** Click on the waveform, which is within the waveform's Editor panel. When you click in a panel, a yellow line outlines the panel.

**6** If you want to see more of the waveform's Editor panel, click the panel's left yellow line, and drag to the left to widen the panel.

**Note:** Panels can have divider lines at the top, bottom, right, and/or left. If a divider icon appears when you hover over one of these lines, you can click and drag to resize the panel. You can also resize the entire workspace by clicking on any edge and dragging.

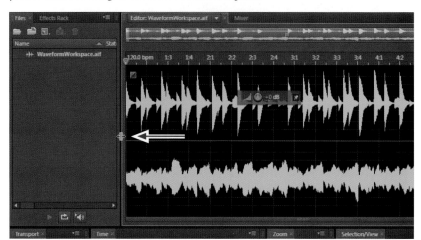

**7** Increase the panel's height by clicking the panel's lower line and dragging down. However, this may cause the panels below the waveform to disappear or become narrow enough to be unusable. So, return the panel's lower line to where it was, and then start to customize the workspace.

Every panel has a tab toward the top of it. The right part of the tab has a Close box, which closes the panel (you can always reopen a panel from the Window menu if you need it later).

**8** The Selection/View panel probably isn't needed right now, so click its Close box to open up some more space. Note how the Zoom panel expands to take up the space.

Every panel is housed in a frame. You can save space by grouping several panels into the same frame to create a collection of panels that has tabs across the top for bringing a particular panel to the "front" of the frame.

**9** On the left part of a panel's tab is a gripper; click the Time panel's gripper and drag it next to the Zoom panel's tab. A strip containing this tab turns blue to indicate it is a "drop zone" where a panel can be dropped.

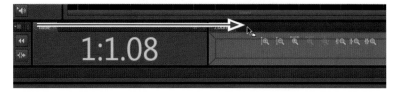

**10** Release the mouse button; the Time and Zoom panels are now within a tabbed frame.

**11** Click the Transport panel's gripper, and drag it into the blue drop zone strip that already has the Zoom and Time tabs. Now the Zoom, Transport, and Time panels are all within a tabbed frame.

**12** Click the Zoom tab, then the Time tab, and then the Transport tab. Note that the original double rows of buttons are now single rows, which allows more space for increasing the Editor panel height.

**13** With the Transport tab showing, click in the Editor panel. Click its lower yellow line and drag down until the Transport panel is just high enough to show all the buttons. Click the Time tab and then the Zoom tab, and note that they've also been resized to fit.

**14** To create even more space, move the Levels panel to the left of the Audition Workspace. Click the Levels panel gripper, and drag it to the Audition Workspace's left edge.

**15** Now you can drag the bottom of the Editor panel down even further.

● **Note:** With narrow frames containing multiple tabs, a tab's Close box may not be visible. You can close tabs via a frame's drop-down menu, which is accessible toward the frame's upper-right corner.

● **Note:** You can click and drag on a tab to change its position among the other tabs.

● **Note:** There are three green drop zones on the left, right, bottom, and top edges of the Audition Workspace. These are different from the blue drop zones because anything dropped into these green drop zones will extend to the main window's full length or height.

## Adding a new panel

So far, you've rearranged existing panels within a workspace. However, you can also add a new panel to a frame.

1 Currently, the Files and Effects Rack panels are in a single frame. This would be a convenient frame for placing the Media Browser panel, so add it to the frame.

2 Click a panel in this frame, like Files.

3 Choose Window > Media Browser. The Media Browser is added to the frame.

However, note that the frame is narrower and you can no longer see all three tabs. When this happens, Audition adds a scroll bar just above the frame.

**Note:** If your mouse has a scroll wheel, you can also hover over any frame tab and scroll from tab to tab using the mouse scroll wheel.

4 Click the scroll bar and drag left and right to reveal the various tabs.

## Dragging panels and frames into panel drop zones

When you click a gripper and drag a panel over another panel, blue "drop zones" appear that indicate where the panel can be dropped. There are five main drop zones.

If the panel drop zone is in the panel center, dropping a panel there is equivalent to dropping it into the bar with the tabs. However, if the panel drop zone shows a bar with beveled edges, the frame will land where the bar is and push the panel with the bar over to make room.

The frame with the Media Browser, Effects Rack, and Files seems unnecessarily tall, and the space at the bottom isn't really necessary. That would be a good place to drag the Time panel.

1   Click the Time panel gripper, and drag it toward the Effects Rack. As it passes over the bottom of the Effects Rack panel, you'll see a blue bar with beveled edges.

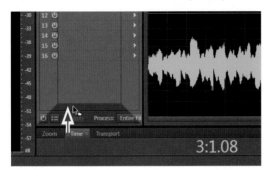

You can also drag frames into drop zones; the frame gripper is in the frame's upper-right corner. Suppose you decide you'd rather have the Time panel above the frame with the Media Browser, Effects Rack, and Files panels. You could drag the Time panel into the frame's upper beveled bar, but there's another way. Neither option is inherently superior, but you might prefer one workflow over the other.

2   Click the frame's gripper, and drag it into the Time panel's lower bar.

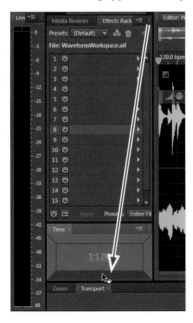

## The Frame drop-down menu

Every frame has a drop-down menu in the upper-right corner. This menu always contains at least five options:

- Undock Panel

- Undock Frame

- Close Panel (same as clicking a tab's Close box)

- Close Frame

- Maximize Frame

There may also be options that relate to specific panels. For example, the Media Browser panel drop-down menu has options for Enable Auto-Play, Enable Loop Preview, and Show Preview Transport. This is handy because even if the Preview Transport isn't shown, it's still possible to enable its Auto-Play and Loop Preview functions.

Undocking allows you to "float" a panel or frame outside of the main window. Here's how it works.

**Note:** You can undock a frame or panel by clicking its gripper and dragging the gripper outside the Audition Workspace.

**Note:** After undocking frames or panels, they will still have grippers that you can use to re-dock them as you would any other frame or panel.

1   Click the drop-down menu for the frame containing the Media Browser, Files, and Effects Rack panels.

2   Choose Undock Frame.

   The frame becomes a separate window that can be moved independently of the Audition Workspace and resized.

3   Click the Media Browser panel.

4   Click the drop-down menu of the frame containing the Media Browser panel.

5   Choose Undock Panel. Now there are three separate windows—the Audition Workspace, the frame with the Files and Effects Rack panels, and the Media Browser panel.

## Tools panel

The Tools panel has some unique attributes compared to the other panels.

1   The Tools panel defaults to being a toolbar—a thin strip of buttons along the top of the Audition Workspace—and has no drop-down menu. Undock it by clicking the gripper in the upper-left corner and dragging it outside the Audition Workspace.

   When undocked, the toolbar takes on the characteristics of a panel: It's housed within a frame, can be combined with other panels within the frame, and contains a frame drop-down menu. It also includes two extra fields—a drop-down menu for choosing a workspace that duplicates the Window > Workspace path and a search box.

● **Note:** The Status Bar at the bottom of the workspace is the one element that is permanent and cannot be floated or docked (however, you can choose whether to show or hide it by choosing View > Status Bar > Show). The Status Bar shows statistics about file size, bit resolution, sample rate, duration, available disk space, and the like.

**2** Re-dock the toolbar along the top of the Audition Workspace before proceeding, and then close Audition.

## Create and save custom workspaces

You are not limited to the workspaces that are included with Audition and can create you own.

**1** Arrange the workspace exactly as desired.

**2** Choose Window > Workspace > New Workspace.

**3** Name the workspace by typing a name into the New Workspace dialog box, and then click OK. Your workspace now joins the list of current workspaces.

**4** To delete a workspace, choose Window > Workspace and select a workspace other than the one you want to delete.

**5** Choose Window > Workspace > Delete Workspace.

**6** When the Delete Workspace dialog box appears, choose the workspace you want to delete from the drop-down menu, and then click OK.

# Navigation

There are three main elements to navigation:

- Navigating to desired files and projects so you can open them, typically using Audition's Media Browser

- Navigation related to playing back and recording audio within the Waveform Editor and Multitrack Editor

- Navigating visually within the Waveform Editor and Multitrack Editor (zooming in and out to specific parts of the file)

## Navigating to files and projects

For both Mac and Windows, Audition adopts standard navigation menu protocols (such as Open and Open Recent) for navigating within the computer to find specific files and projects. The only significant departure is the Open Append menu option, which relates mostly to the Waveform Editor.

**1** Open Audition, navigate to the Lesson02 folder, and open the file WaveformWorkspace.aif.

**2** Choose File > Open Append > To Current.

**3** Navigate to the Lesson02 folder, choose String_Harp.wav, and in the dialog box, click Open.

**4** The file you selected is appended to the end of the current waveform in the Waveform Editor.

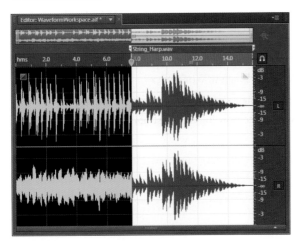

**5** Choose File > Open Append > To New.

**6** Navigate to the Lesson02 folder, choose String_Harp.wav, and open it.

**7** The file you selected is opened in a new Waveform Editor view. It does not replace the previously loaded file, and you can select either one with the Editor panel's drop-down menu.

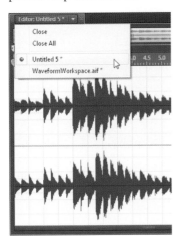

**8** Choose File > Close All, but leave Audition open in preparation for the next lesson.

● **Note:** You can choose Open Append > To New in the Multitrack Editor; however, this will simply open the file in the Waveform Editor, not the Multitrack Editor.

## Navigating with the Media Browser

The Media Browser is an enhanced version of the browsing options offered in the Windows and Macintosh operating systems. If you use Windows, it works similarly to the standard Windows Explorer. If you use the Mac, the Media Browser resembles the list view browser in the left column, but selecting a folder in the left column opens its contents in the right column, like the Mac Finder's column view.

Once you locate a file, you can drag it into the Waveform Editor or Multitrack Editor window.

1   Choose Window > Workspace > Default.

2   Choose Window > Workspace > Reset Default. Click Yes when the confirmation dialog box appears.

3   Click the Media Browser's gripper and drag it outside of the workspace to float it. This isn't strictly necessary, but this makes it easy to extend the size to see all the available options in the Media Browser. Drag the window to the right to extend it.

**Tip:** The Locations drop-down menu in the upper left, above the list of your computer's drives, lets you select any drive. Its contents appear immediately in the right column.

4   The left Media Browser column shows all the drives mounted to your computer. Clicking on any of these displays its contents in the right column. You can also click a drive's disclosure triangle to reveal its contents.

5   In the left column, navigate to the Lesson02 folder. Click its disclosure triangle to expand it, and then click the Moebius_120BPM_F# folder.

The folder's audio files are shown in the right column. Note how additional subcolumns show file attributes, such as duration, sample rate, channels, and more.

**6** You can change subcolumn widths. Click the divider line between two subcolumns, and drag left or right to change width.

**7** You can rearrange the order of subcolumns. Click a column name, like Media Type. Drag it left or right to position it. This feature is helpful because you can drag the columns containing the information you need the most to the left side, so the data is visible even if the window isn't fully extended to the right.

**8** For providing single-click access to specific folders, the Media Browser offers a "virtual drive" along with the other computer drives in the left column that contains shortcuts for often-used folders. To create a shortcut for the Moebius_120BPM_F# folder, click it in the left column.

**9** In the right column, click the + symbol and choose Add Shortcut for "Moebius_120BPM_F#."

**10** Look in the left column, and click the Shortcuts disclosure triangle. Your shortcut now provides one-click access to the designated folder.

**11** Another Media Browser advantage is that you can listen to the files as you browse, thanks to the Preview Transport. If it's not visible, select Show Preview Transport from the upper-right drop-down menu. Click the Auto-Play button with the speaker icon, and you'll hear a file play when you click it.

● **Note:** If enabled, the Loop Playback button to the left of the Auto-Play button will cause the file to play back until you either choose another file or click the Stop button to the left of the Loop Playback button. If you don't want Auto-Play but want to play files manually, deselect Auto-Play and click the Play button (which toggles with the Stop button) to start playback.

**12** Close Audition without saving anything.

## Navigating within files and Sessions

Once you're in the Waveform Editor or Multitrack Editor, you'll want to be able to navigate within the Editor to locate or edit specific sections. Audition has several tools that you can use to do this.

1 Open Audition, navigate to the Lesson02 folder, and open the file WaveformWorkspace.aif.

2 Click the Editor window's gripper and drag it outside of the workspace to float the window.

3 Click the Workspace's lower-left corner and drag diagonally down toward the right until you can see all the Transport and Zoom buttons. Then click around a third of the way into the waveform and drag to about two-thirds of the way through the waveform to create a *selection*. The orange icon at the beginning of the selection is called the *current time indicator (CTI)*, or *playhead* in previous versions of Audition.

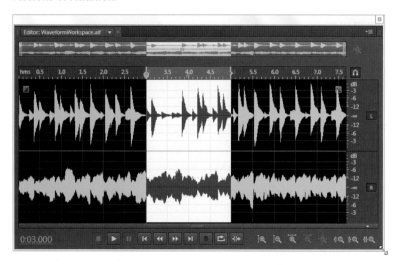

## Navigation via zooming

Zooming acts the same way it does with a camera: Zoom out to see more of an object, and zoom in to see more detail. The Waveform Editor includes zoom buttons, but you can also open a Zoom panel with these same eight buttons if you want to position them elsewhere or float them. The Multitrack Editor includes these same zoom buttons.

1  The Zoom toolbar consists of eight buttons that control zooming. Click two times on the leftmost Zoom In (Amplitude) button. Zooming in on amplitude lets you see low-level signals more easily.

2  Click twice on the next button to the right, the Zoom Out (Amplitude) button. This returns you to the previous amplitude zoom level.

3  Click eight times on the next button to the right, the Zoom In (Time) button. This lets you see very short sections of time on the waveform.

4  Click twice on the next button to the right, the Zoom Out (Time) button. This lets you zoom back out.

5  Click once on the next button to the right, the Zoom Out Full (All Axes) button. This is a "shortcut" button that zooms out the time and amplitude axes to maximum so you can see the complete waveform.

6  Click the next button to the right, the Zoom In at In Point button. This places the selection start (In point) in the middle of the waveform.

7  Click the next button to the right, the Zoom In at Out Point button. This places the selection end (Out point) in the middle of the waveform.

8  Click the rightmost button, the Zoom to Selection button. This causes the selection to fill the window.

9  Click the Zoom Out Full button (the third from the right) to return both axes to zoomed out full.

10  There's an additional Zoom tool at the top of the window that shows a global view of your audio file. Drag the left or right side of the yellow grabber to zoom in or out of an area; the area between the two yellow grabbers is what you'll see in the Editor. Note that you can click the grabber in the middle of the two yellow bars to move the zoom area left or right.

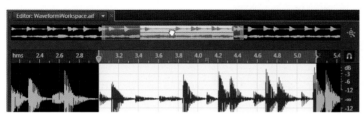

11  To reset the zoom back to the see the entire audio waveform, click the Zoom Out Full button to the right of the upper zoom tool. Close Audition without saving anything.

**Note:** If you zoom in all the way using Zoom In (Time), you can see— as well as edit—the individual samples that make up the waveform.

# Keyboard shortcuts

Keyboard shortcuts can help tremendously with navigation. Once you've memorized important shortcuts, it takes less effort to press a couple of keys than to locate a specific area on the screen, move your mouse to it, access a menu, select an item, and so on.

Audition even lets you create your own keyboard shortcuts for the various commands. Choose Edit > Keyboard Shortcuts, or press Alt+K (Option+K), and then follow the onscreen directions to add and remove shortcuts.

## Navigation with markers

You can place markers (also called cues) within the Waveform Editor and Multitrack Editor to indicate specific places you want to navigate to immediately. For example, in a Multitrack project, you might place markers before a verse and chorus so you can jump back and forth between them. In the Waveform Editor, you might place markers to indicate places where edits are required.

● **Note:** You can rename a marker by right-clicking (Control-clicking) on its white handle in the Waveform Editor and choosing Rename Marker. Or you can click on the marker name in the Markers panel, click again after a slight pause (you don't want to double-click), and then type in a new name. Renaming with either method renames both instances of the marker.

1 Open Audition, navigate to the Lesson02 folder, and open the file WaveformWorkspace.aif.

2 Choose Window > Workspace > Reset "Default." Click Yes to confirm.

3 Choose Window > Markers. The Marker panel appears.

4 Click in the waveform toward the beginning, around 1.0 second.

5 Press M. This adds a marker at the playhead (CTI) location and adds the marker to the list of markers in the marker window.

6 Now click in the waveform around 3.0 seconds. As an alternate way to add a marker, click the Add Cue Marker button in the Markers panel.

7 You can also mark a selection. Click around 5.0 and drag right to 6.0 to create a selection. Press M to mark the selection. Note that the Markers panel shows a different symbol to indicate this Range marker is marking a selection.

8  You can also convert the Range markers to an individual marker at the selection start. Right-click (Control-click) on either the start or end of the Range marker, and then choose Convert to Point.

9  There are several ways to navigate among markers. Double-click the first marker in the Markers panel list, and the playhead jumps to that marker. Double-click the last marker in the Marker panels list, and the playhead jumps to the last marker.

10 Another method for marker navigation involves the Transport. We'll talk about that next. Leave Audition open in preparation for the next lesson.

## Navigation with the Transport

The Transport offers several navigation options, including navigation using markers.

1  Click the Move Playhead to Previous button. The playhead moves to Marker 2.

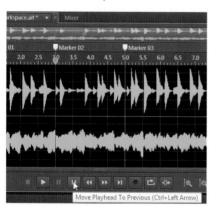

**Note:** If a file contains no markers, Move Playhead to Next jumps to the end; Move Playhead to Previous jumps to the beginning. In the Multitrack Editor, clip start and end points are automatically considered markers by the Transport's Move Playhead to Next and Move Playhead to Previous buttons.

2  Click the Move Playhead to Previous button again. The playhead moves to Marker 1. Click the Move Playhead to Previous button once more, and the playhead moves to the beginning of the file.

3  Click the Move Playhead to Next button (the button to the left of the Record button with the red dot) four times. The playhead steps to each marker until it reaches the end of the file.

4   To move the playhead backward in the file without dragging the playhead or using markers, click and hold the Rewind button until the playhead is in the desired location. You'll hear audio during the scrolling process. Rewind back to the beginning.

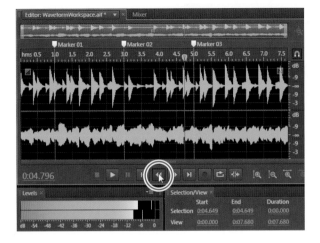

5   Click the Play button (the second Transport button from the left with the right arrow). Playback begins.

6   As soon as the playhead passes the first marker, click the Move Playhead To Next Button. The playhead jumps to the second marker. Click the Move Playhead To Next button again, and the playhead jumps to the third marker.

7   Right-click (Control-click) the Transport Play button and choose Return Playhead to Start Position on Stop. With this option selected, clicking Stop will return the playhead to where it started. With this option deselected, the playhead will stop at the position it had when you clicked the Stop button.

## Review questions

1  What is the difference between a frame and a panel?

2  What is a drop zone?

3  What is a "floated" window?

4  In addition to locating files, name two major advantages of using the Media Browser.

5  What is the purpose of a marker?

## Review answers

1  A frame contains one or more panels.

2  A drop zone indicates where a panel or frame will dock when it's dragged to that zone.

3  A floated window exists outside of an Audition Workspace and can be dragged anywhere on your screen.

4  You can listen to the files you locate, as well as see attributes about them.

5  A marker indicates a place in a file or Session that the playhead can jump to immediately, thus speeding up navigation.

# 3 BASIC EDITING

## Lesson overview

In this lesson, you'll learn how to do the following:

- Select a portion of a waveform for editing

- Cut, copy, paste, mix, and remove silence audio. Learn to eliminate unwanted sounds

- Use multiple clipboards to assemble final audio from individual clips

- Extend and shorten pieces of music

- Add new sounds to an existing piece of music using Mix Paste

- Create loops with music files

- Fade audio regions to create smooth transitions, and remove pops and clicks

 This lesson takes about 75 minutes to complete. Copy the Lesson03 folder into the Lessons folder that you created on your hard drive for these projects (or create it now), if you haven't already done so. Don't be concerned about modifying these files; you can always return to the original versions by copying them from the *Adobe Audition CS6 Classroom in a Book* CD-ROM.

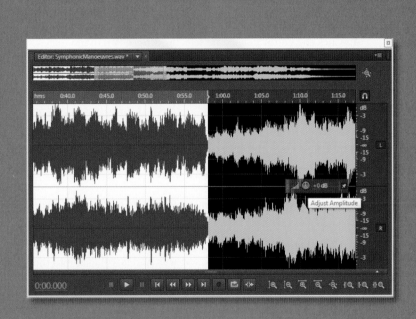

Audition makes it easy to cut, paste, copy, trim, fade, and perform other processes on audio files. You can zoom in to make extremely precise edits, while seeing a zoomed-out version in the overview window at the top.

# Opening a file for editing

You can open multiple files in Adobe Audition, which are stacked behind each other in the main Waveform view. Individual files are selected via the Editor panel drop-down menu.

1 Choose File > Open, navigate to the Lesson03 folder, select the file Narration01, and then click Open.

2 To open multiple files simultaneously, choose File > Open, and navigate to the Lesson03 folder. Select Narration02, and then Shift-click on Narration05. Four files are selected. (To select noncontiguous files, press Ctrl-click [Command-click] on each file you want to load.)

3 Click Open. Audition loads the selected files.

4 Click the Editor panel's file selector drop-down menu (just above the upper left of the waveform) to see a list of the files you loaded. Click on any of these files to select it and open it in the Waveform view. Or, click Close to close the current file in the stack (that is, the one visible in the Editor panel).

# Selecting a region for editing and changing its level

To begin editing your audio, you need to start by choosing a file and specifying which parts of that file you want to edit. This process is called *selection*.

1 Click on the Editor panel drop-down submenu to see a list of recent files loaded into Audition. Select Finish Soft.wav, and it will load into the Editor panel.

2 Click the Transport Play button to hear the file play from start to finish.

3 Note how the words "to finish" are softer than the other words. Sometimes when recording narration, a drop in volume can occur at the end of phrases. You can fix this in Audition CS6.

4 Click at the beginning of the words, and then drag to the end (or click at the end and drag to the beginning). You've now *selected* those words for editing, as indicated by a white background. You can fine-tune the selection by clicking on the region's right or left border, either in the Waveform view or timeline, and dragging. Note that upon selecting a region, a heads-up display with a small volume control appears automatically.

5   Click on the volume control and drag upward to increase the volume level
    to +6dB. To audition this change, click in the timeline above the waveform.
    Click several seconds before the words you just edited so you can hear them
    in context, and then click Play.

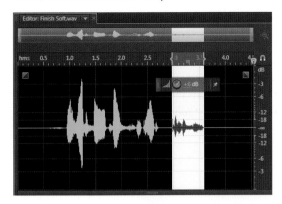

6   If the level is good, you're done. If not, choose Edit > Undo Amplify, or press
    Ctrl+Z (Command+Z). Or, vary the level and audition the results again, as you
    did in the previous step.

7   When you're satisfied with the level, click anywhere in the waveform to deselect
    the region but retain the level changes.

▶ **Tip:** Double-click
anywhere within a file
to select the entire file.
This also returns the
playhead to the file
beginning.

## Cutting, deleting, and pasting audio regions

Cutting, deleting, and pasting audio regions is particularly useful with narration
audio files because you can remove unwanted sounds from your narration, like
coughs or "umms," tighten up spaces, increase spaces between words and phrases,
and even rearrange the dialogue if needed. In this lesson you'll edit the following
narration (file Narration05) so it flows logically and doesn't have unwanted sounds:

"First, once the files are loaded, select the file you, uh, want to edit from the drop-
down menu. Well actually, you need to go to the File menu first, select open; then
choose the file you want to edit. Remember; you can (clears throat) open up, uh,
multiple files at once."

You'll get rid of the uhs and throat clearing, and rearrange the narration to say:

"Go to the File menu first; select open; then choose the file you want to edit.
Remember that you can open up multiple files at once. Once the files are loaded,
select the file you want to edit from the drop-down menu."

1  The file Narration05 should still be open. If not, reopen the file from the Lessons03 folder. If necessary, select the file Narration05 for editing from the Editor panel drop-down submenu. If you've closed and reopened Audition, choose File > Open Recent and then choose Narration05, or navigate to the Lesson03 folder and open Narration05.

2  Play the file until you reach the first "uh." Stop the transport, and click and drag across the "uh" to select it.

3  To hear what the file will sound like after you delete the "uh," click in the timeline several seconds prior to the region, and then click Skip Selection (the rightmost transport button). The file will play up to the region start, and then seamlessly skip to the region end and resume playback. If you hear a click, refer to the sidebar "About zero-crossings."

4  Choose Edit > Delete to delete the "uh."

**Note:** There's a difference between Edit > Cut and Edit > Delete. Cut removes the region but places the region in the currently selected clipboard so it can be pasted elsewhere if desired. Delete also removes the region but does not place it in the clipboard, and leaves whatever is in the clipboard intact.

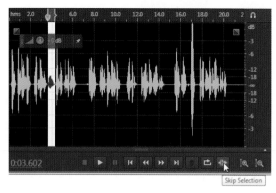

When you invoke this command, you may not see any visual difference when zoomed out, because the adjustments are often very minor. However, Audition is indeed moving the region boundaries as defined by the command; you can verify this by zooming in to the waveform so you can see the results with more accuracy.

5  Now you'll remove the unwanted throat clearing. If you trim right up to the throat-clearing boundaries, when you click the Skip Selection transport button you'll hear a gap. So, select a region that starts somewhat before and ends slightly after the actual throat clearing to tighten that gap. Then choose Edit > Delete.

# About zero-crossings

When you define a region and the boundary occurs where the level is anything other than zero, this may result in a click upon playback.

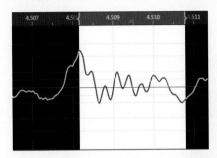

If the boundary occurs on a *zero-crossing*—a place where the waveform transitions from positive to negative, or vice versa—there is no rapid level change; hence, no click.

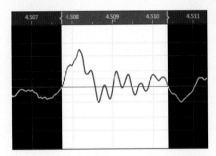

After making a selection, Audition can automatically optimize the region boundaries so they fall on zero-crossings. Choose Edit > Zero Crossings and select one of several options:

- **Adjust selection inward.** Moves the region boundaries closer together so each falls on the nearest zero-crossing.

- **Adjust selection outward.** Moves the region boundaries farther apart so each falls on the nearest zero-crossing.

- **Adjust left side to left.** Moves the left region boundary to the nearest zero-crossing to the left.

- **Adjust left side to right.** Moves the left region boundary to the nearest zero-crossing to the right.

- **Adjust right side to left.** Moves the right region boundary to the nearest zero-crossing to the left.

- **Adjust right side to right.** Moves the left region boundary to the nearest zero-crossing to the right.

6   Now let's remove the second "uh" that's in the audio. Notice that removing this "uh" results in too tight a transition between the words before and after the "uh" (you also have to be careful not to cut off too much of the beginning of the word "multiple"). So, undo your last cut. Instead of deleting the "uh," you'll insert silence instead to produce a better result. To do this, select the "uh" and choose Edit > Insert > Silence. A dialog box appears denoting the length of the silence, which will equal the region length you defined. Click OK.

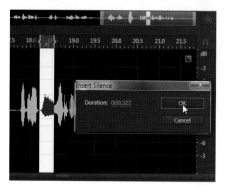

7   The silent gap between words is too long, so define part of the silence as a region. Click Skip Selection to test whether you've deleted the right amount. Lengthen or shorten the silence as needed, and then choose Edit > Delete. The gap is now shorter.

Now that you've fixed some of the verbal glitches, let's change the sentence structure into a more coherent narration. Keep this file open; if you need to interrupt this lesson, choose File > Save As, and save the file as **Narration05_edit**.

## Cutting and pasting with multiple clipboards

You're probably familiar with the computer's clipboard. In a word processing program, you typically copy a sentence to the clipboard and then paste it from the clipboard to somewhere else in the text. Audition's clipboard works similarly but offers five clipboards so you can temporarily store up to five different pieces of audio for later pasting. You'll put that feature to good use when further fixing the Narration05 file beyond just removing the "uhs" and throat clearing.

1   Select the part of the file that says, "Once the files are loaded, select the file you want to edit from the drop-down menu."

2   Choose Edit > Set Current Clipboard and select Clipboard 1. You can also select this clipboard by pressing Ctrl+1 (Command+1).

3   To remove the phrase and store it in Clipboard 1, choose Edit > Cut or press Ctrl+X (Command+X) to place the phrase in Clipboard 1. The word (Empty) will no longer appear next to the Clipboard 1 name.

4   Select the part of the file that says, "Go to the file menu first; select open; then choose the file you want to edit."

5   Press Ctrl+2 (Command+2) to make Clipboard 2 the current clipboard (you could also choose Edit > Set Current Clipboard and select Clipboard 2).

6   Choose Edit > Cut to place the phrase in Clipboard 2.

7   Select the part of the file that says, "Remember; you can open up multiple files at once."

8   Press Ctrl+3 (Command+3) to make Clipboard 3 the current clipboard.

9   Choose Edit > Cut to place the phrase in Clipboard 3. Keep the Narration05 file open.

Now you have a separate clip for each phrase, which will make it easy to place the phrases in a different order. The goal is to end up with "Go to the file menu first; select open; then choose the file you want to edit. Remember; you can open up multiple files at once. Once the files are loaded, select the file you want to edit from the drop-down menu."

1   Select all the leftover bits of audio in the Narration05 file (or simply press Ctrl+A [Command+A]) and press the Delete key. This clears all the audio and places the playhead at the file's beginning.

2   Clipboard 2 contains the introduction you want. Press Ctrl+2 (Command+2) to select that clipboard, and then choose Edit > Paste or press Ctrl+V (Command+V).

3   Play the file to confirm you have the desired audio. The playhead will stop at the file's end if Skip Selection is disabled or return to the file beginning if Skip Selection is enabled.

4   Click within the Waveform view to deselect the pasted audio. Otherwise, subsequent pasting will replace the selected region.

5   Click where you want to insert the next phrase. For this lesson, you'll place it at the end of the audio file.

6   Clipboard 3 has the desired middle section for this project. Press Ctrl+3 (Command+3), and then press Ctrl+V (Command+V).

7   Repeat steps 4 and 5.

8   Clipboard 1 has the desired ending for this project. Press Ctrl+1 (Command+1), and then press Ctrl+V (Command+V).

Play the file to hear the rearranged audio. For further practice, you can:

- Tighten up spaces between words by selecting a region and pressing Ctrl+X (Command+X) or Delete, or choosing Edit > Cut.

- Add more space between words by placing the playhead where you want to insert silence (don't drag, just click), and then choose Edit > Insert > Silence. When a dialog box appears, enter the desired duration of silence in the format minutes:seconds.hundredths of a second.

## Extending and shortening musical selections

Background music often needs to be lengthened or shortened to fit a video's duration. In this lesson you'll lengthen a piece of music by copying one verse and extending it to create two verses.

1 Navigate to the Lesson03 folder, and open the file Ueberschall_PopCharts.wav. ("Pop Charts" is the name of a commercially available sound library from Ueberschall you can use to create your own royalty-free sound tracks and needledrop music.)

2 Start playback. The verse starts at about 7.5 seconds and ends around 23.2 seconds, where it changes key and goes into a bridge.

3 You need to define the precise verse beginning and end, copy that, and then insert it at the end of the first verse. Place the playhead at the approximate beginning of the verse (around 7.5 seconds).

4 Zoom in until you can see an obvious pulse at 7.74 seconds; this corresponds to the downbeat where the kick drum is prominent. Click at the beginning of the downbeat, and then press M to place a marker there.

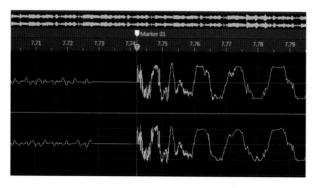

5 Zoom out and locate the end of the verse (around 23.2 seconds).

6 Again, zoom in and place a marker at the beat that happens just after 23.2 seconds.

7 Zoom out until you can see both markers. Choose Edit > Snapping; select Enabled and verify that Snap to Markers is currently enabled.

8   Select the region between the two markers. Note that because you enabled snapping, the markers have a virtual "magnetic field" that "snaps" the region boundaries to the markers when those boundaries are within a certain distance of the markers.

9   Press Ctrl+C (Command+C) or choose Edit > Copy to copy the selected region to the current clipboard.

10  Click within the waveform to deselect the current region, and then click on the second marker. If you click right on the marker, the playhead will snap to it because snapping is enabled. Another option is to click somewhat before the second marker, and then click the transport's Move Playhead to Next button (or press Ctrl+right arrow [Command+right arrow]) to move the playhead directly on top of the marker.

11  Press Ctrl+V (Command+V) or choose Edit > Paste. The pasted verse now follows the first verse before going into the bridge. Play the file from the beginning to verify this.

You can use a similar concept to shorten music. Suppose you want to change the intro's length to half its current length. Note that the intro repeats twice, from 0 seconds to 3.872 seconds and from 3.872 seconds up to the first marker. Here's how to shorten the intro.

1   Place a marker halfway through the intro (this happens at 3.872 seconds). Remember that the marker needs to go at the precise beginning of the beat.

2   Zoom out and select the region between this new marker and the marker that indicates the start of the first verse.

3   Press Ctrl+X (Command+X) or press the Delete key.

4   Play the file to verify that the beginning is now half the original length.

Keep the edited Ueberschall_PopCharts.wav file open and continue. If you need to interrupt this lesson, choose File > Save As and save the file as **Ueberschall_edit**.

# Simultaneous mixing and pasting

Let's add a cymbal to the place where the pasted, second verse begins.

1   With the edited Ueberschall_PopCharts.wav file still open, choose File > Open, navigate to the Lesson03 folder, and open the file Cymbal.wav.

2   Press Ctrl+A (Command+A) to select the entire cymbal sound.

3   Press Ctrl+C (Command+C) to copy the cymbal sound to the current clipboard.

4   From the Editor panel's file selector drop-down menu, choose the Ueberschall_PopCharts.wav file.

5 Click on Marker 01 at 3.5 seconds, which indicates the start of the second verse (the one you pasted in previously).

6 Choose Edit > Mix Paste. A dialog box appears where you can adjust the levels of the copied audio and existing audio.

7 Because you probably don't want an overbearing cymbal sound, set the Copied Audio volume to about 70%, and then click OK.

8 Play the file to hear the cymbal mixed with the original audio to introduce the second verse. Save this file, and then close it before proceeding.

## Repeating part of a waveform to create a loop

Many elements in music are repetitive. A *loop* is a piece of music that lends itself to repetition, like a drum pattern; many companies offer sound libraries of loops that are suitable for creating sound tracks (Lesson 12, "Creating Music with Sound Libraries," covers how to create sound tracks in Audition by using loops). However, it's also possible to create your own loops by extracting a loop from a longer piece of audio.

1 Choose File > Open, navigate to the Lesson03 folder, and open the file Ueberschall_PopCharts.wav.

2 Click the Transport's Loop Playback button, or press Ctrl+L (Command+L).

3 Try to select a region that makes musical sense when looped. You can move the region boundaries during playback. If you have a hard time finding good loop points, set a region to start at 7.742 seconds and end at 9.673. You'll need to zoom in to set these timings accurately.

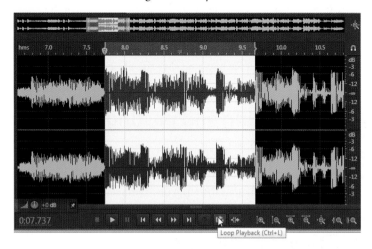

4 Once you've located and selected a suitable loop, choose Edit > Copy to New or press Shift+Alt+C (Shift+Option+C) to copy your loop to a new file that appears in the Editor panel.

You can select between this loop and the original file from which it came using the Editor panel's file selector drop-down menu.

5 With the loop displayed in the Editor panel, choose Edit > Save As or press Shift+Ctrl+S (Shift+Command+S) and navigate to where you want to save the loop. Now you have a loop you can use in other pieces of music.

▶ **Tip:** There are several others ways to save an individual selection. Choose File > Save Selection As to save the selection immediately to disk without having it appear as a file within Audition's Editor panel or be accessible in the Editor panel's file selector drop-down menu. However, note that it's saved to the current clipboard. You can also cut or copy a selection (which of course is saved to the current clipboard), and then choose Edit > Paste to New. This creates a new file that's accessible in the Editor panel's file selector drop-down menu.

## Fading regions to reduce artifacts

Audio may have unintended noises, such as hum or hiss, that are masked when audio like narration is playing but are audible when the narration stops. Other unintended noises can also occur, like "p-pops" (a "popping" sound that happens from the sudden burst of air associated with plosive sounds like "b" or "p"), clicks, mouth noises, and so on. Audition has advanced techniques for removing noise and doing audio restoration, but for simple problems, a fade is often all you need.

1 Choose File > Open, navigate to the Lesson03 folder, and open the file PPop.wav.

2 Zoom in and move the playhead to the start of the file. The keyboard shortcut to do this is Ctrl+left arrow (Command+left arrow). Note the spike at the beginning that corresponds to the "pop."

3 Click the small, square Fade In button in the upper-left corner and drag to the right. You can see the fade attenuating the spike. Dragging the Fade In button up or down alters the fade's shape (up for convex, down for concave). A concave fade is an ideal choice here, because it gets rid of the most objectionable part of the pop but still leaves in the "p" sound.

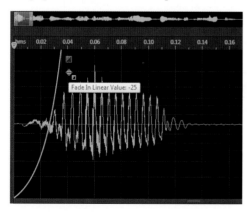

4　There's also another, less objectionable pop at 0.20 seconds. Although you could cut this file to the clipboard, create a new file, add a fade-in, and paste it back into place, an easier solution is simply to select the pop sound as a region and use the HUD's volume control to drop the level by 8 or 9dB.

5　Suppose you want to shorten the file to end with "…that can happen" instead of "that can happen when recording." Zoom in and go to the end of the file. Locate the part that says "when recording," select it as a region, and then press the Delete key.

6　However, now "happen" doesn't end elegantly; there's an audible artifact at the end. You'll use the Fade Out button to reduce this.

7　Click the Fade Out button and drag left to 2.8 seconds. Then drag down to about -30 and release the mouse button to make the fade "stick."

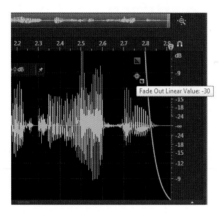

▶ **Tip:** If a file doesn't begin or end on a zero-crossing and you hear a click, adding a very slight fade time will reduce or eliminate the click. Use a convex fade for this application.

8　Play the file to hear that the artifact at the end is gone.

## Review questions

1 What is the easiest way to change level for a selection?

2 Why is it important to have selection boundaries on zero-crossing?

3 How many clipboards does Audition offer?

4 What's the most effective way to eliminate a "p-pop"?

## Review answers

1 As soon as you make a selection, a heads-up display opens with a volume control that lets you change level.

2 Cutting and pasting with selections bounded by zero-crossings tend to minimize clicks.

3 Audition has five individual clipboards that can hold five independent pieces of audio.

4 Placing a fade-in on top of a p-pop lets you determine how much of the pop to minimize and how much to minimize it.

# 4 SIGNAL PROCESSING

## Lesson overview

In this lesson, you'll learn how to do the following:

- Use the Effects Rack to create chains of effects

- Apply effects to audio

- Adjust parameters in various effects to process audio in specific ways

- Alter dynamics, frequency response, ambience, and many other audio attributes

- Simulate guitar amp and effects setups with Guitar Suite effects

- Load third-party plug-in effects with Mac or Windows computers

- Apply single effects rapidly without the Effects Rack by using the Effects menu

- Create favorite presets you can apply immediately to audio simply by selecting them

 This lesson can take several hours to complete, depending on how deeply you want to explore the various processors. Copy the Lesson04 folder that contains the audio examples into the Lessons folder that you created on your hard drive for these projects. Remember that you needn't be concerned about modifying these files, because you can always return to the original versions by copying them from the *Adobe Audition CS6 Classroom in a Book* CD-ROM.

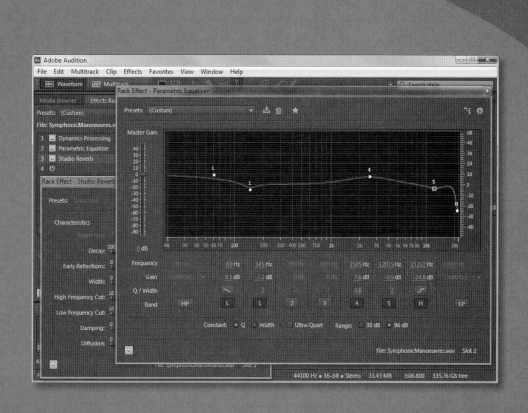

Use signal processors to "sweeten" the audio in multiple ways: fix tonal balance, alter dynamics, add ambience or special effects, and much more. Draw from the extensive collection of effects included in Audition, or use third-party plug-in processors.

# Effects basics

*Effects,* also called *signal processors,* can "sweeten" audio as well as fix problems (such as too much treble or bass). They are the audio equivalent of video effects, like contrast, sharpen, color balance, light rays, pixelate, and so on. In fact, sometimes audio engineers even use similar terms, like "brightness," to describe increased treble.

Adobe Audition includes a wide range of effects. Most can work with the Waveform and Multitrack Editors, but some are available only in the Waveform Editor. There are three main ways of working with effects, which are available in the Waveform and Multitrack Editors.

- **The Effects Rack** allows you to create a chain of up to 16 effects, which you can enable or disable independently. You can add, delete, replace, or reorder effects. The Effects Rack is the most flexible way of working with effects.

- **The Effects menu** allows you to select an individual effect from the Effects menu bar and apply it to whatever audio is selected. When you need to apply only one specific effect, using this menu is quicker than using the Effects Rack. Some effects are available in the Effects menu that are not available in the Effects Rack.

- **The Favorites menu** is the quickest but least flexible way to work with effects. If you come up with a particularly useful effects setting, you can save it as a Favorite preset. The preset is then added to the list of Favorites you can access with the Favorites menu. Selecting it applies that preset instantly to whatever audio is selected; you cannot change any parameter values before applying the effect.

This lesson initially covers using the Effects Rack, which introduces the majority of effects. The second section covers the Effects menu and discusses the remaining effects that are available only via the Effects menu. The final section describes how to work with presets, including Favorites.

# Using the Effects Rack

For all lessons involving the Effects Rack, it is best to use the Default workspace. From the File menu, choose Window > Workspace > Default.

1  Choose File > Open, navigate to the Lesson04 folder, and open the file Drums110.wav.

2  Click the Transport Loop button so the drum pattern plays back continuously. Click the Transport Play button to audition the loop, and then click the Transport Stop button.

**3** Click the Effects Rack tab, and drag the panel's lower splitter bar downward to extend the panel to its full height. You should see 16 "slots," called *inserts*; each of which can hold an individual effect and also includes a power on/off button. A toolbar is located above the inserts, and meters with a second toolbar are below the inserts.

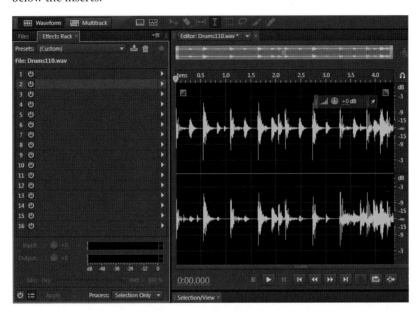

**4** Before exploring individual effects, look at the individual effect's inserts. Although you can't see any graphical connection among them, the effect's inserts are in *series*, meaning that the audio file feeds the first effect input, the first effect output feeds the second effect input, the second effect output feeds the third effect input, and so on until the last effect output goes to your audio interface.

**5** To add an effect to an insert, click the insert's right arrow and choose an effect from the drop-down menu. For the first effect, choose Reverb > Studio Reverb. Inserting an effect turns its power button to "on" (green) and opens the effect's graphic user interface. You may need to move the effect's graphic user interface to load more effects. For the second effect, similarly choose Delay and Echo > Analog Delay.

● **Note:** Effects do not have to go into consecutive inserts. You can leave empty inserts between effects and place effects in these inserts later.

**6** Turn off (bypass) the Analog Delay effect by clicking its power button. Press the spacebar to begin playback, and then turn the Studio Reverb insert's power button on and off to hear how reverb affects the sound.

**7** Click the Rack Effect – Studio Reverb graphic user interface window to bring it to the front. Press the spacebar again to stop playback.

**8** When playback is stopped, you can choose an effect's preset. Click the Studio Reverb's Presets drop-down menu, and select Drum Plate (Large). Begin playback.

You'll hear a more pronounced reverb sound. Note that the effects window has an additional power button in the lower-left corner to make it easy to bypass/compare the processed and unprocessed sound.

**9** Click on the Analog Delay effect graphic user interface to bring it to the front, and then turn on its power button.

You'll hear an echo effect, but it's not in time with the music.

**10** To make the delay follow the rhythm, double-click in the Delay parameter's numeric field, type **545** in place of 200, and then press Enter. The echoes are now in time with the music. (Later in this lesson we'll explain how to choose rhythmically correct delay times.)

Keep this lesson open as you continue.

## Removing, editing, replacing, and moving an effect

Rather than present a structured exercise, try the various bulleted options that follow to see how they work. After each action, choose Edit > Undo [*name of action*] or type Ctrl+Z (Command+Z) to restore the project to its previous state:

- To **remove a *single* effect,** click the effect's insert and press the Delete key, *or* click the insert's right arrow to select Remove Effect from the drop-down menu.

- To **remove *all* effects** in the rack, right-click (Control-click) anywhere on an effect's insert, and then choose Remove All Effects.

- To **remove *some* effects** in the rack, Ctrl-click (Command-click) in each effect insert containing an effect you want to remove. Then right-click (Control-click) anywhere in any selected effect's insert, and choose Remove Selected Effects.

- To **edit an effect** when the effects window is hidden or you closed it, either double-click the effect's insert and click the insert's right arrow to select Edit Effect from the drop-down menu, or right-click (Control-click) anywhere in an effect's insert and choose Edit Selected Effect. Either of these actions brings the effects window to the front and opens it if it was closed.

- To **replace an effect** with a different effect, click the insert's right arrow and select a different effect from the drop-down menu.

- To **move an effect** to a different insert, click the effect's insert and drag to the desired destination insert. If an effect already exists in that insert, the existing effect will be pushed down to the next higher-numbered insert.

## Bypassing all or some effects

You can bypass individual effects, groups of effects, or all effects in the Effects Rack by doing the following:

- The power button in the lower-left corner of the Effects Rack's panel bypasses *all* rack effects that are on. When powered back on, only effects that had been on prior to bypassing return to being on. Bypassed effects remain bypassed regardless of the "all effects" power button setting.

- Right-click (Control-click) on any effect's insert and choose Toggle Power State of Effects Rack.

- To bypass some effects, Ctrl-click (Command-click) on each effect's insert you want to bypass, right-click (Control-click) on any of these inserts, and then choose Toggle Power State of Selected Effects.

## "Gain-staging" effects

Sometimes inserting multiple effects in series causes certain frequencies to "add up" and produce levels that may exceed the available headroom. For example, a filter that emphasizes the midrange could create distortion by increasing levels above acceptable limits.

To set levels, in the lower part of the Effects panel use the Input and Output level controls (with associated meters). These controls can reduce or increase levels as needed.

1 If Audition is open, close it without saving so you can start fresh. Open the program, choose File > Open, navigate to the Lesson04 folder, and open the file Drums110.wav. Do not start playback yet.

2 In any effect's insert, click the right arrow, choose Filter and EQ > Parametric Equalizer from the drop-down menu.

3 When the Parametric EQ window opens, click on the small box labeled 3 and drag it to the graph's top. Close the Parametric EQ window.

**4** *Caution: Turn your monitoring levels way down,* and then press the spacebar to initiate playback. The excessive levels will trigger the output meter's red overload indicators to the meter's right.

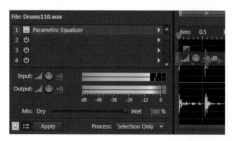

**5** The Input and Output level controls default to +0dB gain, which means neither the signal coming into the Effects Rack, nor the signal leaving it, is amplified or attenuated. However, the massive EQ boost is overloading the output. Turn up the monitoring level enough so you can hear the distortion this causes.

**6** It's generally good practice to keep the Output control at +0dB and compensate for the excessive levels by trimming the Input level. Reduce the Input level until the peaks no longer trigger the red distortion indicators. This will likely require reducing the Input to -35dB or so.

Keep this project open for the next lesson.

## Altering the effect's wet/dry mix

An unprocessed signal is called *dry*, whereas one to which effects have been applied is called *wet*. Sometimes you want a blend of the wet and dry sounds rather than all of one or the other.

**1** With the previous project still open and the levels set properly to avoid distortion, click on the Mix slider below the meters and drag left.

**2** Drag the slider to the right to increase the amount of wet, filtered sound, and drag to the left to increase the amount of dry, unprocessed sound.

## Applying effects

Inserting an effect doesn't change the file but instead plays the original file back through the effect. This is called a *nondestructive* process using a real-time effect, because the original file remains unaltered.

However, you may want to *apply* the effect to the entire file, or only a selection, so that saving the file saves the processed version.

**1** If Audition is open, close it without saving so you can start fresh. Open the program, choose File > Open, navigate to the Lesson04 folder, and open the file Drums110.wav.

> **Tip:** You can click anywhere in the Output meter to reset the red distortion indicators. To reset the Input or Output knob to +0dB, Alt-click (Option-click) on the knob. You can also toggle the Meters/ Controls view with the button to the right of the panel's master on/off switch in the lower left.

> **Tip:** Using the Mix slider to blend in more dry sound provides an easy way to make an effect more subtle.

2   In any effect's insert, click the right arrow and choose Reverb > Studio Reverb.

3   When the Studio Reverb window appears, choose the preset Drum Plate (Small) from the presets drop-down menu.

4   The Process drop-down menu, located in the toolbar at the bottom of the Effects Rack panel, allows you to apply the effect to the entire file or just a selection. For this lesson, choose Entire File.

5   Click the Apply button. This not only applies the effect to the file to process it, but deletes the effect from the Effects Rack so the file isn't "double processed" from the effect being embedded in the file and from a processor remaining in the rack.

6   Close the project without saving by choosing File > Close All.

Let's move on to lessons that show how individual effects change the sound.

# Amplitude and Compression effects

Amplitude and Compression effects change levels or alter dynamics. You'll load each effect individually to hear how each one changes the sound.

## Amplify

Amplify can make a file louder or softer. When increasing amplitude to make a file louder, choose a low enough amount of amplification so that the file remains undistorted.

1   If Audition is open, close it without saving so you can start fresh. Open the program, choose File > Open, navigate to the Lesson04 folder, and open the file Drums+Bass+Arp110.wav.

2   Click an Effects Rack insert's right arrow button, and then choose Amplitude and Compression > Amplify.

**Note:** You can insert additional effects into the Effects Rack to change the sound further, and then apply those effects. The file will then reflect the changes caused by all the effects you've applied. Also note that any changes are still not permanent until you save (using either Save or Save As) the file. At that point, the effects will be embedded permanently in the file.

**3**  Enable looping on the Transport, and then start playback.

Amplify has only one parameter, Gain, which varies from -96dB (maximum attenuation) to +48dB (maximum amplification). With Link Sliders selected, adjusting gain for one channel changes gain equally in the other channel. Deselecting Link Sliders allows for adjusting each channel individually.

**4**  With Link Sliders selected, click the Gain slider and drag left (attenuation) or right (amplification). You can also drag up/down or left/right in the numerical field to change gain in integer increments, or double-click on the numerical field and type in a specific number.

**5**  Using the numerical field, increase the gain to **+2dB**, and observe the Output meters. They do not go into the red so it is safe to increase the gain by this amount. Now increase the gain to **+3dB**. The Output meter goes into the red, which shows that the gain is too high and is overloading the output. Also, try decreasing the level and listen to the results.

**6**  Stop playback, click on the effect's insert with Amplify applied, and press the Delete key. Keep Audition open.

## Channel Mixer

The Channel Mixer alters the amount of left and right channel signal present in the left and right channels. Consider two possible applications: converting stereo to mono and reversing the left and right channels.

**1**  Click an Effects Rack insert's right arrow button, and then choose Amplitude and Compression > Channel Mixer.

**2**  With looping enabled on the Transport, begin playback.

**3**  Click the Channel Mixer's L (left) tab. It's currently set so that the left channel consists entirely of signal from the left channel. You'll convert this stereo signal into a monaural signal by having equal amounts of left and right channel signals in the left and right channels.

**4**  With the L tab still selected, move both the L and R sliders to 50.

**5**  Bypass the Channel Mixer using either the Effects Rack's power on/off button or the one in the Channel Mixer panel's lower left. When bypassed, the stereo image is wider.

**6**  Enable the Channel Mixer by making sure the power button is on, and let's complete converting the signal to mono.

7  Click the R tab and adjust the L and R sliders to 50. Now the signal is monaural. Bypass and enable the Channel Mixer to verify.

8  The Channel Mixer also makes it easy to swap channels. Click the L tab and set the L slider to 0 and the R slider to 100. Now the left channel consists entirely of signal from the right channel.

9  Click the R tab. Set the L slider to 100 and the R slider to 0. Now the right channel consists entirely of signal from the left channel.

10  Bypass and enable the Channel Mixer; doing so reverses the two channels. When bypassed, the hi-hat is in the left channel. When enabled, it's in the right channel.

11  Stop playback, click the effect's insert that contains the Channel Mixer, and then press the Delete key. Keep Audition open.

## DeEsser

Audition's DeEsser reduces vocal sibilants ("ess" sounds). De-essing is a three-step process: Identify the frequencies where sibilants exist, define that range, and then set a threshold, which if exceeded by a sibilant, automatically reduces the gain within the specified range. This makes the sibilant less prominent.

1  If Audition is open, close it without saving so you can start fresh. Choose File > Open, navigate to the Lesson04 folder, and open the file DeEsser.wav.

2  Click an Effects Rack insert's right arrow button, and then choose Amplitude and Compression > DeEsser.

3  Enable looping on the Transport, and then start playback.

4  As the file plays, you'll see a display of the frequency spectrum. Sibilants are high frequencies. Look carefully at the spectrum and confirm that you see peaks in the range around 10000Hz.

5  To make it easier to find the sibilants, set the Threshold to -40dB and Bandwidth to 7500Hz.

**Note:** Converting stereo to mono is a common enough operation that the Channel Mixer preset named All Channels 50% performs this conversion.

6   Vary the Center Frequency. When set to maximum (12000Hz), you can still hear quite a bit of sibilance because this is higher than the sibilants' frequency. Similarly, when set to minimum (500Hz), the sibilants are above this range and are still audible. You'll find a "sweet spot" between 9000 and 10000Hz that reduces sibilants.

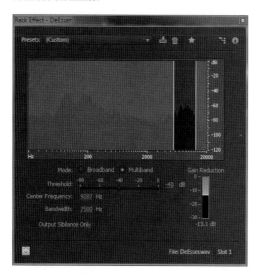

7   To fine-tune this further, select Output Sibilance Only. Now you'll hear only the sibilants. Adjust the Center Frequency to hear the greatest amount of sibilants and the least amount of the voice, which will be around 10400Hz. The Gain Reduction meter shows the sibilant range's attenuation.

8   Deselect Output Sibilance Only, and bypass/enable the DeEsser to hear the difference.

9   Stop playback, click the effect's insert that includes the DeEsser, and press the Delete key.

10  Choose File > Close and don't save the file. Keep Audition open.

## Dynamics processing

With a standard amplifier, the relationship between the input and output is linear. In other words, if there's a gain of 1, the output signal will be the same as the input signal. If there's a gain of 2, the output signal will have twice the level of the input signal, whatever the input signal level may be.

A Dynamics Processor changes the relationship of the output to the input. This change is called *compression* when a large input signal increase produces only a small output signal increase and *expansion* when a small input signal increase produces a large output signal increase. Both can be present at the same time by expanding signals within one range of levels and compressing signals in a different range of levels. The Dynamics Processor's graph shows the input signal on the horizontal axis and the output on the vertical axis.

Compression can make a sound subjectively louder and is the tool that makes TV commercials SO MUCH LOUDER THAN EVERYTHING ELSE. Expansion is less common; one application is to expand objectionable low-level signals (like hiss) to reduce their levels further. There are also many uses for both as special effects.

In the following graph, as the input signal changes from -100dB to -40dB, the output changes from -100dB to only -95dB. As a result, the Dynamics Processor has compressed 60dB of input dynamic range into 5dB of change at the output. But from -40dB to 0dB, the output changes from -95dB to 0dB. Therefore, the Dynamics Processor has expanded 40dB of input dynamic range into 95dB of output dynamic range.

In the graph these ranges are given a segment number, and the area below the graph provides information about each segment:

- The segment number

- The relationship between output and input expressed as a ratio

- Whether the segment is an Expander or Compressor

- The Threshold (range of levels) where the expansion or compression takes effect

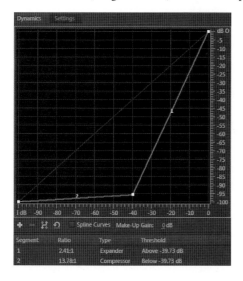

The easiest way to become familiar with dynamics processing is to call up presets, listen to how they affect the sound, and correlate what you hear to what you see on the graph.

1 Choose File > Open, navigate to the Lesson04 folder, and open the file Drums+Bass+Arp110.wav.

**2** Click an Effects Rack insert's right arrow button, and then choose Amplitude and Compression > Dynamics Processing.

**3** Enable looping on the Transport, and then start playback.

**4** Select various presets. Note that you will need to turn down the Effects Rack's Output level with some of the more "aggressive" presets to avoid distortion.

**5** Create your own dynamics processing. Choose the (Default) preset, which provides neither compression nor expansion.

**6** Click on the little white square in the upper right and drag it down slowly to around -10dB. You'll hear how this brings down peaks and makes the sound less dynamic.

**7** Create a less abrupt change. Click in the middle of segment 1 (e.g., where the segment crosses -15dB) to create another square. Drag it up a little bit to around -12dB.

**8** Now you'll use expansion to reduce low-level sounds. Click on the line at -30dB and -40dB to create two more squares. Click on the one at -40dB, and drag it down all the way to -100dB. This effect makes the drums sound more percussive.

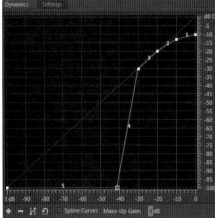

**Note:** Audition's Dynamics Processor is extremely sophisticated. Although you've just experienced the basic concepts in the dynamics processing exercise, the Settings page allows for further customization and effects. Basic compression and expansion can solve most audio problems that need dynamics control, but please refer to the Audition documentation for detailed information on other Dynamics Processor parameters.

**9** Look at the Effects Rack's Output meter. Bypass the dynamics processing, and you'll note that the signal is actually a little louder because compression has reduced the peaks. To compensate for this, click in the Dynamics Processor's Make-Up Gain parameter located just below the curve's horizontal axis. Increase the gain by +4dB.

**10** Bypass and enable the Dynamics Processor. By adding Make-Up gain, the processed signal is now a little bit louder.

**11** Stop playback, click the effect's insert with the Dynamics Processor, and press the Delete key. Don't close the file, and leave Audition open.

## Hard limiter

Like an engine's governor that limits the maximum number of RPMs, a *limiter* restricts an audio signal's maximum output level. For example, if you don't want an audio file to exceed a level of -10dB, yet there are some peaks that reach -2dB, set the limiter's Maximum Amplitude for -10dB and it will "absorb" the peaks so they don't exceed -10dB. This is different from simple attenuation (which lowers the levels of *all* signals), because in this example of limiting, levels below -10dB remain untouched. Levels above -10dB are compressed with an essentially infinite ratio, so *any* input level increase produces no output level increase above -10dB.

This limiter also has an Input Boost parameter, which can make a signal subjectively louder. Here's why: If you set the Maximum Amplitude to 0, you can increase the level of an input signal that already reaches the maximum headroom because the limiter will prevent it from distorting by "clamping" its output to 0. Let's listen to how this affects a mix.

1   With the Drums+Bass+Arp110.wav still loaded, click an Effects Rack insert's right arrow button, and choose Amplitude and Compression > Hard Limiter.

2   Enable looping on the Transport, and then start playback.

3   Look at the Maximum Amplitude numeric field to confirm that the default value is -0.1. This level ensures that the signal won't hit zero, so the output won't trigger the red zone in the Effects Rack panel's Output level meters.

4   Raise the Input Boost amount above 0 while observing the Output level meters. Note that even if you add lots of boost, like 10dB, the output still doesn't go above -0.1, and the Output meters never go into the red.

5   The Release Time sets how long it takes for the limiter to stop limiting after a signal no longer exceeds the maximum amplitude. In most cases the default is fine. With a fair amount of input boost, shorter Release settings—even though they limit the signal more accurately—produce a "choppy" effect. With the Input Boost set to around +16dB, move the Release Time slider all the way to the right to hear this "choppiness." When using the Release Time slider, the rule of thumb is to set it for the most natural sound.

6   The Look-Ahead Time allows the limiter to react to fast transients. With no look-ahead time, the limiter has to react *instantly* to a transient, which is not possible: It has to know a transient exists before it can decide what to do with it. Look-Ahead alerts the limiter when a transient is coming, so the reaction can be instantaneous. Longer settings cause a slight delay through the effect, although in most cases this doesn't matter. The default setting is fine, but experiment with increasing the Look-Ahead Time slider if the transients sound "mushy."

**Note:** There's a point of diminishing returns with hard limiting. Past a certain amount of input boost, the sound will become unnatural. The level at which this will occur varies depending on the input signal source. With voice, you can usually get away with more boost than with a full mix of something like a band.

## Single-Band Compressor

The Single-Band Compressor is a "classic" compressor for dynamic range compression and is an excellent choice for learning about how compression works.

As explained in the "Dynamics processing" section, compression changes the relationship of the output signal to the input signal. The two most important parameters are Threshold (the level above which compression starts to occur) and Ratio, which sets the amount of change in the output signal for a given input signal change. For example, with a 4:1 ratio, a 4dB increase in input level produces a 1dB increase at the output. With an 8:1 ratio, an 8dB increase in input level produces a 1dB increase at the output. In this lesson you'll hear how compression affects the sound.

1  If the Drums+Bass+Arp110.wav is not open, close any currently open files and open it. Also, delete any currently loaded effects.

2  Click the Effects Rack insert's right arrow button, and choose Amplitude and Compression > Single-Band Compressor.

3  Enable looping on the Transport, and then start playback.

4  Assuming the Default preset is loaded, move the Threshold slider over its full range. You won't hear any difference because the Ratio defaults to 1:1, so there's a linear relationship between the output and input.

5  With Threshold at 0, move the Ratio slider over its full range. Again you won't hear any difference, because all audio will lie below the Threshold—so there's nothing above the Threshold that can be affected by the Ratio slider. This shows how the Threshold and Ratio controls interrelate, and explains why you usually need to go back and forth between these two controls to dial in the right amount of compression.

6  Set the Threshold slider to -20dB and the Ratio slider to 1. Slowly increase the Ratio slider by moving it to the right. The farther you move it to the right, the more compressed the sound. Leave the Ratio slider at 10 (i.e., 10:1).

7  Experiment with the Threshold slider. The lower the Threshold, the more compressed the sound; below about -20dB, with a Ratio of 10:1, the sound becomes so compressed as to be unusable. Leave the Threshold slider at -10dB for now.

8  Look at the Effects Rack panel's Output meter. When you bypass the Single-Band Compressor, note that the meters are more animated and have more pronounced peaks. Enable the Single-Band Compressor; the signal's peaks are less dynamic and more uniform.

9   Note the maximum peak level in bypassed mode. Then with the Single-Band Compressor enabled, adjust its Output Gain control to around 2.5-3.0dB, so its peaks match the same level as when bypassed. Now when you compare the bypassed and enabled states, you'll hear that despite having the same peak levels, the compressed version sounds louder. The reason is that reducing peaks allows for increasing the overall output gain without exceeding the available headroom or causing distortion.

10  It's possible to make this difference even more pronounced. Attack sets a delay before the compression occurs after a signal exceeds the threshold. Allowing a slight Attack time, like the default setting of 10ms, lets through percussive transients up to 10ms in duration before the compression kicks in. This retains some of a signal's natural percussiveness. Now set the Attack time to 0.

11  Again, observe the Output level meters. With 0 Attack time, the peaks have been reduced even further, which means the Single-Band Compressor Output Gain can go even higher; set it to 6dB, and when you enable/bypass the Single-Band Compressor, the peak levels are the same—yet the compressed version sounds a lot "bigger."

12  Release determines how long it takes for the compression to stop compressing once the signal falls below the threshold. There are no rules about Release time; basically, set it subjectively for the smoothest, most natural sound, which will usually lie between 200 and 1000ms.

13  Keep Audition open and loaded with the same file.

## Tube-Modeled Compressor

The Tube-Modeled Compressor has the same control complement as the Single-Band Compressor but offers a slightly different, somewhat less "crisp" sonic character. You can use the same basic steps as in the previous lesson to explore the Tube-Modeled Compressor. The one obvious difference is that the Tube-Modeled Compressor has two meters: the one on the left shows the input signal level, and the one on the right shows how much the gain is being reduced to provide the specified amount of compression.

## Multiband Compressor

The Multiband Compressor is another variation on the "classic" Single-Band Compressor. It divides the frequency spectrum into four bands, each with its own compressor. Therefore, it's possible to compress some frequencies more than others, such as adding lots of compression to bass but only a moderate amount of compression in the upper midrange.

Dividing the signal into four bands also embodies elements of equalization (described later), because you can alter a signal's frequency response.

If you think adjusting a Single-Band Compressor is complex, a Multiband Compressor with four bands isn't just four times as complex—all these stages also interact with each other. Rather than describe how to create a multiband compression setting from scratch, you'll load various presets and analyze why they sound the way they do. Note that each band has an S (Solo) button, so you can hear what that band alone is doing.

1  If the Drums+Bass+Arp110.wav is not open, close any currently open files and open it. Also, delete any currently loaded effects.

2  Click an Effects Rack insert's right arrow button, and choose Amplitude and Compression > Multiband Compressor.

3  Enable looping on the Transport, and then start playback.

4  The Default preset doesn't apply any multiband compression, so listen to that first as a point of reference.

5  Load the Broadcast preset, which gives a major boost to the sound. Note that the highest and lowest bands have more gain and a higher compression ratio, which give a little more "sizzle" and "depth," respectively.

6  Load the Enhance Highs preset. This shows how multiband compression can add an element of equalization; the output gain for the two upper bands is considerably higher than the two lower bands.

7  Load the Enhance Lows preset. This is the mirror image of the Enhance Highs preset. The two lower bands' output gain is higher than the two higher bands.

8  Load the Hiss Reduction preset, and notice that there's a lot less highs. The reason is that the highest band has an extremely low threshold of -50dB, so even low-level, high-frequency sounds are compressed.

## Speech Volume Leveler

The Speech Volume Leveler incorporates three processors—leveling, compression, and gating—to even out level variations with narration, as well as reduce background noise with some signals.

1  If Audition is open, close it without saving. Open the program, choose File > Open, navigate to the Lesson04 folder, and open the file NarrationNeedsHelp.wav.

2  Click an Effects Rack insert's right arrow button, and choose Amplitude and Compression > Speech Volume Leveler.

3   Bypass the effect, and listen to the file all the way through. Note the two quiet parts where the narration says, "Most importantly, you need to maintain good backups of your data" and "Recovering that data will be a long and expensive process." The rest is at a reasonable volume. You'll use the Speech Volume Leveler to match the levels.

4   Select the audio that says, "Most importantly, you need to maintain good backups of your data." Move the Speech Volume Leveler sliders for Target Volume Level and Leveling Amount all the way to the left, and then enable the effect.

5   Click the Transport Loop button, and then click Play.

6   Move the Leveling Amount slider to the right while observing the Input and Output meters in the Effects Rack panel. As you move the slider to the right, the output will become louder than the input. Choose a value of about 60 for now. The output will peak at around -6dB.

7   Select the audio that says, "If all your precious music is stored on a hard drive," loop it and play it. Adjust the Target Volume Level until the peaks match the peaks you saw in step 6. The slider should be around -19dB.

8   Double-click on the waveform to select it all, and then listen. There should be fewer volume variations between the soft and loud sections.

9   Click the disclosure triangle next to the Advanced options to reveal two more settings.

10  To even out levels even further, enable the compressor and move the Threshold to the left (more negative numbers) to produce a consistent, natural sound.

11  High Leveling Amount settings can bring up low-level noise, and the Noise Gate can compensate for this. To best hear how this works, with the Leveling Amount at the default setting of 100, select the audio between 2 and 6 seconds, and loop it.

12  Note that the noise becomes very prominent in the space between "data" and "if." Select the Noise Gate, and move the Noise Offset slider all the way to the right (25dB). This doesn't eliminate the noise but reduces it considerably. Move the Leveling Amount back to 60, and the noise goes away.

13  Click the power button to bypass and enable the Speech Volume Leveler a few times so you can hear how the effect alters the sound. Observe the meters, and see if further tweaking can help create a more consistent output. For this particular file, a setting with Compressor and Noise Gate off, Target Volume Level at -18dB, and a Leveling Amount of 50% seems about optimum.

14 To see how this process affects the file's waveform, in the lower part of the Effects Rack panel, choose Process: Entire File from the drop-down menu, and then click Apply. You'll see that the waveform is much more consistent. In the illustration the top waveform is the original file, whereas the lower one has been processed by the Speech Volume Leveler. To compare the two, choose Edit > Undo Apply Effects Rack, and then choose Edit > Redo Apply Effects Rack.

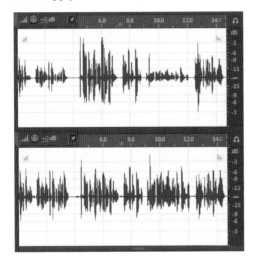

# Delay and echo effects

Adobe Audition has three echo effects with different capabilities. All delay effects store audio in memory and then play it back later. The time that elapses between storing it and playing it back is the delay time.

## Delay

Delay simply repeats the audio, with the repeat's start time specified by the delay amount.

1 If Audition is open, choose File > Close All. Don't save any changes. Choose File > Open, navigate to the Lesson04 folder, and open the file Arpeggio110.wav.

2 Click an Effects Rack insert's right arrow button, and then choose Delay and Echo > Delay.

3 The Mix slider sets the proportion of dry and delayed audio. Set the Right Channel to full Dry and the Left channel to full Wet. This makes it easy to hear the difference between the delayed signal in the left channel and the dry signal in the right channel.

**4**  Set the left channel Delay Time slider full right (500ms). You'll now hear the left channel arpeggio delayed by half a second compared to the right channel.

**5**  Set the left channel Delay Time slider full left (-500ms). You'll now hear the arpeggio start half a second *earlier* in the left channel than in the right channel.

**6**  Set both Mix sliders to 50%, and experiment with different delay times. You'll hear a mix of delayed and dry sounds in each channel. Leave Adobe Audition open for the next lesson.

## Analog Delay

Before digital technology, delay used tape or analog delay chip technology. These produced a more gritty, colored sound compared to digital delay. Audition's Analog Delay provides a single delay for stereo or mono signals and offers three different delay modes: Tape (slight distortion), Tape/Tube (crisper version of tape), and Analog (more muffled). Analog Delay simply repeats the audio with the start time of the repeat specified by the delay amount. Unlike the Delay effect, there are separate controls for Dry and Wet levels instead of a single Mix control. The Delay slider provides the same function as the Delay effect except that the maximum delay time is 8 seconds.

**1**  If Audition is open, choose File > Close All. Don't save any changes. Choose File > Open, navigate to the Lesson04 folder, and open the file Drums110.wav.

**2**  Click an Effects Rack insert's right arrow button, and then choose Delay and Echo > Analog Delay.

**3**  Set Dry Out to 60%, Wet Out to 40%, and Delay to 545ms. Feedback determines the number of repeats as they fade out. No Feedback (a setting of 0) produces a single echo, values moving toward 100 produce more echoes, and values above 100 produce "runaway echoes" (watch your monitor volume!).

**4**  With feedback at 50, set the Trash control to 100. Change the different modes (Tape, Tape/Tube, Analog) to hear how each affects the sound. Vary the feedback, being careful to avoid excessive, runaway feedback.

**5**  Spread at 0% narrows the echoes to mono and at 200% produces a wide stereo effect. Play with the various controls, and you'll hear anything from dance mix drum effects to 1950s sci-fi movie sounds. Keep Audition open for the next lesson.

## Echo

Audition's Echo effect allows for tailoring the echoes' frequency response by inserting a filter in the delay's feedback loop, where the output feeds back to the input to create additional echoes. As a result, each successive echo processes each echo's timbre to a greater degree. For example, if the response is set to be brighter than normal, each echo will be brighter than the previous one.

● **Note:** You can specify delay time (lower-left drop-down menu) in milliseconds, beats, or samples. Beats is most useful in Multitrack view, where the project has a particular tempo. Samples is useful for tuning out short timing differences, because you can specify delays down to 1 sample (at a 44,100Hz sample rate, that's a delay of 22.7 microseconds or 0.00002267 seconds).

▶ **Tip:** With rhythmic material, correlating delay to the rhythm creates a more "musical" effect. Use the formula 60,000/tempo in bpm (beats per minute) to determine the echo for a quarter note. For example, the drum loop tempo is 110 bpm, so the echo time for a quarter note is 60,000/110 = 545.45ms. An eighth note is half that or 272.72ms, a 16th note is 136.36ms, and so on. The Lesson04 folder includes a file called Period vs. Tempo. xls. Enter a tempo in this spreadsheet to see the number of milliseconds and samples that correspond to particular rhythmic values.

**Tip:** To set both channels to the same Delay Time, enable Lock Left and Right. Adjusting either channel will adjust the other to the same value.

1   With the Drum110.wav file open, assuming the Analog Delay effect is still inserted, click its insert's right arrow, and then choose Delay and Echo > Echo.

2   Compared to the previous delay effects, Echo has yet another way of setting the echo mix; each channel has an Echo Level control that dials in the echo amount. The Dry signal is fixed. When using the echo effect, enter the following values for the left channel: Delay Time **545ms**, Feedback **90%**, and Echo Level **70%**. Enter the following values for the right channel: Delay Time **1090ms**, Feedback **70%**, and Echo Level **70%**.

3   Bring all Successive Echo Equalization controls all the way down (-15dB). That makes it easier to hear the difference moving a single slider has on the sound.

4   Raise the 1.4kHz control to 0 (values above 0 produce runaway echo) and note how the sound is more "midrangey."

5   Bring down the 1.4kHz slider and raise the 7.4kHz slider to 0. Now the echoes are brighter.

6   Return the 7.4kHz slider to -15dB, and raise the 172Hz slider to 0. The echoes are now bassy.

7   You can vary more than one slider at a time to create a more complex equalization curve, as well as enable Echo Bounce to have each channel's echo bounce between the left and right channels.

## Filter and EQ effects

Equalization is an extremely important effect for adjusting tonality. For example, you can "brighten" muffled narration by boosting the treble or make tinny, thin-sounding voices sound fuller by increasing the low frequencies. Equalization can also help differentiate among different instruments; for example, bass guitar and a drum kit's kick drum both occupy the low frequencies and can interact in a way that makes each one less distinct. To solve this problem, some engineers might emphasize the bass's highs to bring out pick and string noise, whereas others boost highs on the kick to bring out the "thwack" of the beater.

Adobe Audition has four different equalizer effects, each used for different purposes, that can adjust tonality and solve frequency-response related problems: Parametric Equalizer, Graphic Equalizer, FFT (Fast Fourier Transform) Filter, and Notch Filter.

### Parametric Equalizer

The Parametric Equalizer offers nine stages of equalization. Five stages have a *parametric* response, which can boost (make more prominent) or cut (make less prominent) specific ranges ("bands") of the frequency spectrum. Each parametric equalization stage has three parameters.

*Caution:* In the following lesson, keep monitor levels down as you make adjustments. The Parametric Equalizer is capable of high amounts of gain at the selected frequencies.

1  If Audition is open, close it without saving to start fresh. Open the program, choose File > Open, navigate to the Lesson04 folder, and open the file Drums+Bass+Arp110.wav.

2  In any Effects Rack insert, click the right arrow, and choose Filter and EQ > Parametric Equalizer. Start playback.

3  Note the five numbered boxes. Each represents a controllable parametric stage. Click one of them (e.g., 3) and drag up to boost response, or drag down to reduce response. Drag left to affect lower frequencies or right to affect higher frequencies. Listen to how this changes the sound.

4  In the area below the graph, each parametric stage shows the Frequency, Gain, and Q/Width parameters. Click on the Q/Width parameter and drag up to narrow the range affected by the boost or cut, or drag down to widen the range. You can also click on the stage's number to toggle that stage on or off.

5  Load the Default preset to restore the EQ to having no effect. The L and H squares control a *low shelf* and *high shelf* response, respectively. This starts boosting or cutting at the selected frequency, but the boost or cut extends outward toward the extremes of the audio spectrum. Past a certain frequency, the response hits a "shelf" equal to the maximum amount of cut.

6  Click on the H box and drag it up slightly. Note how this increases the treble. Now drag it to the left, and you'll hear that the boost now affects a wider range of high frequencies. Similarly, click on the L box to hear how this affects the low frequencies. In the Parameter section for the Low and High shelf sections, you can click the Q/Width button to change the steepness of the shelf's slope.

7  Reload the Default preset so the EQ has no effect. There are two additional stages, Highpass and Lowpass, which you enable by clicking on the HP and LP buttons, respectively. Click those buttons now.

8  A Highpass response progressively reduces response below a certain frequency (called the cutoff frequency); the lower the frequency is below the cutoff, the greater the reduction. A Highpass filter is helpful for removing subsonic (very low-frequency) energy. Click on the HP box and drag it to the right to hear how it affects low frequencies.

9  You can also change the filter slope's steepness, in other words, the rate of attenuation compared to frequency. In the HP panel that displays its parameters, click the Gain drop-down menu and choose 6dB/octave. Note how this creates a gradual curve. Then select 48dB/octave to produce a steep curve.

10  Similarly, listen to how the Lowpass filter affects the sound by clicking the LP (Lowpass) button, dragging the LP box left or right, and choosing different curves as accessed from the Gain menu. Keep this project open for the next lesson.

**Note:** The strip along the bottom of the screen has three additional options. Constant Q, where Q is a ratio compared to frequency, is most common, whereas Constant Width means the Q is the same regardless of frequency. The Ultra-Quiet option reduces noise and artifacts but requires much more processing power and can usually be left off. Range sets the maximum amount of boost or cut to 30dB or 96dB. The more common option is 30dB.

All of these responses are available simultaneously. The screen shot shows a steep Highpass slope, a slight parametric boost with stage 2, a narrow parametric cut with stage 3, and a High shelf boost.

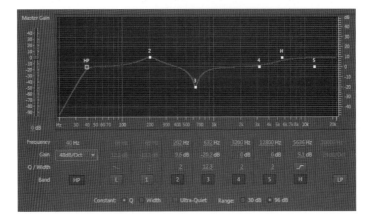

## Graphic Equalizer (10 Bands)

A Graphic Equalizer can boost or cut with a fixed bandwidth at various fixed frequencies. It gets its name because moving the sliders creates a "graph" of the filter's frequency response.

*Caution:* In the following lesson, keep monitor levels down as you make adjustments. The Graphic Equalizer can produce high amounts of gain at specific frequencies.

1 Assuming Audition is still open and the file Drum+Bass+Arp110.wav is still loaded, click the right arrow of the insert that had the Parametric Equalizer loaded, and choose Filter and EQ > Graphic Equalizer (10 Bands).

2 Start playback. Move the various sliders up and down to hear how each affects the timbre through varying the level within their respective frequency bands. In musical terms, each slider is an octave apart. Keep Audition open in preparation for the next lesson.

**Note:** The strip along the bottom of the Graphic Equalizer screen has three additional parameters. Range sets the maximum available amount of boost or cut up to 120dB (which is a lot!). It's easier to make fine adjustments with narrower ranges, like 6–12dB. Accuracy affects low-frequency processing. If you're doing significant amounts of low-frequency boost or cut, raise Accuracy if it improves the sound. Otherwise, leave it at the default of 1000 points to reduce CPU loading. Master gain compensates for Output level changes caused by using the EQ. Turn it down if you added lots of boosting; turn it up if you used lots of cutting.

## Graphic Equalizer (20 Bands)

The Graphic Equalizer (20 Bands) works identically to the Graphic Equalizer (10 Bands) except the bands are half an octave apart, which provides greater resolution. To hear how it works, follow the same basic procedure as the lesson for the 10 Bands version.

## Graphic Equalizer (30 Bands)

The Graphic Equalizer (30 Bands) works identically to the Graphic Equalizer (20 Bands) except the bands are a third of an octave apart, which provides greater resolution. To hear how it works, follow the same basic procedure as the lesson for the 10 Bands version.

## FFT Filter

The FFT Filter is an extremely flexible filter that lets you "draw" the frequency response. The default settings are a practical point of departure. FFT is a highly efficient algorithm commonly used for frequency analysis.

1 Assuming Audition is still open and the file Drum+Bass+Arp110.wav is still loaded, click the right arrow of the insert that had a Graphic Equalizer loaded, and choose Filter and EQ > FFT Filter.

2 Start playback. Click on the graph to create a point; the blue line that indicates frequency response will move up or down as needed to "snap" to that point. You can then drag this point up, down, or sideways. You are not limited to the number of points you can add, which allows you to make very complex—and even truly bizarre—EQ curves and shapes.

3 For a smoother curve, enable Spline Curves. The screen shot on the left shows Spline Curves deselected and the original placement of points, whereas the screen shot on the right shows Spline Curves selected.

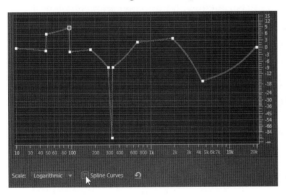 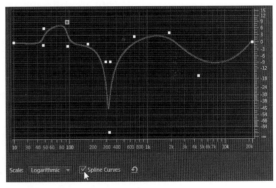

> ● **Note:** As for other FFT Filter parameters, for Scale choose Logarithmic when working primarily with low frequencies because this produces the best resolution for drawing in nodes. Linear has the same advantage at high frequencies. For the Advanced options, for the best accuracy with steep, precise filters, choose higher values like 8192 to 32678. Lower values produce fewer transients with percussive sounds. For Window, Hamming and Blackman are the best overall choices. The choices listed first narrow the shape of the response curve with subsequent choices progressively widening the shape.

## Notch Filter

The Notch Filter is optimized to remove very specific frequencies in an audio file, like hum.

1   If Audition is open, close it without saving to start fresh. Open the program, choose File > Open, navigate to the Lesson04 folder, and open the file ReduceHum.wav.

2   Click the right arrow of an effect's insert, and choose Filter and EQ > Notch Filter.

3   Bypass the Notch Filter, and then start playback. Note the huge amount of hum in the file.

4   Select the Notch Filter. The filter's default setting is a good start (Europeans should select the 50Hz and Harmonics Removal preset instead of the 60Hz-based default), but note that there's some ringing and an unnatural quality. You'll now tweak the settings to reduce hum while retaining a natural sound.

5   There are six notches starting at 60Hz whose frequencies are set to harmonics of 60Hz. Turn off all notches that don't improve the sound by clicking a notch's enable button. Turn off notches 3, 4, 5, and 6. Note that this doesn't increase the amount of hum. Turn off notches 1 and 2. These contribute hum, so reenable them and let's work on optimizing these.

6   Reduce the gain for notches 1 and 2 to around -45dB.

7   For the most natural sound, you want to use the least amount of reduction consistent with reducing hum. Experiment with the Gain parameters for notches 1 and 2. You'll probably be able to get by with about -36dB of cut.

8   Bypass the Notch Filter, and note how the hum increases.

# Modulation effects

Unlike some of the previous effects we've discussed, modulation effects aren't designed to solve problems as much as add "spice" to sounds in the form of special effects. These tend to produce very specific sounds, and the presets included with Adobe Audition are a good place to start. Therefore, with most of these effects, you'll call up presets to hear how they affect the sound. But there will also be some analysis of which parameters are most important for editing.

# Chorus

Chorus can turn a single sound into what seems like an ensemble. This effect uses short delays to create additional "voices" from the original signal. These delays are modulated so that the delay varies slightly over time, which produces a more "animated" sound.

The Chorus effect is optimized for stereo signals, so convert mono signals to stereo for best results. To do this, choose Edit > Convert Sample Type, and from the Channels drop-down menu, choose Stereo. Then click OK.

1  If Audition is open, close it without saving to start fresh. Open the program, choose File > Open, navigate to the Lesson04 folder, and open the file FemaleChoir.wav. Play the file to hear what it sounds like.

2  Click the right arrow of an effect's insert, and choose Modulation > Chorus.

3  Note how with Chorus enabled the Default preset creates a fuller and bigger sound. Select Highest Quality; most modern computers can provide the additional processing power this option needs. If the audio crackles or breaks up, deselect this option.

4  Increase Modulation Depth to 8dB or so. Notice how the sound becomes more animated. To make this more obvious, increase the Modulation Rate to 2.5Hz. Modulation Depth and Rate interact; with a higher Rate, you'll usually want a lower Depth. Return Modulation Depth to 0.

5  To increase the "number of people" in the chorus, click the Voices drop-down menu and choose 16 voices. Because this adds a lot more audio, you may need to bring down the Output control in the Effects Rack panel to avoid distortion.

6  Increasing the Delay Time can also make a bigger sound, but too much Delay Time may produce an "out of tune" effect. Set it to around 40ms for now.

7  Spread increases the stereo image width. Set it to around 152ms. Bypass/enable the Chorus to hear the effect of these edits.

8  With Chorus enabled, note the Dry and Wet Output level controls. For a more subtle effect, set a higher Dry value and lower Wet value, or turn up only the Wet sound for the most "diffused" character.

9  Be careful with Feedback, because even slight amounts can add uncontrolled feedback. Values up to about 10 can produce a more "swirling" sound for the Chorus.

10  The remaining controls apply to stereo imaging. Stereo Field makes the output narrower or wider. For Average Left & Right Channel Output and Add Binaural Cues, simply select these. If you like the sound better, leave them selected. If there's no audible difference, leave them deselected. Leave Average Left & Right Channel Output deselected if the original signal was mono.

**11** To get a sense of how you can also use the Chorus effect for special effects, try working with the other presets. Note that some of the more bizarre sounds combine lots of modulation, feedback, or long delay times.

**12** Leave Audition open in preparation for the lesson on the next effect.

## Flanger

Like Chorus, Flanger uses short delays, but they're even shorter to create phase cancellations that result in an animated, moving, resonant sound. This effect was popularized in the 1960s due to its "psychedelic" properties.

**1** Assuming that Audition is open and the FemaleChoir.wav file is loaded, click the right arrow of the current effect's insert, and choose Modulation > Flanger to replace the Chorus effect. Play the file to hear what it sounds like.

**2** For a more pronounced effect, set the Mix to 50%. Alter the Feedback setting; more feedback produces a more resonant sound.

**3** An important element of Flanging relates to modulating the delay. Stereo Phasing changes the phase relationship of the modulation; when set to 0, the modulation is the same in both channels. Increase the Phasing amount to offset the modulation in the two channels, which creates more of a stereo effect. Vary the Modulation Rate to change the modulation speed.

**4** Initial Delay Time and Final Delay Time set the Flanger sweep range. The "standard" range is 0 to around 5ms; increasing the final Delay Time produces a sound that's more like chorusing when the Flanger delay time reaches the longer delay. Experiment with these options.

**5** The Mode options are used for specialized effects. Selecting Inverted changes the tone. Special Effects changes the flanging "character": Enable it and see if you like what it does. The effect varies depending on the other parameter settings. Finally, Sinusoidal changes the modulation waveform to produce a somewhat more "rolling" modulation effect.

**6** Call up other presets, particularly the vocal flange presets, to get a sense of the range of possibilities that the Flanger can offer. Many of the more radical patches use either high Modulation Rates, large amounts of Feedback, longer Initial or Final Delay Times, or a combination of these.

**7** Leave Audition open in preparation for the lesson on the next effect.

Chorus/Flanger offers a choice of Chorus or Flanger; each is a simpler version of the Chorus and Flanger described previously. Width is essentially the same as varying Delay in the Chorus or Flanger, whereas Width basically determines the wet/dry mix. Speed provides the same function as Modulation Rate. The only different control is Transience, which emphasizes transients to produce a "sharper" sound.

1   Assuming that Audition is open and the FemaleChoir.wav file is loaded, click the right arrow of the current effect's insert, and choose Modulation > Chorus/Flanger to replace the Flanger effect.

2   Load the various presets to hear the types of effects each processor provides.

3   Leave Audition open in preparation for the next lesson.

## Phaser

The Phaser effect is similar to Flanging but has a different, and often more subtle, character because it uses a specific type of filtering called an *allpass* filter to accomplish its effect instead of delays.

1   Assuming that Audition is open and the FemaleChoir.wav file is loaded, click the right arrow of the current effect's insert, and choose Modulation > Phaser to replace the Chorus/Flanger effect. Play the file.

2   Phasing tends to be most effective when processing the midrange. Change the Upper Freq to around 2000Hz.

3   As with Flanging, you can offset the modulation for the left and right channels. The farther you move the Phase Difference away from the center (0) position, the greater the stereo effect. Leave it at 180 for now.

4   Moving Feedback off center to more positive values increases the phaser's sharpness, producing a "whistling" sound. More negative values produce a subtler, "hollower" sound. Leave it at 0.

5   Vary the Mod Rate slider. Note how at faster settings the effect is almost like vibrato. Return it to 0.25Hz before proceeding.

6   The remaining parameters set the degree of "drama" in the phased sound:

    • **More Stages** produces a more profound effect.

    • **Intensity** determines how much phase-shifting the Phaser applies (you'll typically want this above 90 unless you prefer a more "static" sound).

    • **Depth** sets the lower frequency limit that Modulation attains. This complements the Upper Frequency parameter, which is the highest frequency that Modulation attains.

    • **Mix** sets the blend of wet and dry sounds. A 50% value produces the maximum phasing effect by mixing dry and wet signals in equal proportion. Moving the value toward 0 increases the proportion of dry signal to wet signal, whereas moving the value toward 100 increases the proportion of wet signal to dry signal.

    Experiment with these parameters to hear how they affect the sound.

7   Load the various presets to hear the types of effects each processor provides.

# Noise reduction/restoration

Noise reduction and noise restoration are such important topics that these processors are covered in detail in Lesson 5, "Audio Restoration," which describes Adobe Audition's many options for audio restoration. These include the ability to remove noise, delete pops and clicks, minimize the sound caused by scratches in vinyl records, reduce tape hiss, and more.

# Reverb effects

Reverberation imparts an acoustic space's characteristics (room, concert hall, garage, plate reverb) to audio. Two common reverb processes are convolution reverb and algorithmic reverb. Audition includes both.

*Convolution Reverb* is generally the more realistic sounding of the two. It loads an *impulse,* which is an audio signal (typically WAV file format) that embodies the characteristics of a particular, fixed acoustic space. The effect then performs convolution, a mathematical operation that operates on two functions (the impulse and the audio) to create a third function that combines the impulse and the audio, thus impressing the qualities of the acoustic space onto the audio. The trade-off for realism is a lack of flexibility.

*Algorithmic Reverb* creates an algorithm (mathematical model) of a space with variables that allow for changing the nature of that space. It's therefore easy to create different rooms and effects with a single algorithm, whereas for convolution reverb, you would need to load different impulses for fundamentally different sounds. All Audition reverbs other than the Convolution Reverb use algorithmic reverb technology.

Each type of reverb is useful. Some engineers prefer algorithmic reverbs because it's possible to create "idealized" reverb spaces; others prefer convolution due to its "real" feel.

## Convolution Reverb

The convolution type of reverb can produce extremely realistic reverberation effects, and as described later, can also be useful for sound design. However, it is a CPU-intensive process.

1  If Audition is open, close it without saving to start fresh. Open the program, choose File > Open, navigate to the Lesson04 folder, and open the file Drums110.wav. Play the file to hear what it sounds like.

2  Click the right arrow of an effect's insert, and choose Reverb > Convolution Reverb.

3  Load some presets to get a sense of what convolution reverb can do. When you're done, load the Memory Space preset.

**4** Load different impulses from the Impulse drop-down menu. Note how each impulse produces a different reverb character. When you're done, load the Hall impulse so you can check out how the various parameters affect the sound.

**5** Vary Mix to change the ratio of dry to wet sounds.

**6** Room Size changes the size of the hall. Listen carefully to the degree of control this option provides, because you'll be comparing the range available with algorithmic reverb.

**7** Damping LF and Damping HF affect frequency response. Move the Damping LF slider to the left to simulate the effect of a room with lots of sound-absorbing material, which absorbs high frequencies more readily than low frequencies. Move the Damping HF slider to the left to remove lower frequencies, creating a "thinner" but also less "muddy" reverb character.

**8** Pre-Delay sets the time before a sound first occurs and when it reflects off a surface. Move the Pre-Delay slider to the right to increase the pre-delay amount, which implies a longer time for the sound to reflect, hence a bigger space.

**9** Move Width farther to the right to create a wider stereo image; move the slider to the left to narrow the image. Adjust Gain to set the overall gain of the composite wet/dry sound. This will typically be at 0 unless you need to compensate for signal level variations caused by adding the reverb effect.

**10** Leave Audition open for the next lesson.

## Studio Reverb

We're covering these reverbs out of sequence because the Studio Reverb is an algorithmic reverb that's simple, effective, and works in real time so it's easy to hear the results of changing parameters. Many of the Full Reverb and Reverb parameters cannot be adjusted during playback, because they are very CPU-intensive.

**1** Assuming that Audition is open and the Drums110.wav file is loaded, click the right arrow of the current effect's insert, and choose Reverb > Studio Reverb to replace the Convolution Reverb effect.

**2** With the Default preset selected, vary the Decay slider. Note how the range is much wider than the Convolution Reverb's Room Size parameter.

**3** Algorithmic reverbs contain two main components: early reflections and a reverb "tail." The early reflections simulate the discrete echoes caused when a sound first bounces off multiple room surfaces. The tail is the "wash" of composite echoes that have bounced around the room multiple times. Drag the Decay slider all the way to the left, and then vary the Early Reflections slider. Increasing early reflections creates an effect somewhat like a small acoustic space with hard surfaces.

▶ **Tip:** You can use Convolution Reverb to load most WAV files by clicking Load and navigating to a WAV file. Online sources offer free impulses that work with standard convolution reverbs, including Audition's, which make it easy to expand your options. Also, you can load phrases, loops, sound effects, or other "nonacoustic space" files and obtain some pretty wild—and unpredictable—effects. These can be valuable for sound design and special effects.

▶ **Tip:** Low to moderate Early Reflections settings, with Decay set to minimum, can add a little bit of ambience to otherwise "dry" sounds. This can make narration seem more "real."

**4** Set Decay to about 6000ms and Early Reflections to 50%. Adjust the Width control to set the stereo imaging, from narrow (0) to wide (100).

**5** High Frequency Cut works similarly to the Convolution Reverb's Damping LF but covers a wider range. Move the slider more to the left to reduce the high frequencies for a darker sound or more to the right for a brighter sound.

**6** Low Frequency Cut resembles the Convolution Reverb's Damping HF. Move the LF Cut slider to the right to reduce low-frequency content, which can "tighten up" the low end and reduce "muddiness," or more to the left if you want the reverb to affect lower frequencies.

▶ **Tip:** Engineers often reduce the low frequencies on reverb to prevent adding reverb to bass and drums, which can produce a "muddy" sound.

**7** Damping provides the same function as the Convolution Reverb's Damping LF parameter. The difference between damping and High Frequency Cut is that damping applies progressively more high-frequency attenuation the longer a sound decays, whereas the high frequency cut is constant. Experiment with damping.

**8** Vary the Diffusion control. At 0% the echoes are more discrete. At 100% they're blended together into a smoother sound. In general, high-diffusion settings are common with percussive sounds; low-diffusion settings are used with sustaining sounds (e.g., voice, strings, organ, etc.).

**9** The Output level section varies the amount of dry and wet audio. Experiment with these options.

**10** Leave Audition open for the next lesson.

## Reverb

When you call up the Reverb effect, you'll likely see a warning alerting you that this is a CPU-intensive effect and advising you to apply the effect before playback. Also, you cannot adjust the reverb characteristics in real time—only when playback is stopped. You can edit the dry and wet levels at any time.

**1** Assuming that Audition is open and the Drums110.wav file is loaded, click the right arrow of the current effect's insert, and choose Reverb > Reverb to replace the Studio Reverb effect.

**2** Call up various presets and vary the dry and wet sliders. Because you're processing a drum sound, Big Drum Room and Thickener can be very useful; they're designed specifically to enhance drums.

**3** The remaining parameters (Decay Time, Pre-Delay Time, and Diffusion) perform the same function as the like-named parameters in the Studio Reverb and Convolution Reverb. You've already heard the sonic results caused by changing these sliders in the previous lessons, but if you want to hear how they alter the sound in this particular reverb, vary these sliders and listen to how they change the sound. The Perception slider is similar to high-frequency damping; at 0 the sound is "duller" and softer, whereas a setting of 200 simulates more irregularities in the listening environment, so the sound is brighter and "harder." Try different settings of the Perception slider and listen to the results; the difference is relatively subtle. Leave Audition open.

## Full Reverb

Full Reverb is a convolution-based reverb and is the most sophisticated of the various reverbs but also the most impractical to use because of the heavy CPU loading. No parameters other than the level controls for dry, reverb, and early reflections levels can be adjusted during playback, and even then, the level control settings take several seconds to take effect (however, if you stop playback and adjust them, the change occurs immediately on playback). Also, if you change any of the non-level reverb parameters while stopped, it can take several seconds before playback begins. As a result, this is a processor where you'll probably want to start with a preset that's as close as possible to what you want and make a few tweaks as needed.

1 Assuming that Audition is open and the Drums110.wav file is loaded, click the right arrow of the current effect's insert, and choose Reverb > Full Reverb to replace the Reverb effect.

2 Start by calling up some presets to get an idea of the Full Reverb's sonic potential.

3 The Reverberation parameters (Decay Time, Pre-Delay Time, Diffusion, and Perception) are functionally identical to the same controls in the Reverb processor. However, the Early Reflections options are more sophisticated than any of the other reverbs. With playback stopped, turn the Dry and Reverberation Output Level controls to 0 and Early Reflections to 100 so you can easily hear the results of changing the related parameters.

4 Use the Room Size and Dimension controls to create a virtual room. Bigger room sizes create longer reverbs. Dimension sets the ratio of width to depth; values below 0.25 can sound unnatural, but try this for special effect-type sounds (reduce the monitor volume first because the volume may increase unexpectedly).

5 High Pass cutoff works the same way as the High Frequency cutoff control in the Studio Reverb. Move the slider more to the left to reduce the high frequencies for a darker sound or more to the right for a brighter sound. Left/right location moves the early reflections from stereo more toward the left or right by moving the slider more to the left or right, respectively; if you want the source from which the reflections are derived to move with it, choose Include Direct.

6 The Coloration tab opens up a three-band EQ with a high shelf, low shelf, and single parametric stage. You've already learned how equalization works, but there's also a Decay parameter. This sets the time before the coloration EQ takes effect. Set it to 0 as you experiment with the parametric parameters so you can hear the results as quickly as possible. As just one example, reducing highs produces a "warmer" reverb sound.

# Special effects

Two individual effects—Distortion and Vocal Enhancer—are discussed in this section as well as two "multieffects" for Guitar and Mastering that include several compatible effects designed to work together.

## Distortion

Distortion occurs by clipping a signal's peaks, which creates harmonics. Audition's distortion can create different amounts of clipping for positive and negative peaks to produce asymmetrical distortion (which can give a more "jagged" sound) or link the settings for both peaks to produce symmetrical distortion, which tends to sound somewhat smoother.

1 Assuming Audition is open, close it without saving to start fresh. Open the program, choose File > Open, navigate to the Lesson04 folder, and open the file Bass110.wav. Play the file to hear what it sounds like.

2 Click the right arrow of an effect's insert, and choose Special > Distortion.

3 The Default preset has no distortion, because the curves represent a linear relationship between input and output with no clipping. Load various presets to get a sense of the sounds this effect can create, and then return to the Default preset.

4 Now you'll create some light distortion to give the bass some "crunch." Click the Link button (under the cursor in the screen shot) between the two graphs so that adjusting one curve affects the other. (Note that clicking one of the two arrows below the Link button transfers one curve's settings to the other.)

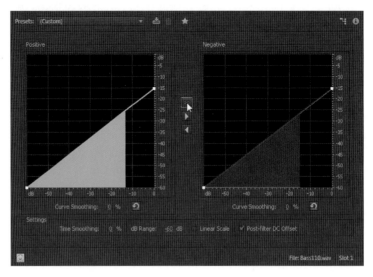

5   With the bass file playing, click the white square in the upper-right corner of a graph's curve. Drag it down to -15 or so, and you'll hear the sound become more distorted as you lower the level where the signal clips. Because more clipping leads to lower levels, you'll need to increase the Effects Rack's Output control to compensate.

6   You can boost lower levels so that they distort more readily. Click at the intersection of the two -30 levels on the X and Y axes. This creates a new node on the curve; you'll hear more distortion.

7   Drag this new node up to increase the volume of low-level signals, thus creating more distortion. Dragging the node to the left also increases distortion by allowing lower levels to distort.

8   To remove a node, right-click (Control-click) on it. Continue adding and moving nodes to hear how this affects the sound. When there are multiple nodes, you can smooth the curve that incorporates them by increasing the Curve Smoothing parameter value.

9   Click a graph's reset button (the spiral arrow). If the graphs are still linked, you'll reset them both simultaneously; otherwise you'd need to reset them individually. With the graphs unlinked, bring the upper-right square for *one* of the graphs down to -20dB. This adds crunch but also preserves the "fullness" of the bass by leaving one set of peaks alone.

10  The Time Smoothing parameter changes the distortion's reaction time to level changes, particularly at lower frequencies. Increase Time Smoothing, and the distortion becomes smoother and less harsh. Choose a value of 30%, and then bypass/enable the distortion to compare the distorted and undistorted sound. Note how the smoothing creates a softer kind of distortion quality that gives the bass a bit of "snarl" but still sounds musical. Processing a bass with a hint of distortion can help it stand out more in a mix.

**Note:** Regarding the other Distortion parameters, dB Range changes the range covered by the graph and limits possible distortion settings to the selected range. Linear scale changes the calibration; logarithmic more closely approximates the way the ear responds. Leave Post-Filter DC Offset selected because it can prevent the addition of a constant offset that can lead to clicks when editing. There's no disadvantage to leaving it on.

## Vocal Enhancer

The Vocal Enhancer effect is one of Audition's easiest effects to use because it has only three options.

1   If Audition is open, close it without saving to start fresh. Open the program, choose File > Open, navigate to the Lesson04 folder, and open the file NarrationNeedsHelp.wav. Play the file.

2   Click the right arrow of an effect's insert, and choose Special > Vocal Enhancer.

3   Click Male to reduce the low end somewhat to minimize p-popping and booming; note that it also helps even out the level variations a bit.

4   Load the file Drum+Bass+Arp110.wav, and insert the Vocal Enhancer in the Effects Rack. Select the Vocal Enhancer's Music option.

5 Bypass the Vocal Enhancer. You'll hear that the music is brighter, which could potentially interfere with vocal intelligibility. Enabling the Vocal Enhancer's Music option creates more "space" for voice-over.

6 With the same file playing, click the Male and Female options. You'll hear how this affects music, which makes the changes in frequency response more obvious.

## Guitar Suite

The Guitar Suite is a "channel strip" that emulates a guitar signal processing chain. It includes four main processors, each of which can be bypassed or enabled individually:

- **Compressor.** Because guitar is a percussive instrument, many guitar players use compression to even out the dynamic range and produce more sustain.

- **Filter.** This shapes the guitar's tone.

- **Distortion.** This is a "condensed" version of the Distortion processor and offers three popular distortion types.

- **Amplifier.** A large part of a guitar's sound is the amplifier through which it plays: The number of speakers and the size of each, as well as the cabinet, have a major effect on the sound. Fifteen types are available, including a cabinet for bass guitar.

However, Guitar Suite is useful for more than guitars—you'll also apply this versatile effects suite to drums.

1 If Audition is open, close it without saving to start fresh. Open the program, choose File > Open, navigate to the Lesson04 folder, and open the file Guitar. wav. Play the file.

2 Click the right arrow of an effect's insert, and choose Special > Guitar Suite.

3 Call up the preset Big and Dumb, which makes a great start for a classic rock guitar sound.

4 Vary the Compressor Amount slider. The sound will be more percussive to the left and more sustained (with a slight volume drop) to the right. Set the Amount to 70 before proceeding.

5 Vary the Distortion Amount slider. The sound is "cleaner" to the left and "dirtier" to the right. Try the three different distortion types from the Distortion Type drop-down menu, and vary the Amount slider. Garage Fuzz is more punk, Smooth Overdrive more rock, and Straight Fuzz emulates the sound of a distortion effect box rather than an amp. Return to Smooth Overdrive, and set the slider to 90.

6 That sound seems a little harsh, but you can make it smoother with the filter. Deselect the Filter bypass check box.

**7** Move the Freq slider to around 1500Hz with Resonance at 0. This removes some of the "edge." Note how increasing Resonance makes the sound "sharper." Leave Resonance at 0 for now.

**8** To hear how different amplifiers affect the sound, choose various options from the Amplifier Box drop-down menu—Classic British Stack, Classic Warm, 1960s American, 1970s Hard Rock, and Deep 4x12 are some of the most realistic emulations. Also note that there are six non-amp and special FX sounds. Bypassing the Amplifier emphasizes just how much speakers and cabinets influence the tone.

**9** Return to the Big and Dumb preset, but choose Classic British Stack for the Amplifier Box parameter. Deselect the Filter bypass check box.

**10** The Filter precedes the Distortion section. Therefore, reducing signal levels due to filtering will result in less distortion. Often, this is the sound you want, but if you feel the overall level is too low, move the Distortion Amount slider to the right to compensate.

**11** With Retro selected as the Filter, choose Bandpass for the Type (this is like a Parametric EQ stage without the boost/cut control). For a big, metal sound, set Freq to around 435Hz and Resonance to 20 to produce a little response peak at that frequency.

**12** You've already worked with Lowpass and Highpass filters in previous sections on equalizers (Lowpass reduces highs; Highpass reduces lows); Resonance is equivalent to the Q control you used with some of the equalizers. Feel free to experiment at this point, but if you're impatient to discover some other filter types, proceed to the next step.

**13** Choose Rez as the Filter and Bandpass as the Type (the other responses work too, but these produce the most obvious effect), and set Resonance to 0. Vary the Freq slider, and you'll hear a resonant effect like a wah pedal. Turn up Resonance if you really want to go overboard.

**14** Each of the remaining five filters has a fixed frequency that corresponds roughly to the mouth's filtering effect when forming various vowels. Change the Freq slider position; note that this doesn't change the TalkBox filter frequency *per se* but acts more like a "window" that sweeps across the filter frequency, making it more or less prominent.

**15** Load the TalkBox U filter and select Bandpass for Type. With Resonance at 0, move the Freq slider across its range. The peak level will be around 1kHz; moving the Freq slider to either side reduces the level somewhat and also changes the timbre.

**16** The Guitar Suite is also suitable for other instruments, particularly drums. Choose File > Open, navigate to the Lesson04 folder, and open the file Drums110.wav.

**17** Click the right arrow of an effect's insert, and choose Special > Guitar Suite. Load the Big And Dumb preset.

**18** Enable the Filter, and move the Freq slider to around 3000Hz. Set Resonance to 20%.

**19** Although you'll hear a good "trash" drum sound, you can tame it by moving the Mix Amount slider to the left (try 30–40%). This adds the dry drum sound in with the "trash" sound so that the overall sound is more defined.

## Mastering

Mastering is another effects "suite." Adobe Audition already excels at mastering, so including a Mastering suite may seem redundant. However, it provides a quick way to master material that doesn't require creating an à la carte set of mastering processors.

The suite includes the following effects:

- **Equalizer.** Includes a low shelf, high shelf, and parametric (peak/notch) stage. Its parameters work similarly to the same parameters in the Parametric Equalizer effect. The Equalizer also includes a real-time graph in the background that shows the current frequency response spectrum. This helps with making EQ adjustments; for example, if you see a huge bass "bump" in the low end, the bass probably needs to be reduced.

- **Reverb.** Adds ambience if needed.

- **Exciter.** Creates high-frequency "sparkle" that's unlike conventional treble-boosting EQ.

- **Widener.** Allows for widening or narrowing the stereo image.

- **Loudness Maximizer.** Is a dynamics processor that increases the average level for a louder sound without exceeding the available headroom.

- **Output Gain.** Can be adjusted to control the effect output and therefore compensate for any level changes due to adding various processes.

You'll use the Mastering Suite to give greater clarity to a piece of music.

**1** If Audition is open, close it without saving to start fresh. Open the program, choose File > Open, navigate to the Lesson04 folder, and open the file DeepTechHouse.wav. Play the file. Note that there are two problems: The bass "booms" a bit too much, and the high end lacks definition.

**2** Click the right arrow of an effect's insert, and then choose Special > Mastering.

**3** Call up the preset Subtle Clarity. Toggle the power button to enable/bypass the preset's effect; note how this indeed produces more clarity.

**4** You'll now fix the bass. Select Low Shelf Enable; a small X appears toward the left, which you click on and drag to change the shelf characteristics. Resume playback.

**5** Drag the Low Shelf marker right to around 240Hz. Then drag down to about -2.5dB. Enable/bypass the Mastering effect, and you'll hear that when Mastering is enabled, the low end is tighter and the high end is more defined.

**6** The Reverb is not intended to provide big hall effects but adds ambience when used subtly. It's set to 20% in the preset; move it left to 0%, and the sound will be a little "dryer." A value of 10% seems to work well for this tune.

**7** Most of the preset's additional "clarity" is due to the slight upper midrange boost around 2033Hz working in conjunction with the Exciter, which affects the highest frequencies. A little bit of Exciter effect goes a long way. Drag its slider to the right, and the sound will become way too bright. Because the song is already fairly bright, disable the Exciter effect by dragging its slider all the way to the left. (Note that the sonic difference among the three characters of Retro, Tape, and Tube becomes most noticeable with dull material and high Exciter amounts.)

**8** Adjust the Widener to taste; end on a setting around 60.

**9** The Loudness Maximizer can increase the apparent loudness for a more "punchy" sound. However, as with the Exciter, you can have too much of a good thing. Excessive maximization can lead to ear fatigue, as well as make the music less interesting by reducing dynamics. For this song, set it to 30 to provide a useful boost without adding a distorted or unnatural sound.

**10** Because the Loudness Maximizer will prevent the level from exceeding 0, you can leave the Output Gain at 0.

**11** Toggle the power button to enable/bypass the effect and listen to the difference. The mastered version has more sparkle, the bass is in proper proportion with respect to level, the stereo image is wider, and there's been a subjective overall level boost.

▶ **Tip:** It might seem logical to set the Widener for the widest possible stereo image to create a more dramatic sound. However, emphasizing the extreme left and right areas of the stereo spectrum can deemphasize the center, thus unbalancing a mix. If you listen closely and move the slider between 0 and 100, you'll usually find a "sweet spot" that provides maximum width without altering the mix's fundamental balance.

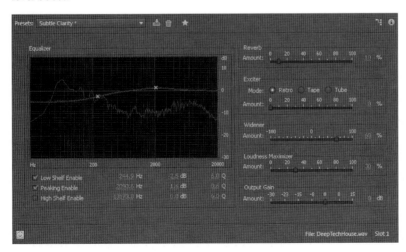

# Stereo imagery effects

Stereo imagery effects alter a file's stereo image. Audition includes two effects for altering stereo image: a Center Channel Extractor and a Graphic Phase Shifter. The latter is a very esoteric tool that you will likely not need to use when doing typical audio projects, so we'll cover only the Center Channel Extractor. For further information on either effect, refer to the Help files.

## Center Channel Extractor

With stereo signals, some sounds are traditionally mixed to center—particularly vocals, bass, and kick drum. Reversing the phase of one channel cancels out any material panned to center while leaving signals panned left and right alone. This is commonly used for karaoke to remove the vocal. By filtering the channel that's out of phase to emphasize voice frequencies, bass and kick aren't affected that much.

However, Audition's Center Channel Extractor is a very sophisticated implementation of this principle that allows for boosting or cutting the center channel, as well as includes precise filtering to help avoid applying the effect where it's not wanted.

1 If Audition is open, close it without saving to start fresh. Open the program, choose File > Open, navigate to the Lesson04 folder, and open the file DeepTechHouse.wav. Don't start playback yet.

2 Click the right arrow of an effect's insert, and choose Stereo Imagery > Center Channel Extractor.

3 Call up the preset Boost Center Channel Bass, but turn down the monitoring level because the bass will be pretty loud.

4 Start playback and slowly turn up the monitoring level. The bass will be excessively loud, and you'll need to pull back on the Effects Rack panel's Output control to around -7dB to avoid distortion.

5 Pull the Center Channel Level control down all the way, and the bass will essentially disappear.

6 Return the Center Channel Level control to 0. Pull the Side Channel Levels control down all the way to isolate the bass.

The next lesson isolates vocals.

1  Choose File > Close. Don't save any changes.

2  Choose File > Open, navigate to the Lesson04 folder, and open the file
ContinentalDrift.wav. Don't start playback yet.

3  Click the right arrow of an effect's insert, and choose Stereo Imagery > Center
Channel Extractor.

4  Call up the preset Vocal Remove. Start playback around 32 seconds. The lead
vocals extend to about 47 seconds, but you won't hear them because they're
being removed (around 45 seconds you'll hear some backup vocals that aren't
removed because they aren't panned to center).

5  Return to around 32 seconds and start playback. Bring up the Center Channel
Level to hear the vocals.

6  You can access several real-time adjustments via the Discrimination tab. Choose
the highest possible Crossover Bleed settings and the lowest possible Phase
Discrimination, Amplitude Discrimination, and Amplitude Bandwidth settings
that are consistent with sound quality and effectiveness. Increasing the Spectral
Decay Rate will often improve sound quality as well.

You've now learned the highlights of the Center Channel Extractor; refer to
Audition's Help file for more details on this relatively esoteric effect.

# Time and Pitch effect

The sole effect under the Time and Pitch effect, Automatic Pitch Correction,
is designed for vocals and corrects the pitch of notes so that they are in tune.
However, be careful when applying this effect; many vocalists deliberately sing
some notes a little flat or sharp to add interest or tension to a vocal; correcting
these can remove a vocal's "human" quality.

## Automatic Pitch Correction

Pitch correction is intended for vocals whose pitch is slightly out of tune. This effect
analyzes the vocal to extract the pitch, calculates how far off a note is from the correct pitch, and then corrects the note by raising or lowering the pitch to compensate.

1  If Audition is open, close it without saving to start fresh. Open the program,
choose File > Open, navigate to the Lesson04 folder, and open the file
OriginalVocal.wav. Don't start playback yet.

2  Click an effect insert's right arrow, and choose Time and Pitch > Automatic
Pitch Correction.

**Note:** Sample Magic produces the Deep Tech House sample library, whereas the Continental Drift sample library is made by Sony. These illustrate the range of music you can create from commercially available sample and loop libraries.

3  Bypass the Automatic Pitch Correction effect, and start playback. Observe the correction meter on the right: The red band indicates how far off the pitch is from the ideal. When the meter moves up, the pitch is sharp. When the meter moves down (see screen shot), the pitch is flat. A centered meter indicates that the vocal is on pitch.

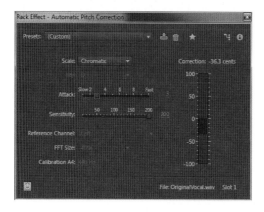

4  The Scale and Key options define the notes to which pitch should be corrected. For example, with a C major scale, the notes will be corrected to C, D, E, F, G, A, and B. However, to use this option, you need to know a vocal's correct scale and key; choose these from the Scale and Key drop-down menus. If you do not know the Scale and Key choose Chromatic from the Scale drop-down menu, which simply corrects to the nearest semitone. (The vocal is in D but uses a flatted 7th note that is not part of the major scale. So, choose Chromatic instead.) In most cases, Chromatic will do the job.

5  Set the Sensitivity slider to 200 to correct all notes. At lower Threshold settings, notes that are off-pitch by more than the pitch threshold will be unaffected.

6  Start playback with Automatic Pitch Correction still bypassed. It's a good idea to loop this example so you don't have to keep clicking Play. Listen for a few iterations of the loop, and then enable the effect.

7  Note how all the notes are on pitch. To compare, either bypass the effect or move the Sensitivity Fader to 0.

8  Move the Attack slider to 10. This produces the fastest response, so the Automatic Pitch Correction will attempt to pitch-correct the vibrato. You'll hear a warbling sound, so use a slow enough setting to allow the vibrato to change pitch naturally. A setting of 2 to 4 is a good compromise between correcting pitch rapidly on sustained notes but not affecting vibrato.

9  Change the scale to Minor and Key to D. You'll hear the vocal take on a more minor quality as notes are shifted to the appropriate pitches for a minor scale.

# Third-party effects (VST and AU)

In addition to using Audition's effects, you can load effects (plug-ins) made by other manufacturers. Audition is compatible with the following formats:

- **VST (Virtual Studio Technology)** is the most common Windows format and is also supported by the Mac. However, you need separate plug-in versions for Mac and Windows. For example, you can't buy a particular VST plug-in for the Mac and use it with Windows.

- **VST3** is an updated version of VST2 that offers more efficient operation and other general improvements. Although not quite as common as standard VST, it's gaining in popularity.

- **AU (Audio Units)** is Mac-specific, was introduced with OS X, and is the most popular and common format for the Mac.

On either platform, plug-ins are installed in specific hard drive folders. You need to let Audition know where to find these plug-ins. The information in the following sections applies to both Windows and Macs unless otherwise specified.

## The Audio Plug-In Manager

Audition's Audio Plug-In Manager provides several functions:

- It scans your computer for plug-ins so Audition can use them and creates a list showing the name, type, status, and file path (where the plug-ins are located on your computer).

- It allows you to specify additional folders that contain plug-ins, and then re-scan these added folders. Most plug-ins install to default folders, and Audition scans these folders first. However, some plug-ins may install into a different folder, or you might want to create more than one folder of plug-ins.

- It lets you enable or disable plug-ins.

When you first open Audition, you'll need to tell it to scan for plug-ins before they can be used in a project.

1 From the Effects option in the menu bar, choose Audio Plug-In Manager.

2 Click Scan for Plug-Ins. Audition must inspect your hard drive, so this can take a while.

   When scanning is complete, you'll see the plug-in listing and status, which usually indicates the manager is done. However, if needed, also complete the following steps.

3 To add an additional folder with plug-ins, click Add and navigate to the folder.

4 To enable or disable a particular plug-in, select the check box to the left of the plug-in's name.

**Note:** Both Windows and Mac offer 64-bit operating systems (Windows Vista and 7, Mac OS X Lion and Mountain Lion), which can use 64-bit versions of plug-ins. Although Audition can run on 64-bit operating systems, it is a 32-bit application and is not compatible with 64-bit plug-ins on either Mac or Windows. However, very few plug-ins are 64-bit only; almost all are available in 32-bit versions that are compatible with Audition CS6.

**Note:** Many free, legal plug-ins in a variety of formats are available on the Internet. These range from poorly coded effects made by beginning programmers to plug-ins that are every bit as good—and sometimes better—than commercially available, professional products.

5   To re-scan the existing plug-ins, click Re-Scan Existing Plug-Ins.

Note that you can enable or disable all plug-ins by clicking the appropriate button.

6   When you're finished with the Audio Plug-In Manager, click OK.

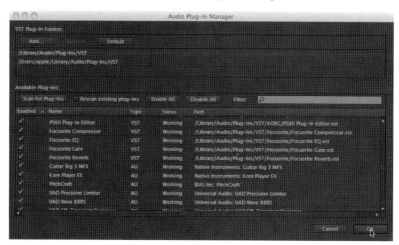

## Using VST and AU plug-ins

VST and AU plug-ins appear as part of the same drop-down menu that opens when you click an Effects Rack insert's right arrow. For example, with Windows you'll see entries for VST and VST3 effects along with the other entries for Modulation, Filter and EQ, Reverb, and the like; the Mac adds another entry for AU effects. Here's how to use these effects in Audition.

1   Click an Effects Rack insert's right arrow.

2   Choose the entry (VST, VST3, or on the Mac, AU) containing the effect you want to insert.

3   Click the effect you want to insert, as you would with any of the effects included with Audition.

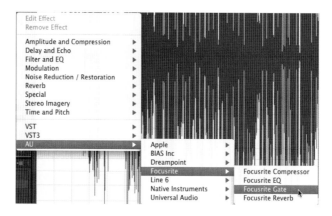

# Using the Effects menu

You can process any audio selected in the Waveform or Multitrack Editor by choosing the desired effect from the Effects menu. Unlike with the Effects Rack, you can apply only one effect at a time.

This section covers effects that are available only from the Effects menu. Any effects you can also access from the Effects Rack work the same way when opened from the Effects menu with three exceptions:

- The Invert, Reverse, and Silence effects are applied to the audio as soon as you select them. You can use the Undo command to undo the effects.

- Most effects chosen via the effects categories (Amplitude and Compression, Delay and Echo, etc.) have an Apply and a Close button. Clicking Apply applies the effect to the selected audio.

- Unlike the Effects Rack, editing is destructive (although the changes aren't made permanent unless and until the file is saved). However, you can still audition any changes before applying them, because most effects chosen via the effects categories have a Play and Loop button to the right of the effect's power on/off button. Loop repeats the selected portion of the audio when you click Play.

## Invert, Reverse, and Silence effects

Invert changes the signal's polarity (commonly called *phase*) and produces no audible difference. Reverse flips an audio selection so that the beginning occurs at the end and the end at the beginning. Silence replaces the selected audio with silence.

1  If Audition is open, close it without saving to start fresh. Open the program, choose File > Open, navigate to the Lesson04 folder, and open the file NarrationNeedsHelp.wav.

2  Play the file to hear what it sounds like, and then select the part at the beginning that says, "Most importantly, you need to maintain good backups of your data."

3  Choose Effects > Invert. Note that the positive and negative sections are flipped, so the positive peaks are now negative and vice versa. However, if you play this, you'll hear no audible difference.

4  Choose Effects > Reverse. Play back the selection, and you'll hear reversed speech.

5  Select the same section. Choose Effects > Silence to convert the audio to silence.

6  Close the File without saving it, but leave Audition open.

## Additional Amplitude and Compression effects

Three Effects menu functions are not available with the Effects Rack: Normalize, Fade Envelope, and Gain Envelope.

1  Choose File > Open, navigate to the Lesson04 folder, and open the file Bass110.wav.

2  Select a single bass note, and choose Effects > Amplitude and Compression > Normalize (process).

3  Normalization adjusts a selection's level so that its peak (highest level) attains a particular percentage of the overall level. Set Normalize to 25% and click OK; the note's peak will reach 25% of the maximum available level.

**Note:** You can show the peak as either a percentage of the signal or the level in dB, referenced to the maximum available headroom. For example, if you select the dB radio button, 25% normalization is equivalent to a peak that reaches -12dB. Normalize All Channels Equally treats the peaks for both channels similarly, and DC Bias Adjust ensures that a level of 0 is truly a value of 0. There's no practical reason not to select this option.

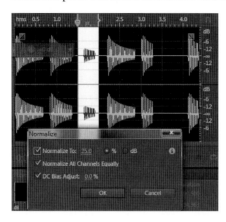

4  Choose Edit > Undo or press Ctrl+Z (Command+Z) to restore the bass note to its previous level.

5  Select the right half of the waveform (the first three notes), and choose Effects > Amplitude and Compression > Fade Envelope (process).

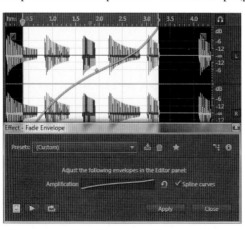

6   Load the Linear Fade In preset. A line that indicates amplitude appears superimposed on the selection. Play the file, either by clicking the Fade Envelope dialog box's Play button or by pressing the spacebar, and you'll hear the bass notes fade in.

7   You can adjust the fade shape by clicking on the line to create new nodes, as you did toward the end of Lesson 3, "Basic Editing." A thumbnail in the Fade Envelope dialog box shows the shape; select the Spline Curves check box to round the fade line.

8   Select a different region. The curve now adapts to fit within the selection. Regardless of the size of the selection, the curve adapts proportionally to fit.

9   Click Close in the Fade Envelope dialog box without applying the fade.

10   Select part of the waveform, and choose Effects > Amplitude and Compression > Gain Envelope.

11   Select +3dB Hard Bump. A line that indicates amplitude appears superimposed on the selection. You can adjust the gain curve shape by clicking on the line to create new nodes, and as with the fade, a thumbnail in the Gain Envelope dialog box shows the shape. If desired, select the Spline Curves check box to round the fade line.

12   Select a different region. As with the Fade Envelope, the curve adapts to fit within the selection.

## Diagnostic effects

Diagnostic effects will be covered in Lesson 5 along with the real-time, nondestructive noise reduction and restoration tools. The Diagnostic effects produce the same sonic results but are destructive, DSP-based processes.

## Doppler Shifter effect

The Doppler Shifter effect is an unusual effect that changes pitch and amplitude to make signals sound "three dimensional" as they circle around you, whiz by from left to right, and do other effects that alter spatial placement.

1   If Audition is open, close it without saving to start fresh. Open the program, choose File > Open, navigate to the Lesson04 folder, and open the file FemaleChoir.wav.

2   Choose Effects > Special > Doppler Shifter. Click the dialog box's Play button to hear the default effect. Like all of the Doppler Shifter presets, this effect is particularly dramatic on headphones.

3   Choose various presets. You may need to stop and restart Play between presets.

**4** The best way to understand how this effect works is to choose a Path Type (straight or circular), and then vary the parameters to hear how changes to specific parameters affect the sound. Take a few moments to do this now. You can get some really wild effects with this processor; note that you may need to stop and restart Play with major edits.

**5** When you're finished, close Audition without saving the file.

## Manual Pitch Correction effect

The Manual Pitch Correction effect is one of two Time and Pitch effects that are available only from the Effects menu.

**1** If Audition is open, close it without saving to start fresh. Open the program, choose File > Open, navigate to the Lesson04 folder, and open the file Drum+Bass+Arp110.wav.

**2** Choose Effects > Time and Pitch > Manual Pitch Correction. The Waveform Editor changes to Spectral view, and the Manual Pitch Correction dialog box appears. Play the file as a reference.

**3** The HUD has an additional control for pitch along with the standard volume control. Click on this control and drag down to lower pitch; drag up to raise pitch. For now, drag down to -200 cents (2 semitones). A yellow line superimposed on the Waveform overview shows the amount of pitch change.

**4** Click Play to hear the sound transposed down to a lower pitch.

● **Note:** The Pitch Curve Resolution parameter trades off better accuracy (higher numbers) for faster response and lower CPU loading (lower numbers). For the Reference Channel, try both options and use whichever produces the highest-quality sound.

**5** Drag the HUD so it's not on top of the yellow line. Click on the yellow line to create a node, which you can drag up or down to further change pitch. As with other Audition envelopes, you can insert multiple nodes and make complex curves, as well as round them off by selecting the Spline curves check box.

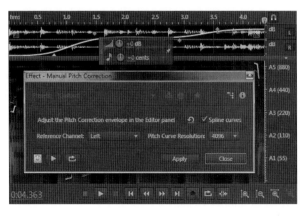

**6** Click Close without applying the effect. Leave Audition open for the next lesson.

# Stretch and Pitch effect

The Stretch and Pitch effect is the other Time and Pitch effect that's available only from the Effects menu. It offers high-quality time and pitch stretching.

1  Assuming the Drum+Bass+Arp110.wav file is still open, choose Effects > Time and Pitch > Stretch and Pitch.

2  The default preset changes neither time nor pitch. Set the Stretch slider to 200%, click the dialog box's Loop button, and then click Play. The file will now play at half speed.

3  Set the Stretch slider to 50%, and then click Play. The file now plays at double-speed. After auditioning this change, reset the Stretch fader to 100%.

4  Vary the Pitch Shift slider and note how this affects the sound. There's a slight delay before any pitch change takes effect, because Audition has to do a lot of calculations. You can shorten this time by selecting a level of Precision other than the default setting of High.

5  Select Lock Stretch and Pitch Shift. This links the two parameters so that if, for example, you shift pitch up an octave, the speed doubles; shifting pitch down an octave halves the speed. For an interesting "slowdown" effect, set Stretch to 100%. Click Play, and then slowly move the Stretch slider to the right. With Stretch and Pitch Shift still locked, return the Stretch slider to 100% before proceeding.

6  You can also use the Stretch effect to change a file's length. For example, the current file is 4.363 seconds long. Suppose it needs to be 5.00 seconds long. Select the Lock Stretch Settings to New Duration check box, and enter **5.00** for the New Duration parameter. Click Play; now the loop is exactly 5.00 seconds long.

7  Because the stretch settings are locked to duration, the pitch will be somewhat lower because the file is longer. To preserve the pitch, deselect Lock Stretch Settings to New Duration, make sure Lock Stretch and Pitch Shift aren't selected, and then set Pitch Shift to 0 semitones. When you're finished, close Audition without saving the file.

8  The Advanced parameters are mostly important when manipulating voice; make sure the Solo Instrument or Voice and Preserve Speech Characteristics check boxes are selected, and adjust the Pitch Coherence slider for the best sound quality (this will be subtle). You can try deselecting Solo Instrument or Voice and Preserve Speech Characteristics with audio other than voice, but you may not hear much difference.

9  Click Close.

**Note:** There are two algorithm choices in the Stretch and Pitch window, iZotope Radius and Audition. The Audition algorithm is less CPU-intensive, but the Radius algorithm has much better fidelity, and most modern computers will have no problem handling the extra CPU load.

# Managing presets

When you create a particular effect you like, or even a complete Effects Rack configuration with multiple effects, you can save it as a preset for later recall. The preset header is similar for both individual effects and the Effects Rack.

## Create and select a preset

Here's how to create and save a preset for the Amplify effect that boosts gain by +2.5dB.

1   Open Audition, navigate to the Lesson04 folder, and open any audio file you'd like.

2   Choose Effects > Amplitude and Compression > Amplify. Enter **+2.5dB** in the Left and Right Gain numeric fields.

3   Click the Save Settings as a Preset button to the right of the Presets field. A Save Effect Preset dialog box appears.

4   Enter a name for the preset, such as **+2.5dB increase**, and click OK. The preset name will then appear in the list of presets.

## Delete a preset

To delete a preset, select it, and then click the Trash Can button to the right of the Save Settings as a Preset button.

## Create and select a favorite

If you create a preset you expect to use a lot, you can save it as a favorite.

1   When the preset settings are as desired, click the star button toward the upper-right corner of the effect window.

2   Name this favorite preset in the dialog box that appears.

3   Click OK.

4   To access the favorite, select the audio you want to process, choose Favorites, and then select your favorite to apply the preset settings immediately to the selected audio.

# Review questions

1   What are the advantages of the Effects Rack, the Effects menu, and Favorites?

2   Is it possible to expand the roster of effects available to Audition?

3   Why is "gain-staging" important with the Effects Rack?

4   What is the difference between "dry" and "wet" audio?

5   What is the name of the process that allows for transposing pitch or lengthening/shortening files?

# Review answers

1   The Effects Rack allows you to make complex effects chains, the Effects menu includes additional effects and can apply single effects rapidly, and the Favorites presets can apply settings to audio immediately upon choosing the preset.

2   Audition can load third-party VST, VST3, and for the Mac, AU effects as well.

3   Effects can increase gain, thus causing distortion within the Effects Rack. By adjusting levels going into and out of the rack, it's possible to avoid distortion.

4   Dry audio is unprocessed, whereas wet audio has been processed. Many effects let you alter the proportion of the two types of audio.

5   The processes are called high-quality time- and pitch-stretching, respectively.

# 5 AUDIO RESTORATION

## Lesson overview

In this lesson, you'll learn how to do the following:

- Remove hiss, like tape hiss or preamp noise

- Reduce the level of clicks and pops automatically

- Minimize or even remove constant background noises like hum, air conditioning, ventilation system noise, and the like

- Remove undesired artifacts, like someone coughing in the middle of a live recording

- Do highly effective manual click and pop removal

- Use restoration tools to completely modify a drum loop

This lesson takes about 45 minutes to complete. This assumes you've copied the Lesson05 folder that contains the audio examples into the Lessons folder that you created on your hard drive for these projects. Remember that you needn't be concerned about modifying these files, because you can always return to the original versions by copying them from the *Adobe Audition CS6 Classroom in a Book* CD-ROM.

Audition offers tools for reducing hiss, hum, clicks, pops, and other types of noise. But you can also remove undesired artifacts by defining sections to be removed based on amplitude, time, *and* frequency.

# About audio restoration

Sometimes you'll work with audio that needs restoration, like music from vinyl or cassette, or audio with hum, hiss, or other artifacts. Audition has multiple tools for solving these problems, including specialized signal processors and graphic waveform editing options.

However, audio restoration involves trade-offs. For example, removing the crackles from vinyl recordings may remove part of the sound that occurs during the crackles. So you may have to reconcile solving a problem with the infamous "law of unintended consequences."

Nonetheless, as these lessons demonstrate, it's possible to clean up audio significantly while retaining sound quality.

# Reducing hiss

Hiss is a natural by-product of electronic circuits, particularly high-gain circuits. Analog tape recordings always had some inherent hiss, but so do mic preamps and other signal sources. Audition provides two ways of reducing hiss (also see the section "Reducing noise"); we'll start with the easiest option.

▶ **Tip:** When mixing music that will be mastered, don't trim a file up to the beginning; leave some of the track before the music begins. This can provide a noise floor reference if noise reduction is needed.

1 With Audition open to the Waveform Editor, choose File > Open, navigate to the Lesson05 folder, and open the file Hiss.wav.

2 Click the Transport Play button, and you'll hear obvious hiss, especially during quiet sections. Click the Transport Stop button.

3 Select the first two seconds of the audio file, which contain only noise (the "noise floor"). Audition will take a "noise print" (like a noise "fingerprint") of this signal and subtract audio with only these hiss characteristics from the audio file.

4 Choose Effects > Noise Reduction/Restoration > Hiss Reduction (process).

**5** Click the Capture Noise Floor button. A curve appears that shows the noise's spectral distribution.

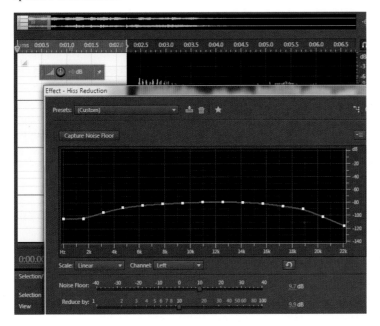

**6** Extend the audio selection in the Waveform Editor to around 5 seconds, and click the Transport Loop button. This also turns on the Hiss Reduction dialog box's Loop button.

**7** Click the Hiss Reduction dialog box's Play button. You'll hear less noise.

**8** You generally want to use the minimum acceptable amount of noise reduction to avoid altering the rest of the signal; reducing hiss may also reduce high frequencies. Move the Reduce by slider to the left and the hiss will return. Move it right to 100dB, and although there will be no hiss, the transients will lose some high frequencies.

**9** Move the Reduce by slider to find a compromise setting between noise reduction and high-frequency response. For now, leave it at 10dB.

**10** The Noise Floor slider tells Audition where to draw the line between the noise floor and the signal. As with the Reduce by slider, moving the slider farther to the left increases noise and farther to the right reduces noise and high-frequency response. Leave it set to 10dB for now.

**11** Revisit the Reduce by slider and move it to 20dB. The hiss is gone, but there's a little less "snap" to the transients compared to the 10dB setting. You'll need to decide which quality is more important to you, but for now choose 15dB as a compromise setting.

▶ **Tip:** You typically adjust the Reduce by parameter first to set the overall amount of noise reduction, and then adjust the Noise Floor parameter to determine the noise reduction characteristics. However, re-tweaking each slider can optimize the sound further. Also note that selecting Output Noise Only will play back only what's being removed from the audio. This can help determine whether any desirable audio is being removed along with the hiss.

**12** Click the Transport Stop button. Turn off the Transport Loop button, click once within the Waveform Editor to deselect the loop, and then choose Edit > Select > Select All.

**13** Click the Transport Play button. Enable and disable the Hiss Reduction dialog box's Power State button to hear the file with and without noise reduction; the difference is significant, especially at the beginning and end where there's no signal to mask the hiss. Stop playback.

**14** Click the Hiss Reduction dialog box's Close button.

**15** If there's no noise floor, Audition can still help remove noise. While still in the Waveform Editor, choose File > Open, navigate to the Lesson05 folder, and open the file HissTruncated.wav.

**16** Choose Effects > Noise Reduction/Restoration > Hiss Reduction (process).

**17** Click the Transport Play button. Despite not capturing a noise print, you can verify that there's less noise by clicking the Hiss Reduction dialog box's Power State button to listen to the enabled and bypassed states.

**18** Move the Reduce by slider to around 20dB, which is a typical amount for noise reduction. Now vary the Noise Floor slider for the best compromise between hiss reduction and high-frequency response; -2dB is a good choice.

**19** Click the Hiss Reduction dialog box's Power State button to listen to the enabled and bypassed states. Although the noise reduction doesn't have quite the finesse obtainable by working with a noise print, it still makes a huge improvement without any significant audio degradation.

**20** Close the Hiss Reduction dialog box, and stop playback in preparation for the next lesson.

## Reducing clicks

Clicks can consist of the little ticks and pops you hear with vinyl recordings, occasional digital clocking errors in digital audio signals, a bad physical audio connection, and so on. Although it's difficult to remove these completely without affecting the audio, Audition can help attenuate lower-level clicks and crackles.

**1** With Audition open to the Waveform Editor, choose File > Open, navigate to the Lesson05 folder, and open the file Crackles.wav.

**2** Click the Transport Loop and Play buttons, and you'll hear clicks and crackles, especially during the quiet parts between drum hits in the beginning.

**3** Choose Effects > Noise Reduction/Restoration > Automatic Click Remover.

**4** The Threshold slider sets the sensitivity to clicks; lower values will "trap" more clicks but may also reduce lower-level transients you want to keep. Move the Threshold slider to 0; the processor will interpret almost anything as a click, so you'll hear the program sputter as it tries to make an excessive number of real-time calculations. Conversely, a setting of 100 lets through too many clicks. Choose a setting of 20 to reduce most clicks while minimally affecting the audio.

**5** Complexity sets how complex a click Audition will process. Higher settings allow Audition to recognize more complex clicks but requires more computation and may degrade the audio somewhat. This is not a real-time control, so you need to adjust it, play the audio, adjust, play, and so on. For now, click the Transport Stop button, and then move the slider to 80.

**6** Click the Transport Play button. Because this is a computation-intensive process, during real-time playback Audition may not be able to process a click prior to playing it back. The only way to be certain how processing will affect the sound is to click the Automatic Click Remover dialog box's Apply button; click it now. Note that this closes the Automatic Click Remover processor.

**7** Click the Transport Play button. Although the clicks are lower in volume, the removal process affects the audio, so we'll try again. Choose Edit > Undo Automatic Click Remover.

**8** Choose Effects > Noise Reduction/Restoration > Automatic Click Remover; the settings will be as you left them. If Complexity is grayed out, click the Automatic Click Remover dialog box's Play button and then the Stop button. Move the complexity slider to 35, and click Apply again.

**9** Click the Transport Play button. The new setting produces better results than the original default value of 16 or the higher value you tried of 80. To compare the "repaired" sound with the original, choose Edit > Undo Automatic Click Remover, and then choose Edit > Redo Automatic Click Remover. Click the Transport Stop button when you're done comparing the two.

● **Note:** There's not a lot of difference between minor Complexity setting variations. For example, if you had chosen 40 or 30 instead of 35, you probably wouldn't notice any difference compared to a setting of 35.

# Reducing noise

Although you can reduce hiss with the Hiss Reduction effect, there are other types of noise you'll want to reduce as well, like hum, air conditioning noise, and ventilation sounds. If these sounds are relatively constant, Audition can reduce or remove them using the Noise Reduction process. This process can also reduce hiss and allow for more detailed editing compared to the Hiss Reduction option.

1 With Audition open to the Waveform Editor, choose File > Open, navigate to the Lesson05 folder, and open the file Hum.wav.

2 Click the Transport Play button to hear the hum that was caused by a bad electrical connection (this kind of hum can also occur with unbalanced audio cables and high-gain circuits).

3 Select the first second of the audio file, which contains only hum. As with reducing hiss, Audition will take a noise print of the hum and subtract only this objectionable noise from the file.

4 Choose Effects > Noise Reduction/Restoration > Noise Reduction (process).

5 Click the Capture Noise Print button. A curve appears that shows the noise floor's spectral distribution.

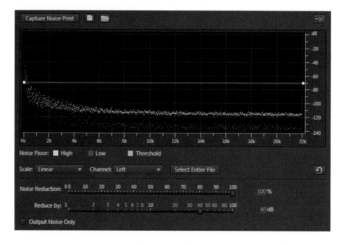

6 Select about the first 20 seconds of the file, and click the Transport Loop button if it is not already enabled.

7 Click the Noise Reduction dialog box's Play button. The hum will be gone during silent sections.

8  You may hear a little hum immediately after a drum sound decays. The reason is that noise reduction doesn't apply as much reduction when the sound is being masked and takes some time to return to full reduction when audio is no longer present. To remove more of the hum, move the Noise Reduction slider all the way to 100%.

9  The Reduce by slider sets the amount by which the noise will be reduced. A setting between 10 and 20dB is a good compromise between affecting the audio and reducing the noise. Set this slider to 15dB for now.

10 You'll still hear a little hum after a drum sound decays. Click the Advanced disclosure triangle for more options.

11 The Spectral Decay Rate parameter determines how long it takes for the noise reduction to return to maximum when the audio goes from signal to silence. Reduce the Spectral Decay Rate to 20% to speed up the noise reduction response, thus eliminating the hum at the end of the drum sounds.

12 Toggle the Noise Reduction dialog box's Power State button, and you'll hear the effectiveness of the noise reduction process. Close Audition without saving anything (click No to All) in preparation for the next lesson.

# Removing artifacts

Sometimes particular sounds will need to be removed, like a cough in the middle of a live performance. Audition can do this using the Spectral Frequency Display, which allows for editing based on not just amplitude and time (as with the standard Waveform Editor), but also frequency. You can switch between these two displays by pressing Shift+D. This exercise shows you how to remove a cough in a performance by classical harpsichordist Kathleen McIntosh.

1  Open Audition to the Waveform Editor, choose File > Open, navigate to the Lesson05 folder, and open the file Cough.wav.

2  Click the Transport Play button, and you'll hear a cough in the background at around 1.65 seconds.

3  Choose View > Show Spectral Frequency Display. Because you'll be doing detailed work, make the Waveform Editor window as large as possible by dragging the horizontal and vertical dividers.

**4** Zoom in and look closely at the spectrum at around 1.65 seconds. Unlike the linear bands of audio in various frequencies you see in the rest of the file, there's something that looks almost like a "cloud"; that's the cough.

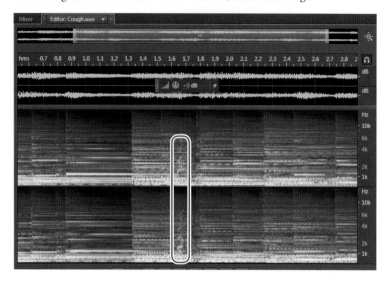

**5** Choose the rightmost button in the top toolbar (Spot Healing Brush tool), or type **B** to choose it. A circular cursor (that looks somewhat like a bandage icon) appears.

● **Note:** The required Size parameter setting will vary depending on the Spectral Frequency Display's zoom level.

**6** Upon selecting the Spot Healing Brush tool, a Size parameter appears next to the Spot Healing Brush tool's toolbar button. Adjust the size so that the circular cursor is as wide as the cough.

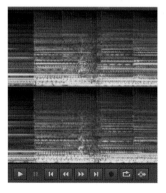

**7** In one channel, drag the circular cursor over the area with the cough; the same area will be selected automatically in the other channel. The area over which you dragged with be "ghosted" in white. Be careful to drag over only the cough.

**Tip:** To drag in a straight line, hold down the computer keyboard's Shift key while dragging.

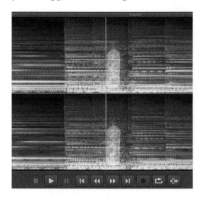

**8** Release the mouse button, and then click the Transport Play button. The cough will be gone, and Audition will have "healed" (reconstructed) the audio behind the cough. (The healing process takes audio on either side of the deleted audio, and through a complex process of copying and crossfading, fills in the gap caused by removing the artifact.)

**Tip:** If you don't remove all of an artifact with this process, you can try multiple times, or even use this process on successive, small selections of an artifact.

**9** Close Audition without saving anything in preparation for the next lesson.

## Alternate click removal

You can use the Spectral Frequency Display to remove clicks. Although this is a manual process that is more time-consuming than using the Automatic Click Remover effect, the removal process will be more accurate and have less impact on the audio quality.

**1** Open Audition to the Waveform Editor, choose Edit > File > Open, navigate to the Lesson05 folder, and open the file Crackles.wav.

**2** Because you had the Spectral Frequency Display open in the previous lesson, Audition should open with the Spectral Frequency Display visible. If not, choose View > Show Spectral Frequency Display (or press Shift+D).

**3** Zoom in until you can see the clicks toward the file's beginning as thin, solid vertical lines (outlined in white in the screen shot for clarity).

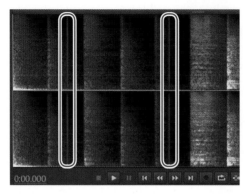

**4** Type **B** to choose the Spot Healing Brush tool, and set its pixel size to the same width as a click.

**5** Hold down the Shift key, and then click at the top of the click (noise) and drag down. This selects the noise in both channels.

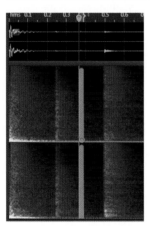

**6** Release the mouse button; the click will be gone and the audio behind it "healed." Repeat steps 5 and 6 for each click you want to remove.

**7** Return the playhead to the beginning of the file if necessary, and then click the Transport Play button. The file sounds as if the clicks had never been there.

**8** Keep Audition open in preparation for the next lesson.

# Creative removal

Audition's restoration tools aren't just for fixing problems; you can also use them in creative ways and for sound design. This lesson takes a drum loop and uses the Spectral Frequency Display to remove four drum hits.

1   With Audition open to the Waveform Editor, choose File > Open, navigate to the Lesson05 folder, and open the file DrumLoop.wav.

2   Click the Transport Play button. Note that there are four white noise "hits" at about 0.47, 1.45, 2.39, and 3.35 seconds. We'll remove them.

3   As with the previous lessons, zoom in until the hit you want to remove is big enough so it's easy to define.

4   Because we want to remove the audio completely, not "heal" it in the context of other audio, choose the Marquee Selection tool from the Waveform Editor's top toolbar, or type **E**.

5   Draw a rectangle around the first drum hit.

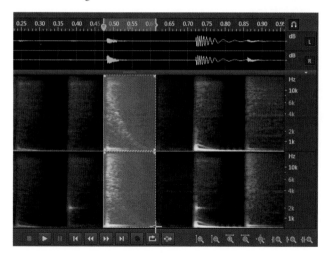

6   Choose Effects > Amplitude and Compression > Amplify. Move both Gain sliders full left, and click Apply.

7   Locate the second hit, and again draw a rectangle around it, but this time *don't include the yellow section at the bottom of the hit,* because that represents the kick drum sound.

8   Choose Effects > Amplitude and Compression > Amplify. With both Gain sliders full left, click Apply.

9   Draw a rectangle around the third drum hit, as you did in step 5.

10  Choose Effects > Amplitude and Compression > Amplify. With both Gain sliders full left, click Apply.

**11** Locate the fourth hit, and again draw a rectangle around it, but as in step 7 don't include the yellow section at the bottom of the hit, which is the kick drum sound.

**12** Choose Effects > Amplitude and Compression > Amplify. With both Gain sliders full left, click Apply.

**13** Click in the Waveform Editor outside of the area you selected to deselect it. Return the playhead to the file's beginning, and then click the Transport Play button. Most of the sound from the hits is gone, but you can still hear a little bit of noise on the second and fourth hits.

**14** Choose the Lasso Selection tool from the Waveform Editor's upper toolbar, or type **D**.

**15** Go to the second hit, and carefully draw a lasso around the red/violet part of the waveform that sits above the yellow kick drum audio.

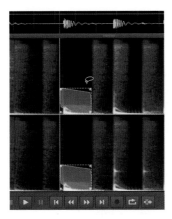

**16** Choose Edit > Cut, or press the Delete key.

**17** Go to the fourth hit, and carefully draw a lasso around the violet part of the waveform that sits above the yellow kick drum audio. Then choose Edit > Cut, or press the Delete key.

**18** Click the Transport Play button. The drum loop is the same as the original but without the four hits.

● **Note:** The technique of drawing a lasso around artifacts can remove sounds like finger squeaks on guitar strings, clicks or pops, breathing while a person plays an instrument, and many other artifacts. It takes experience to recognize what's an artifact and what's part of the sound, and also whether to choose the Spot Healing Brush tool and drag across the sound or choose the Lasso tool and either cut or reduce the artifact level. However, with sufficient practice, this type of restoration is extremely effective.

## Review questions

1 Which is more effective, automatic or manual click removal?

2 What is a "noise print"?

3 Is noise reduction good only for removing hiss?

4 What does "healing" do?

5 Are Audition's restoration tools amazing, or what? Name two ways other than restoration where these tools can be useful.

## Review answers

1 Automatic click removal is faster, but manual click removal can be more effective.

2 It's like a "fingerprint" that represents the specific sonic character of a section of noise. Subtracting this from the audio file removes the noise.

3 Noise reduction can minimize or even remove any constant background sound, as long as there's an isolated section where you can capture a noise print.

4 "Healing" replaces audio removed by the Spot Healing Brush tool with crossfaded, "good" audio from either side of the artifact.

5 Indeed they are; not only can you use them for fixing audio problems, but you can even use them in highly creative ways, like removing specific drum hits from drum loops or doing sound design.

# 6 MASTERING

## Lesson overview

In this lesson, you'll learn how to do the following:

- Use effects to improve the sound of a mixed, stereo piece of music

- Apply EQ to reduce "mud," emphasize the kick drum, and make cymbals more articulated

- Apply dynamics to give music more apparent level, which can also help overcome background noise in cars and other environments

- Create ambience for music that has a "dry," sterile sound

- Alter stereo imaging to create a wider stereo effect

- Make small edits to emphasize particular parts of a piece of music

 This lesson takes about 45 minutes to complete. This assumes you've copied the Lesson06 folder that contains the audio examples into the Lessons folder that you created on your hard drive for these projects. Remember that you needn't be concerned about modifying these files, because you can always return to the original versions by copying them from the *Adobe Audition CS6 Classroom in a Book* CD-ROM.

Mastering is the stage between mixing and distribution. By tasteful application of EQ, dynamics, waveform editing, widening, and other techniques, you can shape a piece of music into a refined audio experience that's ready for distribution or posting online.

# Mastering basics

Mastering is the process that occurs after mixing but before distribution. It's where you add any final edits or enhancements (equalization, dynamics, fade in or out, etc.) to a stereo or surround mixed file. With album projects (whether a CD or collection of music posted online), mastering also involves determining the correct order of the songs in the album ("sequencing" the songs) and matching their levels and timbres for a cohesive listening experience.

As the final link in the music production chain, mastering can make or break a project. As a result, people often hand off projects to veteran mastering engineers, not just for their technical expertise, but to enlist a fresh, objective set of ears.

However, if your goal with mastering is simply to make a good mix better, Audition provides the tools required for professional-level mastering. The more you work with mastering, the more your skills will improve. But it can't be emphasized enough that the most important mastering tool is a good set of ears that can analyze where a piece of music is deficient, coupled with the technical expertise of knowing what processing will compensate for those deficiencies.

In addition, remember that ideally the purpose of mastering is not to salvage a recording, but to enhance an already superb mix. If there's a problem with the mix, remix the tune; don't count on mastering to solve the problem.

In Lesson 4, "Signal Processing," you learned how to do basic mastering with the mastering suite of effects in the Special menu. This lesson takes a more "component" approach by using individual effects, which are presented in the order in which you would typically apply these effects (equalization, dynamics, ambience, stereo imaging), and waveform "touchup." Note that sometimes touching up the waveform occurs first if there are known problems that need to be fixed, such as a portion of the track is too quiet and needs to be raised in level with the Amplify effect.

# Step 1: equalization

Usually, the first step of mastering involves adjusting equalization to create a pleasing tonal balance.

1  With Audition open to the Waveform Editor, choose File > Open, navigate to the Lesson06 folder, and open the file KeepTheFunk.wav.

2  In the Effects Rack, click insert 1's right arrow and choose Filter and EQ > Parametric Equalizer.

3  If necessary, choose the Default preset from the Presets drop-down menu, and then select the 30dB Range radio button in the lower-right corner.

**4** Click the Transport Play button and listen. The music sounds a little "muddy" in the low frequencies and lacks crispness in the highs. Loop the file by clicking the Transport's loop button so it keeps playing while you make the following adjustments.

**5** One way to identify problem areas is to boost a parametric stage's Gain, sweep its Frequency, and listen to whether any frequencies jump out as excessive. So, click the Band 2 box, drag it all way up to +15dB, and drag the box left and right. Note that the sound is "tubby" around 150Hz.

**6** Drag the Band 2 box down to around -5dB at around 150Hz. Note how this tightens up the low end. The difference is subtle, but often mastering is about the cumulative effect of multiple subtle changes.

**7** The kick drum seems like it should be stronger and have more of a deep "thud" for this kind of music; use Band 1 to dial in the drum's frequency and add a narrow boost. Set Band 1's Q to 8, and drag the Band 1 box up to +15dB. Sweep the Frequency back and forth between 20 and 100Hz, and note that the kick really stands out around 45Hz.

**8** Bring the Band 1 level back down to around 5-6dB so the kick isn't too prominent.

**9** The hi-hat and cymbals seem kind of dull, but increasing the high-frequency response can improve that. Set Band 4's Q to 1.5, set Frequency to 8kHz, and drag the Band 4 box up to around +2dB.

**10** Toggle the power state button again for comparison. Note that in the screen shot, unused bands have been turned off for clarity. Keep Audition open for the next lesson.

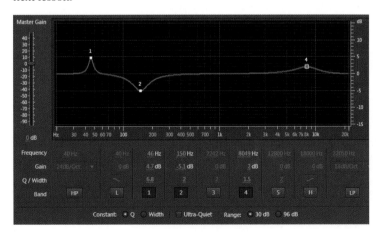

# Step 2: dynamics

Dynamics processing can make a piece of music "jump out" of the speakers because it acquires more punch and makes low-level sounds louder. This can also help the music overcome background noises found in many different listening environments. To avoid listener fatigue, you don't want to add *too* much processing and kill the dynamics, but some processing can produce a nice, lively lift.

This lesson uses the Multiband Compressor to control dynamics. In addition to offering compression in four frequency bands, there's an overall output limiter.

● **Note:** Dynamics is usually the last processor in a mastering chain because it sets the maximum allowable level. Adding effects afterward could increase or decrease the overall level.

● **Note:** The meters to the immediate right of each band's Threshold slider (whose position follows the numeric Threshold field) indicate the amount of compression. The further down the red "virtual LED" goes, the more compression is being applied.

1  In the Effects Rack, click insert 4's right arrow and choose Amplitude and Compression > Multiband Compressor. (The reason for choosing insert 4 is because you'll want to add some effects later between the EQ and dynamics.)

2  Choose the Pop Master preset from the Presets menu to give the music *much* more apparent loudness.

3  If you listen for a while, you'll hear that the dynamics have been reduced dramatically—in fact, too much. To restore some dynamics, set each band's Threshold parameter to -18.0dB.

4  Click in the limiter's Threshold field and drag down to -20dB. The sound becomes overly limited, squashed, and uneven. Now drag up to 0. No limiting is being applied, and the sound lacks "punch." Drag down to a good compromise setting between these two extremes, like -8.0dB.

5  Toggle the Effects Rack's power state to compare the sound with and without the EQ and Multiband Compressor. The processed sound is fuller, tighter, more distinct, and louder. Also note that the Multiband Dynamics has emphasized the EQ changes made previously.

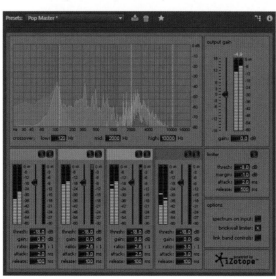

# Step 3: ambience

Although reverb is seldom added during mastering, the music seems a little "dry." So, you'll add some ambience to give the illusion of the music being played in an acoustic space.

1   In the Effects Rack, click insert 2's right arrow and choose Reverb > Studio Reverb.

2   Choose the Room Ambience 1 preset from the Presets menu. You'll need to stop the Transport to choose a preset. After choosing the preset, click the Transport Play button.

3   Set the Dry slider to 0 and the Wet slider to 40% so it's easy to hear the results of any edits.

4   Set Decay to 500ms, Early Reflections to 20%, Width to 100, High Frequency Cut to 6000Hz, Low Frequency Cut to 100Hz, and both Damping and Diffusion to 100%.

5   Adjust the blend of Dry and Wet signals. Set Dry to 90% and Wet to 50%.

6   Toggle the Reverb's power state; you won't hear much difference unless you listen very carefully, because this adds just a tiny bit of "spice." The added ambience is most noticeable when the drums hit by themselves.

▶ **Tip:** With albums that contain tracks recorded at different times or in different studios, sometimes adding a subtle overall ambience produces a more cohesive feeling.

● **Note:** The Studio Reverb trades off sound quality for real-time adjustment. For critical applications, one of the other reverbs is preferable, but for learning how reverb affects the sound, the Studio Reverb is a better choice due to its immediacy in changing settings.

# Step 4: stereo imaging

As with reverb, stereo imaging isn't added often, but it's appropriate for this particular lesson. Stereo imaging stretches the stereo image so the left channel moves more to the left, and the right channel moves more to the right. In this lesson, increasing the stereo image helps separate the two guitars in the opposite channels even more.

1   In the Effects Rack, click insert 3's right arrow and choose Special > Mastering. Only the Widener will be used.

**2** If necessary, choose the Default preset from the Presets menu.

**3** Set the Widener slider to 85%.

**4** Toggle the Effects Rack's power state to compare the sound with and without the various mastering processors—the results speak for themselves. Also, try turning the power state on and off for the individual processors to hear each processor's overall contribution to the sound.

# Step 5: "push" the drum hits; then apply the changes

Four drum hits happen between 23.25 and 24 seconds. You'll boost them just a bit to give them more emphasis.

**1** Click the Transport Stop button. Select the four hits (zoom in if necessary) and add +3.9dB of gain with the HUD (heads-up display).

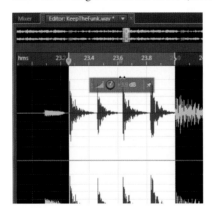

**2** Play the file to hear the result of boosting these four drum hits.

**3** You'll apply all these effects to make them a permanent part of the file, which will also redraw the waveform to show the changes caused by mastering. In the Effects Rack, choose Entire File from the Process drop-down menu.

**4** Click Apply. Audition applies the result of all the effects to the file and removes the effects from the Effects Rack.

**Note:** Making edits to the waveform can be done prior to adding effects or after adding effects if a particular issue doesn't become obvious until after you've applied effects that change the overall sound in a subtle, or even dramatic, way.

**Note:** The Apply function resets all effects to their default value. If you don't like the results of using Apply, choose Edit > Undo to restore the effects and the settings you edited.

**Note:** It can take years to become good at the art and science of mastering, especially if the file has problems that need to be fixed. Nonetheless, most mastering simply revolves around EQ, dynamics, and some selected other processors.

# Review questions

1 At what stage of the music production process does mastering occur?

2 Is mastering only about optimizing individual tracks?

3 What are the most essential processors used in mastering?

4 Is adding ambience recommended when mastering?

5 What is the main disadvantage of excessive dynamics compression?

# Review answers

1 Mastering occurs after mixing but before music distribution.

2 With album projects, mastering also sequences the songs in the correct order and aims for sonic consistency from track to track.

3 Typically, EQ and dynamics processors are the main effects used in the mastering process.

4 No. Normally ambience is added during the mixing process but can sometimes improve the sound when added while mastering.

5 The main disadvantage is a lack of dynamics, which can lead to listener fatigue because there are no significant variations between loud and soft passages.

# 7 SOUND DESIGN

## Lesson overview

In this lesson, you'll learn how to do the following:

- Apply extreme processing to everyday sounds

- Create special effects

- Change the environments in which sounds occur

- Use pitch shifting and filtering to alter sounds

- Use the Doppler Effect to add motion

 This lesson takes approximately 45 minutes to complete. This assumes you've copied the Lesson07 folder that contains the audio examples into the Lessons folder that you created on your hard drive for these projects. Remember that you needn't be concerned about modifying these files, because you can always return to the original versions by copying them from the *Adobe Audition CS6 Classroom in a Book* CD-ROM.

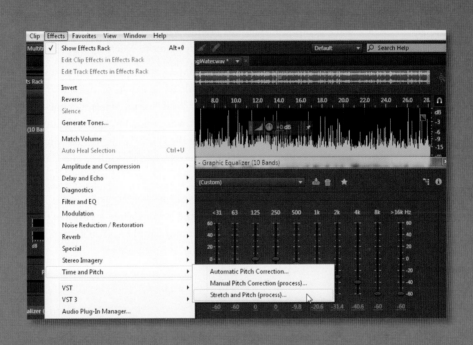

With Audition's array of signal processors, it's possible to modify common, everyday sounds into something completely different—like transforming a wall fan into a spaceship's engine room or a running faucet into crickets at night.

# About sound design

*Sound design* is the process of capturing, recording, and/or manipulating the audio elements used in movies, television, video games, museum installations, theater, postproduction, and other art forms that require sound. Sound design can refer to music, but this lesson emphasizes sound effects and ambience. These types of sounds are also common in sonic logos (like the sound you hear to identify Intel Inside or NBC) or the sounds layered in movie scenes to create a particular mood.

For example, a scene in a science-fiction movie might have the characters in a spaceship's engine room where the drone of the engine provides a suspenseful backdrop as the protagonists search for the cause of a radiation leak. Occasionally, against this engine sound backdrop, sudden, sharp sounds might appear to indicate a new leak breaking through the engine wall. Of course, no one is in space recording these sounds; it's up to the sound designer to create appropriate effects.

Sound effects libraries are available from several companies, but a sound designer will often modify these or record sounds using a field recorder. For example, in the beginning of the movie *Raiders of the Lost Ark,* a giant boulder rolls toward Indiana Jones. The sound of the rolling boulder was created by taping a microphone to the rear bumper of a Honda and recording the sound of the car backing down a gravel driveway. Subsequent sound design work turned this into a huge, ominous sound. Another example involves the TIE fighters in *Star Wars*: The sound of them diving is a modified elephant cry.

Two files were recorded for the following lessons using a portable digital recorder: water running into a sink from a faucet and a wall fan. You'll learn how to turn these sounds into a variety of sound effects and ambience.

# Creating rain sounds

With sound design, it helps to start with a sound in the same genre. To create rain, the running water would most likely produce a better end result than the recording of the fan.

1   Choose File > Open, navigate to the Lesson07 folder, and open the file RunningWater.wav.

2   Click the Transport Loop button so the water sound plays back continuously. Click the Transport Play button to audition the loop.

3   You'll first change this sound to a light, spring rain. Click the Effects Rack tab, and drag the panel's lower splitter bar downward to extend the panel to its full height because you'll be using several effects.

4   Click Effects Rack insert 1's right arrow button and choose Filter and EQ > Graphic Equalizer (10 Bands). Ensure that Range is 48dB and Master Gain is 0.

5   Pull the sliders for all bands other than 4k and 8k all the way down to -24dB.

6   Bring the 4k sand 8k sliders down to -10dB.

7   Toggle the effect's power state on and off a few times to compare how the EQ has changed the overall sound. With the EQ power on, you now have a light spring rain. You might find the effect more realistic if you bring the 8k slider down to -15dB.

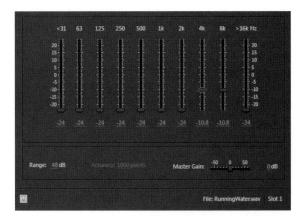

8   Suppose you wanted to do sound design for a scene where the character is inside a house, and it is raining outside. In this case there would be fewer high frequencies due to the house walls and windows blocking the highs. Pull the 8k slider down all the way, and the rain sounds more like it's outside.

9   To surround the character with rain if the character, say, opens the door, leaves the house, and is in the middle of the rain, click insert 2's right arrow button and choose Delay and Echo > Delay.

10  The Default patch spreads out the sound, but it's too separated: Rain wouldn't fall only to the character's right and left, but all around. Change both Mix controls to 50% so there's a convincing panorama of rain.

11  It's important that the delay not create any kind of rhythm. Set the Left Channel Delay Time to around 420ms and the Right Channel Delay Time to 500ms. These delays are long enough that you won't perceive a rhythm.

12  If the character then goes outside again, return to the Graphic Equalizer window by double-clicking its insert in the Effects Rack, and increase the 8kHz slider to around -14kHz. Keep this project open as you move to the next lesson.

# Creating a babbling brook

Changing the scene from rain to a babbling brook in the distance simply involves removing the delay and changing the EQ setting.

1   Click the Delay insert's arrow, and choose Remove Effect. A babbling brook has a more distinct sound than sheets of rain, so you don't need the additional "rain drops" created by the Delay.

2   Click on the Graphic Equalizer's window to select it. Set Range to 120dB and Master Gain to 0dB.

3   Set the Graphic Equalizer sliders as follows: <31, 63, 8k, and >16k all to -60dB. Set 125 and 250 to 0, 500 to -10, 1k to -20, 2k to -30, and 4k to -40.

4   The babbling brook is now in the distance. As the character moves closer to the brook, increase 2k to -20 and 4k to -30. Now the brook sounds closer. Keep this project open as you move on to the next lesson.

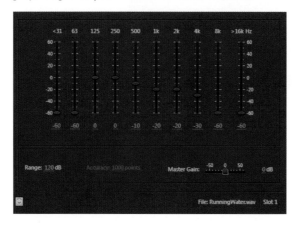

# Creating insects at night

It's even possible to use the running water to create a nighttime insect/crickets sound. This lesson demonstrates how signal processing can turn one sound into something completely different.

1   Double-click in the Waveform Editor to select the entire waveform.

2   From the Effects menu near the top of the window, choose Time and Pitch > Stretch and Pitch (process).

3   In the Stretch and Pitch window, select the Default preset if it is not already selected.

4   Move the Pitch Shift slider all the way to the left (-36 semitones), and then click OK. It will take several seconds for processing to occur.

5   Click on the Graphic Equalizer window to select it. With Range still at 120dB, move all sliders to -60dB except set 4k to 10dB. Click the Transport Play button to hear the processed sound.

6   You can smooth out the sound and make it sound a little more distant by adding reverb. In the Effects Rack's insert 3, click the right arrow button and choose Reverb > Studio Reverb. Stop playback by clicking the Transport Stop button so you can select a reverb preset.

7   Click the Presets drop-down menu and choose Great Hall.

8   Click the Transport Play button, and listen to your refined insects at night sound.

● **Note:** Extreme pitch shifting can add anomalies, like volume spikes or clicks, at the file's beginning and end. If so, make an audio selection that excludes the first and last two seconds, and then choose Edit > Crop. Extreme shifting may also lower the volume, so you might want to increase the Effects Rack's Output control.

## Creating an alien choir

For the last effect using the running water sound, you'll create a totally abstract sound that's ethereal and quite evocative.

1   If the entire waveform isn't already selected, double-click in the Waveform Editor.

2   Choose Effects > Time and Pitch > Stretch and Pitch (process). The settings should be the same as they were previously, but if not, choose the preset Default from the drop-down menu.

3   If needed, move the Pitch Shift slider all the way to the left (-36 semitones), and then click OK. It will take several seconds for processing to occur.

4   Make an audio selection that excludes the first and last two seconds, and then choose Edit > Crop.

5   The level will be very low, so let's bring it up. With the waveform still selected, choose Effects >Amplitude and Compression > Normalize (process).

6   Select Normalize To and enter **50%**. Normalize All Channels Equally should also be selected. Click OK.

7   Bypass the Graphic Equalizer. The Reverb should still have the Great Hall preset selected. Move the Decay, Width, Diffusion, and Wet sliders all the way to the right. Move the Dry slider all the way to the left. When you click the Transport Play button, you should now hear an ethereal, animated pad.

8   Now add some animation for the final touch. In an Effects Rack's insert after the Studio Reverb, click the insert's right arrow and choose Delay and Echo > Echo. Select the preset Spooky.

**9** In an Effects Rack's insert after the Echo, click the insert's right arrow and choose Modulation > Chorus. Select the preset 10 Voices. You may need to turn down the Effects Rack's Output control to avoid clipping. Note how extensive pitch stretching coupled with effects from the Studio Reverb, Echo, and Chorus can turn running water into an alien soundscape.

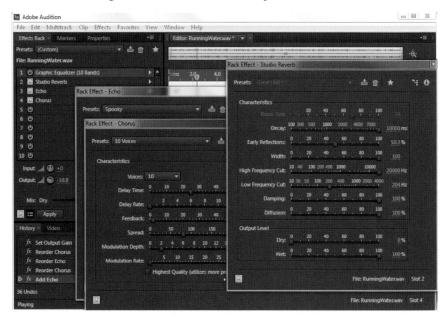

# Creating sci-fi machine effects

Just as you used running water to generate water-based effects, the fan sound makes a good basis for machine and mechanical sounds. This lesson describes how to turn an ordinary wall fan sound into a variety of science-fiction, spaceship sound effects.

**1** If Audition is open, close it without saving to start fresh. Open the program, choose File > Open, navigate to the Lesson07 folder, and open the file Fan.wav. Click the Transport Play button to hear what the file sounds like.

**2** Double-click inside the Waveform Editor to select the entire waveform.

**3** Choose Effects > Time and Pitch > Stretch and Pitch (process).

**4** Select the preset Default if it is not already selected.

**5** Set the Pitch Shift slider to -24 semitones. Lowering the pitch makes the engine sound "bigger," but lowering beyond -24 semitones makes the sound indistinct. Click OK; processing will take a few seconds.

**6** As in the previous lessons, for the smoothest sound, make an audio selection that excludes the first and last two seconds, and then choose Edit > Crop.

**7** Click the Effects Rack insert 1's right arrow button and choose Special > Guitar Suite. From the Presets drop-down menu, choose Drum Suite. Click the Transport Play button, and note how the sound becomes more metallic and machine-like.

**8** Click the Effects Rack insert 2's right arrow button and choose Filter and EQ > Parametric Equalizer. If the preset Default is not already selected, choose it from the Presets drop-down menu.

**9** Deselect bands 1–5 to leave only the L (low) and H (high) bands active.

**10** Click the L and H Q/Width button to select the steepest (the button's center line is most vertical) slope.

**11** If the file isn't already playing, click the Transport Play button. Pull the H box all the way down and left to around 3kHz.

**12** Pull the L box up to 20 and right to about 300Hz.

**13** Add some character to the engine with a resonant peak that increases the level in a narrow band of frequencies. Click the Band 2 button to enable that parametric stage. Edit Frequency to 500Hz, Gain to 10dB, and Q/Width to around 20. The Guitar Suite and Parametric EQ effects provide the main engine sound.

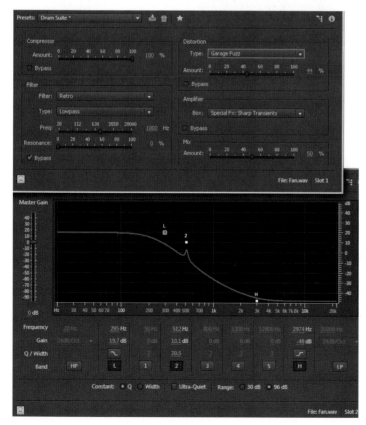

**14** Now let's travel to a different section of the virtual spaceship, away from the main hum of the machine room but where you can still hear the engine rumble. Click the Effects Rack insert 3's right arrow button, and choose Reverb > Studio Reverb.

**15** Click the Transport Stop button to change the Studio Reverb preset, and then choose Great Hall from the Presets drop-down menu.

**16** You'll now add lots of reverb but only to the low frequencies to emphasize the rumble. Set the Decay, Width, Diffusion, and Wet sliders all the way to the right. Set the High Frequency Cut slider to 200Hz, the Low Frequency Cut slider full left, and the Dry slider full left. Click the Transport Play button.

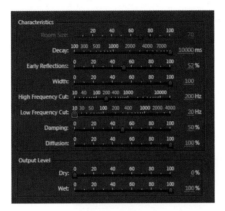

**17** Bypass the Studio Reverb to return to the engine room sound, or enable it to move farther away to a different part of the spaceship. Leave this project open in preparation for the next lesson.

## Creating an alien drone flyby

In addition to creating static sound effects, Audition includes a Doppler Shifter processor that imparts motion—from left to right, around in circles, tracing an arc, and so on. In this lesson you'll take advantage of the Doppler Shifter processor to "animate" the sound of an alien drone.

**1** If the waveform isn't already selected, double-click within the Waveform Editor to select the entire waveform.

**2** Choose Effects > Time and Pitch > Stretch and Pitch (process).

**3** Choose the preset Default from the Presets menu. Set the Stretch slider to 200%. Click OK; processing will take a few seconds.

**4** Either bypass the Parametric Equalizer effect, or click its insert's arrow and choose Remove Effect.

**5** Either bypass the Studio Reverb effect, or click its insert's arrow and choose Remove Effect.

**6** If the Guitar Suite window isn't open already, double-click its insert in the Effects Rack. Choose the preset Lowest Fidelity from the Presets drop-down menu.

**7** With the entire waveform still selected, choose Effects > Special > Doppler Shifter (process).

**8** Choose the preset Whizzing by From Left to Right from the Doppler Shifter's Presets drop-down menu, and then click OK. Click the Transport Play button to hear the drone fly by from left to right.

**9** Because the sound is most effective if it fades up from nothing and fades out to nothing, in the Waveform Editor click the Fade In button in the upper-left corner, and drag it to the right about two seconds.

**10** Similarly, click the Fade Out button in the Waveform Editor's upper right, and drag it left to about eight seconds.

**11** To enhance the Doppler Shifter effect, click an Effects Rack insert's right arrow and choose Modulation > Flanger.

**12** In the Flanger window, choose the preset Heavy Flange from the Presets drop-down menu.

**13** Click on the Modulation Rate parameter, type **0.1**, and then press Enter. Using the slider would make it almost impossible to choose this precise a value.

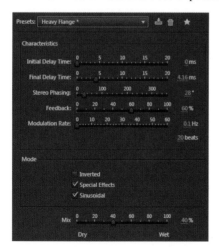

**14** Click the Transport Play button, and the alien drone will sound even more realistic as it flies by from left to right.

# Review questions

1 What is sound design?

2 What effects can provide spatial placement within Audition?

3 What artifacts can extreme pitch shifting add?

4 Is the Guitar Suite useful only for guitar effects?

5 Do you need to use commercial sound libraries to create sound effects?

# Review answers

1 Sound design is the process of capturing, recording, and/or manipulating the audio elements used in movies, television, video games, museum installations, theater, postproduction, and other art forms that require sound.

2 EQ, reverb, delay/echo, and the Doppler Shifter can all contribute to placing a sound in the stereo or surround field.

3 Extreme pitch shifting may cause unpredictable amplitude spikes at the beginning and/ or end of the file, as well as lower the file's overall level.

4 The Guitar Suite offers huge possibilities for sound design; this lesson has tapped only a bit of its potential.

5 Not always. Because of Audition's rich selection of signal processors, ordinary sounds can be transformed into entirely different sounds.

# 8 CREATING AND RECORDING FILES

## Lesson overview

In this lesson, you'll learn how to do the following:

- Record into the Waveform Editor

- Record into the Multitrack Editor

- Drag and drop files into the Multitrack Editor

- Import tracks from CDs into the Waveform Editor

- Create custom templates for the Multitrack Editor

 This lesson takes approximately 30 minutes to complete. This assumes you've copied the Lesson08 folder that contains the audio examples into the Lessons folder you created on your hard drive for these projects. Remember that you needn't be concerned about modifying these files, because you can always return to the original versions by copying them from the *Adobe Audition CS6 Classroom in a Book* CD-ROM.

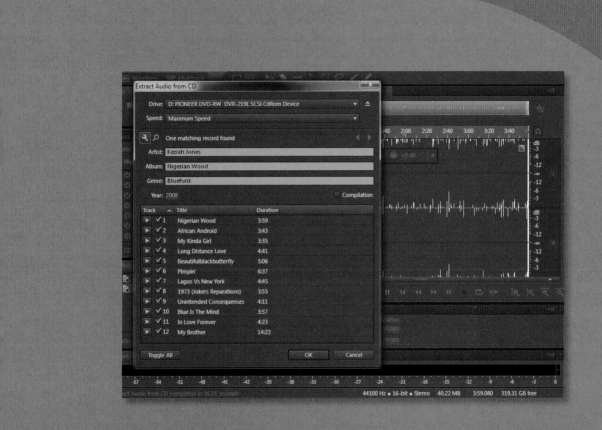

Not only can you record audio into Audition's
Waveform Editor or Multitrack Editor, you can also
extract audio from standard Red Book Compact Discs
or drag files from the desktop directly into either
Audition Editor.

# Recording into the Waveform Editor

**Note:** You will need an audio CD to do one of these lessons.

Lesson 1, "Audio Interfacing," covered audio interfaces and how to map the interface's physical inputs and outputs to Audition's virtual inputs and outputs. This lesson covers how to record and import audio into Audition, as well as how to extract audio from CDs. If necessary, review Lesson 1 to make sure you understand the principles behind interfacing. This lesson assumes you know how to map inputs and outputs. You'll start by recording audio into the Waveform Editor.

1 Connect a microphone, guitar, portable music player output, cell phone audio output, or other signal source into a compatible audio interface input or internal audio input on your computer.

**Note:** The optimum input level should never go into the red on a level meter. Today's digital recording technology allows for sufficient headroom, so it's not necessary to have the highest levels possible. Also, once you've recorded in Audition, you can use the Amplify or Normalize effects to bring up the level as needed.

2 Adjust the interface's Input level control for an appropriate signal level. The interface will have either a physical meter or dedicated control panel software that monitors the inputs and outputs, and displays signal strength. You'll need to rely on the interface's meters when setting levels because Audition's Waveform Editor indicates levels only when recording or paused, not when stopped.

3 Open Audition. Choose File > New > Audio File.

4 A dialog box appears with an editable File Name field, and three fields with drop-down menus. Enter the File Name **RecordNarration**.

5 Audition defaults to a 48000Hz sample rate, which is standard for video. However, for this lesson choose 44100Hz—the standard for CD audio—as the sample rate from the drop-down menu. The most common choices for sample rates include:

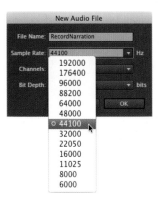

- **44100Hz** is the same rate used for CDs and is the most "universal" sample rate for audio.

- **48000Hz** is the standard choice for video projects.

- **32000Hz** is common in broadcast and satellite transmissions.

- **22050Hz** was a popular choice for games and low-resolution digital audio. Sample rates lower than 22050Hz are of very low fidelity and are generally used for speech, dictation, toys, and so on.

- **Sample rates above 48000** are rarely used, although some studios record at 88200 or 96000, believing that it has the potential to improve sound quality or provides a better archival medium. Most studies show that few people can accurately tell the difference between 44100 and 48000 or higher sample rates. Higher sample rates also require more storage space; that is, a one-minute 96kHz file will require twice the space as the same file at 48kHz.

6   Choose the desired number of channels from the Channels drop-down menu. For a mic or electric guitar, choose Mono. For a portable music player or other stereo signal source, choose Stereo. The option 5.1 is for recording in surround sound.

7   Choose 24 bits from the Bit Depth drop-down menu. Here is a list of the choices and their descriptions:

- **8 bits** is low resolution and is not used for professional audio. It's common for games and consumer devices.

- **16 bits** is the resolution for CDs and offers industry-standard audio quality.

- **24 bits** is preferred by most recording engineers because it provides more headroom, and setting levels is less critical because there is greater dynamic range. Files that are 24-bits take up 50 percent more space than 16-bit files, but given the low cost of hard disk storage, this is an acceptable trade-off.

- **32 (float)** results in the highest resolution but offers no significant advantage over 24-bit files. They take up more space, and many programs are not compatible with 32-bit float files.

8   After making the selections in steps 4–7, click OK.

9   Assuming you're using an external audio interface, choose Edit > Preferences (Audition > Preferences) > Audio Hardware. Verify that the correct Device Class, I/O Buffer size, and Sample Rate are selected. For Windows users, also verify that the Device Class and Device settings are correct. Click OK.

10  To see levels in Audition while recording, choose Window > Level Meters if the meters are not already in your workspace. Dock the meters horizontally along the bottom of your workspace for the best meter resolution.

**11** Click the Transport's red Record button. Recording begins immediately. Speak into the mic or play back whatever sound source connects to your interface. You'll see the waveform being drawn in the Waveform Editor in real time, and the meters will reflect the current input signal level.

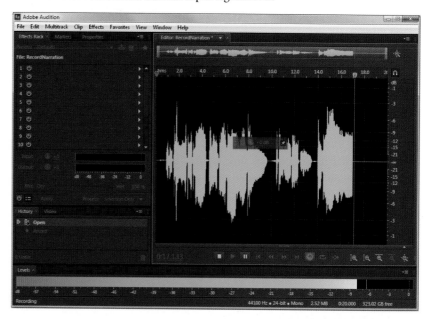

**12** Click the Transport Pause button. Recording will pause, but the meters will still show the incoming signal level.

**13** To resume recording, click the Pause button or Record button.

**14** Click the Stop button to stop recording. The waveform you recorded will be selected.

▶ **Tip:** Being able to record over previously recorded material can speed up the recording of narration. If you make a mistake in a particular line, click at the beginning of the line and re-record it.

**15** Click somewhere in the middle of the Waveform Editor (i.e., where you've already recorded something), and then click the Record button to record over the previously recorded material.

**16** Record for a few seconds, and click Stop. The audio between where you started and stopped recording will be selected.

**17** Leave Audition open and your signal source and interface set up in preparation for the next lesson.

# Recording into the Multitrack Editor

Audition not only integrates the Waveform Editor and Multitrack Editor, but can transfer files easily between the two. This lesson shows you how to record into the Multitrack Editor, explains how to transfer your recording into the Waveform Editor for editing, and then describes how to return it to the Multitrack Editor.

1 Choose File > New > Multitrack Session.

A dialog box appears with fields for an editable File Name, Folder Location for storing the project, and project Template. The dialog box also includes Sample Rate and Bit Depth fields identical to those in the New Audio File dialog box, and a Master field that determines whether the output is Mono, Stereo, or a surround format (if supported by your interface).

2 Enter the Session Name **MultitrackRecording**.

3 The default folder location for saving projects is within the User's Documents folder (Windows or Mac). For this tutorial, accept the default folder.

4 Choose the 24 Track Music Session template. Later in this lesson we'll cover how you can create your own templates.

5 Click OK. The Multitrack Editor opens.

6 Each track has an Input field; an arrow to its left points right toward the input field. For Track 1, choose the interface input to which your signal source connects from the Input field's drop-down menu. A track can be stereo or mono.

ADOBE AUDITION CS6 CLASSROOM IN A BOOK  **147**

---

**Tip:** It's good practice to have a separate, high-speed (at least 7200 rpm) drive with a dedicated folder for storing your projects. This separates streaming audio on the audio drive from program operations on your main drive. Also, backing up the audio drive backs up all of your projects.

**Note:** Sample Rate, Bit Depth, and the Master output are stored with the Template, so once you've chosen a template, these options are grayed out. If you want to edit these settings, select None for Template.

**Note:** If the Input field is not visible, click the double-arrow button in the upper left of the Multitrack Editor's toolbar.

**7** As soon as you select an input, a track's R button becomes available to Arm For Record (*arming* means the track is ready to record as soon as you click the Transport's Record button). Click the R button and talk into the mic; note that the track's meter indicates the incoming level.

**8** Click the Transport Record button to begin recording. Record your signal source for at least 15–20 seconds. As when recording in the Waveform Editor, you can pause and resume recording by clicking the Pause button. After you've finished recording, click the Transport Stop button.

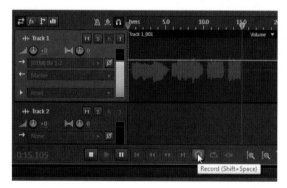

**9** Place the playhead around 5 seconds into the file.

**10** Click the Transport Record button, and record for about 5 seconds or so. Then click Stop.

**11** Click on the track where you just recorded (i.e., between the 5- and 10-second marks). Notice that there is a separate layer recorded on top of the previously recorded track. By clicking on it, you can drag it left or right, as well as drag it down into Track 2.

⬤ **Note:** Audition makes it easy to transfer files back and forth between the Multitrack Editor and Waveform Editor. To open a Multitrack Editor audio file in the Waveform Editor, double-click the clip in the Multitrack Editor or right-click (Control-click) on it and choose Edit Source File.

⬤ **Note:** To transfer the file back into the Multitrack Editor at the position from which it came, click the Multitrack button or type 0. To transfer it elsewhere in the session, or even to a different session, right-click (Control-click) in the Waveform Editor and choose Insert into Multitrack > [name of Multitrack Session]. The file will start at the Multitrack Editor's playhead position and be inserted into the first available track where no audio is recorded at the playhead position.

**12** In preparation for the next lesson, click on each recorded audio selection, and press the Delete key to remove all audio from the project. Click the Transport's Move Playhead to Previous button.

# Drag and drop into an Audition Editor

In addition to recording files into Audition, you can drag and drop files from the desktop or any open computer folder (whose contents are visible) into the Waveform Editor or a Multitrack Editor track. The file can be in any file format that Audition recognizes; in the Multitrack Editor, it will automatically be converted to the project settings. For example, if you created a project with 24-bit resolution, you can bring it in as a 16-bit WAV file or even an MP3 format file.

With the Waveform Editor, you simply drag the file from the desktop into the editor. This lesson demonstrates how to drag and drop a file into the Multitrack Editor.

**1** This lesson assumes the Multitrack Editor from the previous lesson is still open. If not, choose File > New > Multitrack Session. Leave the default folder location as is, and select 24 Track Music Session as the template.

**2** Make sure the Lesson08 folder is on your desktop, and open it to reveal its three files. If needed, resize Audition's window so you can see Audition's tracks and the open Lesson08 folder at the same time.

**3** Drag the file Caliente Bass.wav to the start of Track 1. A yellow line appears where the dragged file will start; this should be flush with the beginning of the track. Note that if you drag slightly past (to the left of) the track's beginning, the yellow line will "snap" to the track's start. Release the mouse button.

● **Note:** The line that separates the bottom of one track and the top of another is a *splitter bar*. You can click on this line and drag up or down to decrease or increase, respectively, the above track's height.

**4** Similarly, drag the file Caliente Drums.wav into Track 2 and the file Caliente Guitar.wav into Track 3.

**5** Click the Transport Play button to hear the tracks play back simultaneously.

**6** These tracks were recorded at a high volume, and they are overloading the output. Adjust each track's volume control to -6dB (the Transport can either be playing or stopped).

**7** Click the Transport's Move Playhead to Previous button until the playhead is at the beginning of the song.

**8** Click Play. The sound is now undistorted, and none of the meters go into the red (clipping) zone.

# Importing a track from an audio CD

Because the tracks on audio CDs are in a specific file format, they cannot be dragged directly into Audition without processing. However, you can access a function that extracts audio from CDs and places it into the Waveform Editor. You can then edit it or transfer it to the Multitrack Editor as described previously.

You need a standard audio CD to complete this lesson.

1  Close Audition and don't save anything in order to start fresh.

2  Open Audition. You can extract audio from CDs in either the Waveform Editor or Multitrack Editor, or even if no project is open.

3  Insert a standard audio CD into your computer's optical drive.

4  Choose File > Extract Audio from CD.

   A dialog box appears that shows the drive, and if the computer is connected to the Internet, Audition retrieves information from the freedb database to populate the Track, Title, and Duration fields.

5  The Speed drop-down menu lets you choose the extraction speed. Leave it at the default (Maximum Speed); if errors occur during the extraction process, choose a slower speed.

6  All CD tracks are selected as the default. They will be extracted one at a time, each as a separate file. You need to extract only one track for this lesson, so click the Toggle All button to deselect all tracks, and then select one track.

7  Click OK. The extraction process begins and places the audio in the Waveform Editor. Leave Audition open in preparation for the next lesson.

# Saving a template

A *template* is a snapshot of all the session settings at the time of saving the template. Audition includes several template files for Multitrack Sessions, but you can also create your own.

1  Choose File > New > Multitrack Session.

2  The Session Name and Folder Location don't matter.

3  Choose None as the Template from the drop-down menu, and then choose the desired Sample Rate, Bit Depth, and Master Output. Click OK.

4  Arrange the Multitrack Session session as desired including the number of tracks, layout, processors in the tracks, levels, and so on. These settings will be incorporated into the template.

5  After you have everything set to your liking and are ready to make a template, choose File > Save As.

6  Name the session with the desired template name (e.g., VO + Stereo Sound Track).

7  For the Location, click Browse. On Windows, navigate to Computer > C: Drive > Users > Public > Public Documents > Adobe > Audition > 6.0. Click Session Templates, click Open, and then click Save. On a Mac, browse to root drive > Users > Shared > Adobe > Audition > 5.0. Click Session Templates, and then click Save. Next time you open a new Multitrack Session, the template you created will be available in the drop-down menu of templates.

# Review questions

1   Can you monitor input levels with Audition's metering when the Transport is stopped?

2   What is the most common sample rate for digital audio?

3   What is the preferred bit resolution for professional audio?

4   How can you add audio to the Waveform Editor or Multitrack Editor without employing the process of recording?

5   Is there a way to create a custom template so your session is already preconfigured the way you want it to be?


# Review answers

1   You can monitor input levels with Audition's metering when the Transport is stopped in the Multitrack Editor but not the Waveform Editor.

2   The most common sample rate is 44100Hz, which is used for CDs and many other digital audio applications.

3   Most engineers prefer to record with 24-bit resolution, although recording with 16-bit resolution is also common.

4   You can drag and drop files to either editor and extract audio from audio CD tracks into the Waveform Editor.

5   Yes, you can create as many custom templates as you like for various applications.

# 9 MULTITRACK EDITOR ORIENTATION

## Lesson overview

In this lesson, you'll learn how to do the following:

- Integrate the Waveform and Multitrack Editors so you can switch back and forth between the two

- Play back a specific part of music repeatedly (looped playback)

- Edit track level and position in the stereo field

- Apply EQ, effect, and send areas in tracks

- Apply EQ to tracks using the Multitrack Editor's built-in parametric EQ

- Apply effects to individual tracks

- Process multiple tracks with a single effect to save CPU power and produce more consistent results

- Map effects channels so that outputs can feed different audio channels than the default settings

- Set up side-chain effects so that one track can control the effect in another track

 This lesson takes about 70 minutes to complete. This assumes you've copied the Lesson09 folder that contains the audio examples into the Lessons folder that you created on your hard drive for these projects. Remember that you needn't be concerned about modifying these files, because you can always return to the original versions by copying them from the *Adobe Audition CS6 Classroom in a Book* CD-ROM.

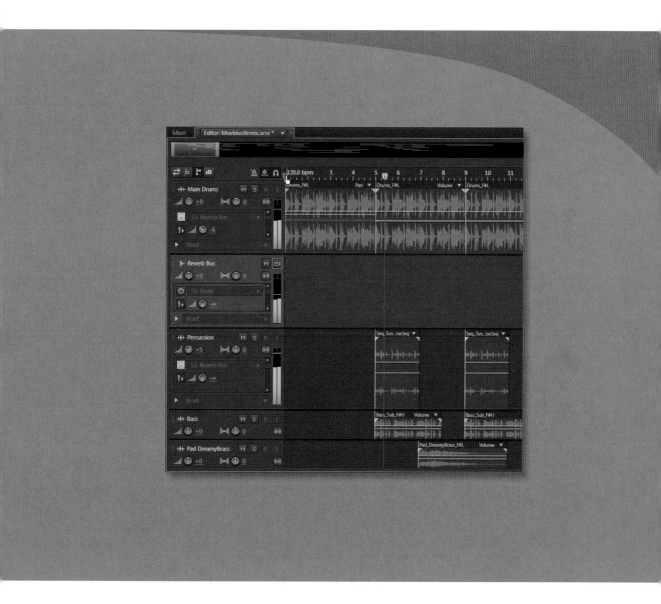

The Multitrack Editor is where you assemble clips, add
effects, change levels and panning, and create buses
for routing tracks to various effects.

# About multitrack production

Before beginning the lessons, it's important to understand a Multitrack Session's workflow so the lessons have a context.

In the Waveform Editor, a single clip is the only audio element. A multitrack production assembles multiple audio clips to create a musical composition. The audio resides in *tracks*, which you can think of as "containers" for clips. For example, one track could contain drum sounds, another bass, a third vocals, and so on. A track can contain a single long clip or multiple short clips that can be identical or different. A clip can even be positioned on top of another clip in a track (however, only the clip that is on top will play back), or clips can overlap to create crossfades (described in Lesson 11).

The production process consists of four main stages:

- **Tracking.** This involves recording or importing audio into the Multitrack Session. For example, with a rock band, tracking could consist of recording drums, bass, guitar, and vocals. These might be recorded individually (each player records a track, typically while listening to a metronome for reference) in particular combinations (e.g., drums and bass recorded simultaneously) or as an ensemble (all instruments play live and are recorded as they play).

- **Overdubbing.** This is the process of recording additional tracks. For example, a singer might sing a harmony line to supplement the original vocal.

- **Editing.** After recording the tracks, editing can polish them. For example, with a vocal track you could remove the audio between verses and choruses to reduce any residual noise or leakage from other instruments. You might even alter the arrangement, like cut a solo section to half its original length.

> **Note:** Some processes are available only in one editor or the other. If a menu option is gray in either editor, that option is not available.

- **Mixing.** After editing, the tracks are blended together into a final stereo or surround file. The mixing process primarily involves adjusting levels and adding effects. A Multitrack Session in Audition CS6 provides the tools to do basic editing tasks during the mixing process, but if detailed edits are needed, Session audio can be transferred to the Waveform Editor for further editing.

# Multitrack and Waveform Editor integration

A unique Adobe Audition feature is that it offers different environments for waveform editing and multitrack production. In addition, these are not isolated from each other. Audio in the Multitrack Editor is catalogued in the Waveform Editor's file selector and can be opened in the Waveform Editor for editing. This lesson illustrates how the Multitrack and Waveform Editors work together.

1 With Audition open, navigate to the Lesson09 folder, and open the Multitrack Session MoebiusRemix.sesx from the MoebiusRemix folder.

2 Place the playhead at the beginning of the file, and click the Transport Play button. Like the Waveform Editor, the Multitrack Editor plays linearly from start to finish. However, because the Multitrack Editor consists of multiple, parallel *tracks*, each of which can play back a clip, multiple clips can play back simultaneously. Play the song to become familiar with it.

3 To check out the Waveform and Multitrack Editor integration, click the first clip in the Main Drums track (Drums_F#L) to select it.

4 Click the Waveform tab to switch to the Waveform Editor.

5 The clip you clicked on appears in the Waveform Editor, ready for editing.

6 Click the Waveform Editor's file selector drop-down menu. It shows all the clips in the Multitrack Session so that you can choose any of them for editing.

● **Note:** You'll often see multiple versions of the same clip in the Multitrack Editor. However, there is only one physical clip, which is stored in RAM; the graphic clips in the Multitrack Editor just reference the physical clip. For example, if there are four copies of the same clip in a row, four separate clips don't play back sequentially—the clip stored in RAM plays four times, as instructed by the Multitrack Editor.

7 Choose the file Bass_Sub_F#H for editing. It sounds a bit too loud in the track, so you'll reduce the level by 1dB.

8 Press Ctrl+A (Control+A) to select the entire file.

9 Choose Effects > Amplitude and Compression > Amplify.

10 Reduce the right and left channels by typing in the value **-1dB**, and then click Apply.

11 Click the Multitrack tab to return to the Multitrack Session. All the Bass_Sub_F#H clip levels have been reduced by 1dB.

12 Keep the project open for the next lesson.

● **Note:** You could adjust the level of each clip in the Multitrack Editor or lower the level while mixing, but sometimes it's simpler just to modify the clip so all instances that "point" to this clip use the edited version.

# Looped playback

In several of these lessons, you'll be hearing what happens when several tracks with parallel clips play back simultaneously. As a result, you'll likely want to loop sections containing these clips for playback so that you don't have to wait through parts of the music that don't contain the clips you want to hear. Here's how to select a section of music for looped playback.

1   Choose the Time Selection tool from the main program toolbar, or press T.

2   In an empty part of the Multitrack Editor (e.g., the Master Track at the bottom of the Multitrack Editor), drag the white handles in the timeline to set the In and Out loop points, or drag across the portion of the music you want to loop.

3   Click the Transport Loop Playback button.

4   Click the Transport Play button. The looped area will play continuously.

5   Click the Transport Stop button, and click the Transport Loop Playback button to deselect it.

6   Return to the Move tool by choosing it from the main program toolbar, or press V.

# Track controls

▶ **Tip:** You can resize the heights of all tracks simultaneously by placing the cursor over the track controls area and using the mouse scroll wheel.

Each track has multiple controls arranged as two sections, which primarily affect playback. One section has a fixed set of controls, whereas the other section is an *area* whose controls change according to a particular selected function. To reveal these controls, complete the following steps.

1   Click the splitter bar between the Main Drums track and Bass track, and continue holding down the mouse button.

2   Drag down to extend the height of the Main Drums track.

## Main track controls

● **Note:** If both the Mute and Solo buttons are enabled, the Mute button has priority.

The main track controls are the most commonly adjusted parameters for mixing.

1   Click the Transport Play button to begin playback.

2   Click the Main Drums track's M (Mute) button to silence it. Note that the Mute button is green when active and gray when it is off (not muted).

3   Click the Mute button again to unmute.

**4** Click the track's S button to solo the track. Only the Main Drums track will sound. (The R button is for recording; do not click it for now.) Leave the Main Drums track soloed for all the following lessons unless instructed to do otherwise.

● **Note:** There are two solo modes—Exclusive (soloing one track mutes all other tracks) and Non-Exclusive (the default; you can solo multiple tracks simultaneously). To override either mode, Ctrl-click (Command-click) on the Solo button. To choose one mode or the other as a default, choose Edit > Preferences > Multitrack (Audition > Preferences > Multitrack) and select the desired Track Solo preference.

**5** You can move tracks to reorganize them in a way that makes sense to you. For example, you might prefer to have the Percussion track below the Main Drums track instead of the Bass track. On the same row as the Mute and Solo buttons, click the waveform icon to the left of the Percussion track, and drag it up until a yellow line appears at the bottom of the Main Drums track. This line indicates where the top of the dragged track will "land." Release the mouse button to leave the Percussion track below the Main Drums track.

▶ **Tip:** If a track's signal goes "into the red," the track meters' red lights will remain lit so you know the track exceeded the maximum level, even if you weren't looking at it. To reset the red lights and turn them off, click on the lights.

● **Note:** If dragging the Pan knob left places in the audio to the right, check the connections going to your speakers and audio interface.

▶ **Tip:** A shortcut to return the Volume or Pan control to the default of 0 is to Alt-click (Option-click) on the control that you want to reset.

**6** With the transport playing, click the Volume knob immediately below the left part of the Main Drums name, and then drag up/down or left/right to vary the playback volume. The track meters will go "into the red" if you turn this up too high. For now, leave the Volume at 0.

**7** Click the Pan knob to its right. This changes the track position in the stereo field. Drag left, and you'll hear the audio coming out of only the left speaker or headphone. Drag right, and the audio will play from only the right speaker or headphone.

**8** Click the Sum to Mono button to the right. This "collapses" the stereo field to the center so the stereo file plays back in mono. Click on it again to return to stereo.

**9** Return the Pan control to 0.

# Track area

Extending a track's height, either by click-dragging the track's lower splitter bar downward or clicking in the Track Editor area and rotating the mouse scroll wheel, reveals an area below the main track controls. You can display one of four sets of controls in this area, as determined by the four buttons in the left section of the Multitrack Editor's toolbar:

- Input and outputs
- Track Effects Rack
- Sends
- EQ

## The EQ area

EQ is widely considered one of the most important effects for multitrack production, because it allows each track to "carve out" its own sonic space in the audio frequency spectrum (see Lesson 15, "Mixing," for an in-depth discussion of applying EQ during multitrack production). As a result, each track has the option to insert a Parametric EQ effect. Let's do that now.

1 Drag the Main Drums track's lower splitter bar downward to show the track area, and click the toolbar's EQ button (the rightmost button with vertical lines). The EQ area displays an EQ graph; it's currently a straight line, because no changes have been made.

2 Click the pencil button to the left of the EQ graph.

3 The Parametric EQ effect appears. This is identical to the Parametric EQ effect covered in the "Filter and EQ effects" section in Lesson 4.

4 Choose Acoustic Guitar from the Presets menu—just because it's named Acoustic Guitar doesn't mean it can't be used for drums!

5   Close the EQ window. Note that the EQ area now shows the EQ curve. Click the EQ area's power state toggle button; the EQ frequency response curve turns blue to show that the EQ is active, and the power state button glows green. Leave the EQ enabled.

● **Note:** If before closing the Parametric EQ's window you toggle the Parametric EQ window's power state button so the power is on, the power will already be on in the EQ area.

6   Click the Transport Play button. You'll hear that the EQ makes the drums sound a little more defined.

### The Effects Rack area

Each track has its own Effects Rack so you can add signal processing to individual tracks; this Effects Rack is almost identical to the Waveform Editor Effects Rack covered in Lesson 4. This lesson covers using the features that differ.

1   Click the fx button in the Multitrack Editor's main four-button toolbar.

2   The track's Effects Rack area appears. Increase the track height so you see 16 slots—just like the Effects Rack in the Waveform Editor. You can choose from the same effects, including VST (Windows or Mac) and AU (Mac-only) effects.

3   The main difference compared to the Waveform Editor Effects Rack is that you can change the position of the effects in the Multitrack Editor's signal flow. To hear how this works, click the Main Drums track's insert 1 right arrow, and then choose Delay and Echo > Analog Delay.

4   Choose Canyon Echos from the Presets menu, and then set Feedback to 70. Click the Transport Play button; you should hear lots of repeating echoes.

5   Three buttons are located above the inserts. The leftmost button is a master effects on/off button, which is enabled automatically when you insert an effect. Click it to turn off the Analog Delay effect, and then click it again to turn the Analog Delay effect back on.

6   The next button to the right is the FX Pre-Fader/Post-Fader control, which selects whether the Effects Rack is before (the default) or after the track's Volume control. With the track playing, turn down the track's Volume control. Note that this turns down the echoes as well, because the effect is pre-fader— in other words, "upstream" of the fader.

**7** Turn the track Volume control back to 0, and then click the FX Pre-Fader/ Post-Fader button. It turns red to indicate that the effect is now post-fader.

● **Note:** If the track Volume control remains turned down, eventually the echoes will stop because there won't be any more audio going into the Analog Delay, so there won't be any audio subject to being delayed.

**8** Let the track play for several seconds, and then turn down the track's Volume control. The echoes continue because you've turned down only the signal going to the Analog Delay, not the signal coming out of it.

**9** Click on the first insert's right triangle, and then choose Remove Effect so that the Analog Delay effect is no longer inserted.

**10** Turn off the Main Drums track's Solo button so you can hear all tracks play simultaneously.

### The Master Track output

Before you look at the Sends area in the next section, you first need to understand the concept of a *bus*. Although buses appear in the Multitrack Editor like tracks and have several elements in common, they serve a different purpose.

A bus does not contain audio clips but instead carries a specific mix of one or more tracks. Every Multitrack Session has at least one bus—the Master bus, which provides the Master Track output. This can be mono, stereo, or 5.1 surround, as specified by the Master parameter when you open a new Multitrack Session.

All tracks feed into the Master bus, and therefore, the Master Track's Volume control regulates the master volume of all tracks. This is essential because as you add more tracks to a composition, the output level increases. Eventually, it will likely start distorting, but you can use the Master Track Volume control to adjust the output level and prevent distortion.

# About Buses

In addition to the capabilities provided by a Master bus, buses have two other main functions: adding effects and creating monitor mixes.

## Adding effects

You'll often want to add an effect to several tracks. A common example is reverb, which creates the illusion of those tracks playing in a common acoustical space, like a concert hall. Although you could add a reverb for each track, this has two main disadvantages:

- Each reverb requires CPU power. With older computers or highly complex projects, using more effects can slow down performance and possibly even reduce the total track count.

- It's more difficult to create the illusion of a single acoustic space if there are multiple acoustic spaces distributed among various tracks.

The solution is to send audio from each track that should have reverb to a bus and insert a *single* reverb in the bus's Effects Rack. This greatly reduces the amount of CPU load, and because there's only a single reverb, it sounds more like a single acoustic space. The amount of audio sent to the bus controls the amount of reverb; for example, if you want a vocalist to have lots of reverb, you would turn up the vocal track's send control to the reverb.

## Creating mixes (also called monitor mixes)

When musicians record a part, they often want to hear a specific mix in their headphones as they play. For example, the bass player will want to lock the rhythm to the drums and will likely want to hear louder drums compared to the other instruments. However, the vocalist, who is paying more attention to the melody, will likely want to hear more melodic instruments, like piano and guitar.

To accommodate each player, you would create two buses and send each bus's output to a separate headphone amp. The bus going to the vocalist would have more send from the piano and guitar, whereas the bus going to the bass player would have more send from the drums.

1  Scroll down to the bottom of the Multitrack Editor and locate the Master Track.

2  Expand the Master Track height sufficiently to see the output meters.

3  Click the Play button to start playback. Note that the Master Track Volume control is set to -4.5dB; the project was saved this way so when you opened the file and started to play it, you wouldn't hear distortion. At no point does the Master Track output meter go into the red.

4  Stop playback, and then return the playhead to the file's beginning.

5  Alt-click (Option-click) the Master Track Volume control to return it to zero, and then click Play to start playback.

▶ **Tip:** Most engineers agree that you don't want to have to reduce a Master Volume control too much. If it becomes necessary to lower it much more than -12dB or so, reduce the Volume controls for individual tracks to reduce the output level. This allows the Master bus Volume control to remain between 0 and -6dB.

**6** Note that the meter goes into the red starting around measure 5 when the Main Drums are joined by other tracks.

**7** Click Stop to stop playback. Return the Master Track Volume control to -4.5dB.

### The Sends area

Each track has a Sends area. You can create buses in this area, as well as control bus levels and other parameters.

**1** Click the Sends button (the one between the fx and EQ buttons) in the Multitrack Editor's main four-button toolbar. The track's Sends area appears.

**2** Increase the Main Drums and Percussion track heights so you can see the Send area's controls.

**3** To add stereo reverb to both tracks, click the Main Drums' Send area drop-down menu and choose Add Bus > Stereo. This creates a Bus immediately below the Main Drums track.

**4** Click in the Bus A name field and type **Reverb Bus**. Note that the bus name changes automatically in the Main Drums Send area drop-down menu.

**5** Click the Percussion Send area drop-down menu. Because you created a Reverb bus, it appears in the list of available send destinations. Choose Reverb bus.

**6** Now insert a reverb in the Reverb bus. Start by clicking the fx button in the track toolbar.

**7** An Effects Rack appears in the Reverb bus that works identically to the Effects Rack in individual tracks.

**8** Click the right triangle in the Reverb bus's first insert, and then choose Reverb > Studio Reverb.

**9** When the Studio Reverb dialog box appears, choose Drum Plate (large) from the Presets drop-down menu. Set the Dry slider to 0 and Wet to 100%. Close the Studio Reverb dialog box.

**10** Return to the Sends area by clicking the Sends button in the toolbar.

**11** Solo the Main Drums and Percussion tracks to make it easy to hear the effect of adding reverb. Audition "knows" to solo the Reverb bus automatically, because the Main Drums and Percussion tracks send signal to it.

**12** Click the Transport Play button to begin playback.

**13** Turn up the Main Drums send Volume control to around -6dB. You'll now hear reverb added to the Main Drums track.

● **Note:** When you're using effects with Wet/ Dry controls as send effects, the tracks providing the sends are already providing dry audio to the Master bus. Therefore, the effects are set to full wet audio and no dry audio. The bus Volume control sets the overall amount of wet signal present in the Master bus.

**14** Turn up the Percussion send Volume control to around +5dB. When the Percussion clips play, you'll hear lots of reverb. The reason is that more audio is being sent to the Reverb bus compared to the Main Drums.

**15** You can set the overall amount of wet (reverb) sound with the Reverb bus Volume control. Vary this control between -8dB and +8dB to hear how this affects the sound. Then Alt-click (Option-click) this control to return it to 0.

**16** You can also pan a bus in the stereo field. Vary the Reverb bus Pan control from L100 to R100, and you'll hear the reverb effect move from left to right, respectively. Alt-click (Option-click) this control to return it to 0.

**Tip:** A track's Send area also includes an FX Pre-Fader/Post-Fader button. This determines whether the signal going to the Send volume control is pre or post the Track Volume control. The default is post-fader, because if you reduce the track level, you generally don't want to still hear the wet sound at the same level as when the track level was higher. If you do (perhaps for a special effect where a track goes from dry+wet to full wet), click the FX Pre-Fader/Post-Fader button so that the button is not red.

**17** Turn off the Solo buttons for the Main Drums and Percussion tracks. In preparation for the next lesson, leave this project open with the various track and bus controls set as shown.

### Sending buses to buses

Buses can also send audio to other buses, which multiplies your signal processing options even further. In this lesson, you'll send two tracks to a Delay bus, and that bus will feed the Reverb bus created in the previous lesson.

**1** Right-click on a blank space in the Pad DreamyBrass track, and choose Track > Add Stereo Bus Track to create a bus immediately below the Pad DreamyBrass track.

**2** Click in the Bus B name field and type **Delay Bus**.

**3** If necessary, extend the heights of the Pad DreamyBrass, Delay Bus, and Organ Church tracks so you can see their Send areas.

**4** Click the Pad DreamyBrass Send drop-down menu and choose Delay Bus.

**5** Click the Organ Church Send drop-down menu and choose Delay Bus.

**6** Now insert a Delay in the Delay bus. Start by clicking on the Multitrack Editor's main toolbar's fx button.

**7** Click the right triangle in the Delay bus's first insert, and then choose Delay and Echo > Analog Delay.

**8** When the Analog Delay dialog box appears, choose Round-robin Delay from the Presets drop-down menu. Set the Dry Out slider to 0, Wet to 100%, and Spread to 200%; enter exactly **2000**ms for Delay, and set Trash to 0. Close the Analog Delay dialog box.

**9** Return to the Sends area by clicking the Sends button in the toolbar.

**10** Solo the Pad DreamyBrass and Organ Church tracks, and then set each of these track's send Volume controls to around -8dB to add just a bit of delay.

**11** Position the playhead at the start of measure 7, and then click the Transport Play button to begin playback and hear the effect of the added delay.

**12** Now that the delay effect is set up, choose Reverb Bus from the Delay Bus send drop-down menu. This sends the Delay bus output to the Reverb bus, and you'll hear delay going through reverb.

**Note:** The Delay value of 2000ms (in the "Sending buses to buses" section) is chosen so that the delay correlates to the tempo. For details on how to arrive at this number, review the "Analog Delay" section in Lesson 4.

**13** Turn up the Delay bus Send control to around +4dB. You'll now hear reverberated delay.

**14** To contrast the delay sound with and without reverb, toggle the Delay bus power state button.

**15** Close Adobe Audition *without* saving your changes (choose No to All in the dialog box) in preparation for the next lesson.

# Channel mapping in the Multitrack Editor

The channel mapping feature is available for all effects in the Waveform Editor and the Multitrack Editor but is most appropriate for multitrack productions. It allows for mapping any effect input to any effect input and any effect output to any effect output. This is primarily of interest for surround mixes, because you can place an effect output into a particular surround channel. However, this lesson shows that channel mapping can also be useful with stereo effects for altering the stereo image.

**1** Open Audition and choose File > Open Recent > MoebiusRemix.sesx.

**2** Click the Main Drums Solo button, and click the fx button in the toolbar. Extend the Main Drums track enough to see the Effects Rack inserts.

**3** Click insert 1's right arrow and choose Reverb > Convolution Reverb.

**4** From the Impulse (not Presets) drop-down menu, choose Massive Cavern. Set Width to 300% and Mix to 70%.

**5** Loop a portion of the Main Drums track, and click the Transport Play button.

**6** Click the Convolution Reverb effect's Channel Map Editor button.

**Note:** Because both outputs can't be assigned to the same audio channel in the Channel Map Editor, the Right Effect Output, which had been assigned to Right, is now assigned to (None). Therefore, you will hear the Right channel Effect Output in the Left audio channel, and no effect output in the Right audio channel.

**7** The Channel Map Editor opens. Click the Left Effect Output field drop-down menu, and choose Right.

**8** Click the Right Effect Output field drop-down menu, and choose Left. The output channels are now reversed, which reverses the reverb output's stereo image. The image is wider, because some of the left input now appears in the right output, and some of the right input is now in the left output.

**9** To hear the difference, click the Channel Map Editor's Reset Routing button. If you listen on headphones, you'll hear a definite collapsing (narrowing) of the stereo image; this will be more subtle on speakers.

## Applying the Channel Map Editor in the Multitrack Editor

The applications for the Channel Map Editor are obvious for 5.1 surround, because you can direct effect outputs to various audio channels: left, right, front, back, center, or even the sub-woofer.

With stereo, the Channel Map Editor is relevant only with effects that generate different audio for the left and right outputs, such as Reverb, Echo, and the various Modulation effects. The main uses in the Multitrack Editor are to create more interesting stereo images with individual tracks or when using the same effect in more than one place (e.g., the same effect in two buses, in one track and one bus, in two tracks, etc.), because reversing the imaging on one of the effects can add more variety.

# Side-chaining effects

The side-chaining effects-related technique is available only in the Multitrack Editor, because it requires at least two tracks.

Side-chaining uses the output from one track to control an effect in a different track. In this lesson, you'll use side-chaining to automatically reduce the level of a background music bed when narration occurs.

1   With Audition open, navigate to the Lesson09 folder, and open the Multitrack Session Side-chaining.sesx located in the Side-chaining folder.

2   Click the Transport Play button. Note how the background music drowns out the narration.

3   Click the Multitrack Editor's main toolbar fx button to open the Effects area.

4   Click the right arrow in the BackgroundMusic track's first effects insert, and then choose Amplitude and Compression > Dynamics Processing.

5   When the Dynamics Processing interface opens, choose Broadcast Limiter from the Presets menu.

6   Click the Set Side-Chain Input button and choose Stereo. Leave the Dynamics Processing effect open, because you'll need to tweak its settings.

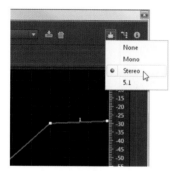

7   Click the Multitrack Editor's main toolbar Sends button to open the Sends area.

8   In the Narration track, click the send and choose Side-Chain > Dynamics Processing (Background Music – Slot 1).

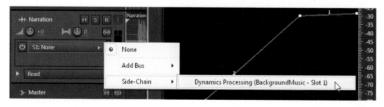

9   Return the playhead to the beginning, and click the Transport Play button.

**10** The background music does get softer when narration occurs, but it follows the narration too closely; the sound isn't smooth, because the background music spikes higher in level during even brief pauses in narration. To fix this, click the Dynamics Processing Settings tab to change various settings.

**11** Select Noise Gating under the general header Attack and Release, because expanding levels downward will exceed 50:1, and more of a gating action—where the background music is either "loud" or "soft"—is the desired type of response.

**12** Click the Link Channels button (in the Gain Processor section under the Settings tab) to ensure that changes in one channel are imposed on the other channel, so there aren't significant level variations between the two channels.

**13** Set the Level Detector and Gain Processor Attack Times to 0ms. This will cause compression to start as soon as the Dynamics Processing side-chain input detects narration.

**14** Increasing release times retains the compression action for the specified time in the absence of narration. Set the Level Detector Release Time to around 500ms.

**15** Adjust the Gain Processor Release Time slider for the most even response. A setting of approximately 1200ms seems about optimum.

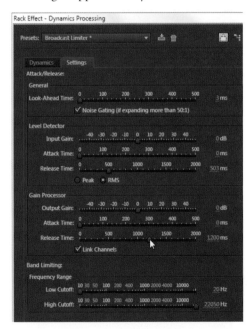

**16** Click the Transport Play button. Note how when the narration stops, the background music fades up, based on the Release Time settings. When the narration resumes, compression lowers the level of the background music.

# Review questions

1  What is the main difference between the Waveform Editor and Multitrack Editor?

2  What's the advantage of sending tracks to a single effect through a bus instead of inserting the same effect multiple times, once for each track?

3  Is it possible to have buses send signal to other buses?

4  On what type of project is channel mapping most useful?

5  What are the most common effects used for side-chaining?

# Review answers

1  The Waveform Editor can play back one file at a time, whereas the Multitrack Editor can play multiple files simultaneously.

2  Using a bus saves CPU power and is desirable when you want to apply the same effect (e.g., a specific acoustic space) to multiple tracks.

3  Yes, any bus can send audio to any other bus.

4  Channel mapping is most useful on surround productions, although channel mapping can also be used with stereo.

5  The most common effects used are dynamics processors like Compressors and Noise Gates.

# 10 THE MULTITRACK MIXER VIEW

## Lesson overview

In this lesson, you'll learn how to do the following:

- Switch from the Multitrack Editor to the Mixer view

- Adjust the Mixer fader heights to allow for greater resolution when setting levels

- Show/hide various areas to customize the Mixer size and configuration

- Scroll through different Effects Racks inserts and Sends within their respective areas

- Scroll to view different groups of channels if the Mixer window isn't wide enough to show them all

- Differentiate among channel types via color coding

- Rearrange the Mixer channel order

 This lesson takes about 25 minutes to complete. This assumes you've copied the Lesson10 folder that contains the project example into the Lessons folder that you created on your hard drive for these projects. Remember that you needn't be concerned about modifying these files, because you can always return to the original versions by copying them from the *Adobe Audition CS6 Classroom in a Book* CD-ROM.

The Mixer view is an alternate way to look at a
multitrack project; it's optimized for mixing rather
than editing the multitrack project's tracks.

# Mixer view basics

Multitrack projects can have two different views. So far, you've been working with the Multitrack Editor, which as its name implies, is optimized for editing. However, the Mixer tab (to the left of the Multitrack Editor tab) accesses another way to work with multitrack projects and is optimized for mixing.

The Multitrack Editor shows the clips within various tracks. The Mixer does not show clips but has a corresponding Mixer channel for each Multitrack Editor track. The reason for calling a Mixer channel a "channel" instead of a track is because hardware mixers use that term; in physical studios, there isn't necessarily a one-to-one correlation between tracks and channels (e.g., one tape recorder track could feed more than one mixer channel).

Although the Multitrack Editor provides mixing functions, such as altering levels and panning (a track's position in the stereo field), several mixing functions (sends, EQ, effects, and ins/outs) share a common area and you can only see the settings for one of these functions at a time. With the Mixer, all of these functions are arranged as rows and can be viewed simultaneously.

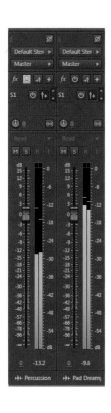

Mixing typically occurs after the various tracks are recorded and edited, and you're ready to concentrate solely on blending all the tracks together to create a cohesive listening experience. However, even when editing, there are often times when it makes more sense from a workflow standpoint to temporarily switch over to the Mixer.

1 With Audition open, navigate to the Lesson10 folder, and open the Multitrack Session Mixer.sesx.

2 After clicking the Multitrack button (if necessary), click the Mixer tab.

3 The Mixer uses faders instead of rotary controls to adjust level. The higher you can extend the Mixer, the longer the faders. Click the splitter bar toward the bottom of the Mixer panel, and drag down as far as possible to make the faders as long as possible.

**4** Click on the same splitter bar, and drag up. Note that the faders get shorter. Continue dragging up; eventually the faders will collapse. Return the faders to the longest size allowed by your screen, consistent with still being able to access the Transport buttons.

▶ **Tip:** Undocking the Mixer window is very convenient, because it can be a consistent size and you don't have to be concerned about resizing it. Undocking is also a natural for two-monitor setups, because you can put the Mixer in its own dedicated monitor and the editor section in the other monitor.

**5** Keep the project open in preparation for the next lesson.

● **Note:** Long-throw hardware faders are desirable in hardware mixers because it's easier to do precise, "high-resolution" mixing moves. The same is true of "virtual" faders in software. When Audition's faders are extended to their greatest height, you can edit levels easily in 0.1dB steps. In the Multitrack Editor, the most resolution you can achieve with the rotary Volume controls is 0.3dB, and that requires a precise touch.

## Using hardware controllers

Although being able to mix onscreen is convenient, many engineers prefer the "human touch" of using physical faders. Audition supports various *control surfaces*—hardware devices that include faders and can control the onscreen faders. Many control surfaces can also control the Mute and Solo buttons, transport, arm tracks for record, and more.

Audition supports several control surface protocols: Mackie Control, Avid/Euphonix EUCON, PreSonus FaderPort, and ADS Tech RedRover. Of these, Mackie Control is by far the most popular, and several control surfaces from multiple manufacturers are compatible with this protocol.

Adding a control surface is easy. Choose Edit > Preferences > Control Surface. Under Device Class, choose the type (e.g., Mackie Control), and then click Configure. This brings up a dialog box where you can add the control surface and specify the MIDI ports (input and output) to which the control surface connects.

## Mixer show/hide options

● **Note:** Two Mixer sections cannot be hidden: the I/O section at the top (polarity switch, Input Assign drop-down menu, and Output Assign drop-down menu) and the channel's Pan and Sum to Mono controls.

Most rows of Mixer modules have an expand/collapse disclosure triangle. You can customize how much space the Mixer takes up on the screen and automatically change the relative fader height by showing or hiding different parts of the Mixer.

1   With the fx area closed, you can still see the fx area's master fx power state button, the FX Pre-Fader/Post-Fader button, and the pre-render track button that's often used to save CPU power when mixing complex projects (pre-rendering is covered in detail in Lesson 15, "Mixing").

Click the fx area disclosure triangle to expand its options. Note that the faders become shorter because the fx area now takes up more space.

2   In all channels, you can now see three Effects Rack inserts. You cannot drag this area downward to reveal more inserts, but the scroll bar to the right of the inserts lets you see all available inserts. Click on the rectangle within the scroll bar and drag up or down to see the other inserts; you can also click on the scroll bar's top and bottom arrows to step up or down respectively through one insert at a time.

**3** With the Sends area closed, you can see the number of the currently selected sends in the upper-left corner, the power state button, and FX Pre-Fader/Post-Fader button. Click the Sends area disclosure triangle to expand it. Note that again the faders become shorter because the Sends area now takes up more space.

**4** One send is shown at a time along with its power state button, FX Pre-Fader/Post-Fader, Send Volume, Stereo Balance controls, and drop-down menu for reassigning the send to a different send (or creating a new send bus or side-chain send). Like the fx area, a scroll bar is available for choosing the current send. In the second channel from the left (labeled Bass), click on the rectangle within the scroll bar and drag up or down to see the other sends; you can also click on the scroll bar's top and bottom arrows to step up or down, respectively, through one send at a time.

**5** With the EQ area closed, no aspect of the EQ area is visible. Click the EQ area disclosure triangle to expand it. As with expanding the fx and Sends areas, the faders become even shorter to compensate for having less available space.

**6** The EQ section works similarly to how it works in the Multitrack Editor. The power state button can enable/bypass the EQ. Click the button with the pencil icon; you'll open the channel's Parametric Equalizer (you can also open it by double-clicking on the EQ graph). Click the Parametric EQ's close box, because you won't be making any adjustments.

**7** Close the fader section by clicking its disclosure triangle. The faders section collapses to show the Mute, Solo, Arm for Record, and Monitor Input buttons, and also reduces the fader to a Volume control identical to the one found in the Multitrack Editor.

## Channel scrolling

With projects that have many channels, your monitor may not be wide enough to show them all. However, you can scroll though the various channels, as well as see which ones are buses, standard tracks, or the Master Track Output bus.

1   Click on the right edge of the Audition window and drag left to narrow the Mixer. Make sure that you can't see all channels in the Mixer.

2   A scroll bar appears along the bottom of the Mixer panel if the panel isn't wide enough to show all channels. Click on the scroll bar rectangle, and drag all the way to the right. Now you can see the rightmost group of channels.

3   Drag the scroll bar rectangle full left in preparation for the next lesson.

**Note:** Channel faders have different colors to indicate their function. Standard tracks have gray faders; buses have yellow faders and a yellow Mixer symbol to the left of the bus name. The Master Track Output has a blue fader and a blue Mixer symbol to the left of the Master Track name.

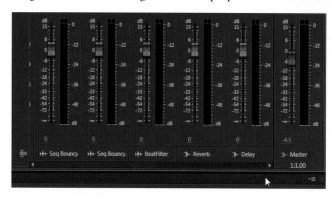

## Rearranging Mixer channel order

You're not limited to an existing left-to-right track order. For example, you may have recorded drums first in Multitrack Editor Track 1 and a percussion part in Multitrack Editor Track 3; these appear in Mixer channels 1 and 3, respectively. However, suppose you'd rather have the Percussion channel next to the Drums channel. You can move channels horizontally to anywhere within the Mixer.

1   Hover the cursor over the track you want to move until the cursor turns into a hand. There are several places in the channel where this happens, such as right below the meter.

**2** Click and drag left until a yellow line appears to the right of the Main Drums channel. This is where the left side of the channel will be moved. (Note that if you drag right until you see a yellow line, the right side of the channel will be moved there.)

**3** Release the mouse button, and the Percussion channel will relocate to the right of the Main Drums channel.

**4** Click the Editor tab to return to the Multitrack Editor. Note that the track order has changed to reflect the channel change you made in the Mixer.

● **Note:** The Mixer view reflects changes in track order made in the Multitrack Editor, and the Multitrack Editor reflects changes in track order made in the Mixer view.

# Review questions

1 What are the main advantages of the Mixer view compared to the Multitrack Editor?

2 What is the Mixer view's main limitation?

3 How can you see all the Mixer channels if your monitor isn't wide enough?

4 How can you differentiate a bus from a track at a glance?

5 Is it possible to rearrange the left-to-right channel order to create a more logical workflow?

# Review answers

1 The faders can have extremely high resolution, and if desired, you can see the fx, Sends, and EQ areas simultaneously.

2 You cannot edit clip properties in the Mixer view.

3 A scroll bar along the bottom of the Mixer panel lets you view different groups of channels.

4 The bus has a yellow fader, and a standard track has a gray fader.

5 Yes; you can drag and drop channels horizontally anywhere you want within the Mixer.

# 11 EDITING CLIPS

## Lesson overview

In this lesson, you'll learn how to do the following:

- Use crossfading—both symmetrical and asymmetrical—to create remixes from individual clips

- Export the mix as a single file

- Pan individual clips on a per-clip basis

- Edit a clip to fit a specific length of time (e.g., for a commercial)

- Apply global clip stretching to fine-tune a piece of music's specific length

- Change volume on a per-clip basis

- Add effects to individual clips

- Extend a clip via looping

 This lesson takes about 50 minutes to complete. This assumes you've copied the Lesson11 folder that contains the audio examples into the Lessons folder that you created on your hard drive for these projects. Remember that you needn't be concerned about modifying these files, because you can always return to the original versions by copying them from the *Adobe Audition CS6 Classroom in a Book* CD-ROM.

You can apply a variety of operations to individual clips, including combining them with crossfading to create a perfect DJ-style continuous mix of music, and then bounce the mix to a single file suitable for exporting, burning to CD, uploading to the web, and so on.

# Creating a DJ-style continuous music mix with crossfading

Crossfading between clips can provide for smooth transitions between the end of one clip and the start of another. However, crossfading is also a crucial element of creating a DJ mix. Here, you'll take five clips and create a dance mix.

1  With Audition open, navigate to the Lesson11 folder, and open the Multitrack Session DJ Mix.sesx located in the DJ Mix folder.

2  With the Editor panel open, right-click (Control-click) on the timeline and choose Time Display > Bars and Beats.

3  Right-click (Control-click) on the timeline and choose Time Display > Edit Tempo. Enter **120** in the Tempo field and then click OK.

**Note:** The name for each piece of music in the Multitrack Session DJ Mix lesson starts with the name of the company that created the song and released the sound library; the song title is the name of the library.

4  Click on any clip, and then verify that Automatic Crossfades Enabled (Clip > Automatic Crossfades Enabled) is selected so that overlapping one clip with another creates a crossfade in the overlapping section.

5  Place the playhead at the project's beginning and click Play. Listen to the song "Poptronica," and as you listen, make a mental note of where you might like another song to start playing. The theme returns at measure 57 and then repeats at measure 65 before fading out. So, measure 65 is a good candidate for another song to kick in.

6  Now listen to the song "UK Grime." The first eight measures are an introduction; the main part of the song doesn't start until measure 9.

▶ **Tip:** If snapping seems ineffective, zoom in to increase the resolution and thus the snapping "sensitivity." It's *very* important in the crossfading lesson that clips snap precisely to the beat, or you'll hear what DJs refer to as a "train wreck" transition because the clips are out of sync with each other where they overlap. When you move a clip, zoom in to verify that the edge is aligned with a beat.

7  Enable snapping by clicking the Snap button (indicated by a magnet icon) to the left of the timeline. Drag "UK Grime" into Track 1 so it overlaps "Poptronica" starting at measure 65. This is ideal, because "Poptronica" will fade out over eight measures, "UK Grime" will fade in over eight measures, and when "Poptronica" finishes fading out, the main part of "UK Grime" will start.

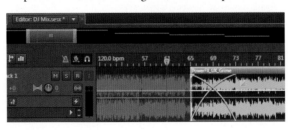

8  Position the playhead before measure 65, and then click the Play button to hear the transition.

9  Proceed to creating the next transition. Listen to the end of "UK Grime"; it goes on for a long time, so you'll probably want to trim it. As the song starts getting repetitive at measure 122, you'll have the clip end at measure 130 to allow for an eight-measure crossfade.

**10** Hover over the right edge of the "UK Grime" clip so the cursor turns into a Trim tool (a red right bracket). Drag left until the right edge of "UK Grime" snaps to measure 130.

**11** Move the playhead to the beginning of the song "Electro Patterns," and then click Play to hear it. With "Electro Patterns," the first eight measures would be good for a fade in, because the main theme starts at the beginning of the ninth measure.

**12** Drag "Electro Patterns" into Track 1 so it overlaps "UK Grime" starting at measure 122. Play this transition.

**13** It would sound stronger if the kick in "Electro Patterns" came in sooner and was louder. You can alter the crossfade to do this. Click the Fade In control square in the "Electro Patterns" file, and drag it straight up so the tooltip displays Fade In Linear Value: 100.

**14** Click Play and listen to the transition; it's much stronger.

**15** Listen to the end of "Electro Patterns" and the beginning of "Iced." "Iced" doesn't really get going until after 16 measures, whereas the ending for "Electro Patterns" starts at measure 166. From a musical standpoint, the "Electro Patterns" measures that play after measure 166 are kind of heavy and bassy, whereas the first part of "Iced" is "lighter." It's unclear what would make a good transition, so drag "Iced" into Track 1 starting at measure 166 so it overlaps "Electro Patterns," and you'll tweak it from there.

**16** Click on "Electro Patterns" to select it. Hover over its right edge so the cursor turns into a Trim tool. Drag left to trim the clip, but leave enough to make a good transition area into the next clip; I recommend dragging left to measure 174.

**17** For the final transition, you'll try a "mashup" (i.e., two pieces of music playing at the same time for a fairly long amount of time). Drag "Acid Jazz City" into Track 1 starting at measure 192. Return the playhead to the beginning, click Play, and enjoy your mix.

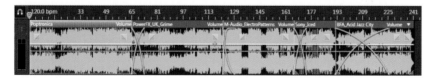

**18** Keep this project open, so you can save your work as a single file in the next lesson.

# Mixing or exporting a collection of clips as a single file

When creating a DJ mix or chopping up a clip to fit it to a specific length (as covered in the next lesson), you might want to save a collection of edited clips as a single file that incorporates all the edits you've made.

You have two options for doing this. The first option, which converts the clips into a single file that appears in the Waveform Editor, is ideal if you want to make some overall tweaks on the final, composite file.

1  Right-click (Control-click) in an empty space in the track (in this case, Track 1) containing the clips you want to bounce (mix) together into a single, new clip.

2  Choose Mixdown Session to New File > Entire Session. This creates a new file in the Waveform Editor and automatically switches to the Waveform Editor.

The second option exports the mix as a single file to your desktop or other designated folder without going through the Multitrack Editor. Exporting is covered in more detail in Lesson 15, "Mixing," because in almost all cases you'll want to export a final mix to a mono, stereo, or surround file.

1  Right-click (Control-click) in an empty space in the track containing the clips you want to bounce (mix) together.

2  Choose Export Mixdown > Entire Session.

   A dialog box appears in which you can specify several attributes of the mixed file, such as the folder location where the file will be stored, format, sample rate, bit resolution, and the like.

3  Select the desired attributes in the dialog box, and then click OK.

4  Close Audition, and when the Save Changes dialog box appears, click No To All.

# Editing for length

Music often needs to be cut to fit a specific amount of time—for example, a 30-second commercial. In this lesson, you'll use many of Audition's clip editing tools to trim down a 45-second music clip to make the background for a 30-second commercial.

1 With Audition open, navigate to the Lesson11 folder, and open the Multitrack Session 30SecondSpot.sesx located in the 30SecondSpot folder.

2 Right-click (Control-click) on the timeline and choose Time Display > Decimal (mm:ss.ddd) to verify that the music is about 45 seconds long. Then right-click (Control-click) on the timeline and choose Time Display > Bars and Beats for editing.

3 Right-click (Control-click) on the timeline and choose Time Display > Edit Tempo. Enter **125** in the Tempo field, and then click OK.

   The first two measures and next four measures are similar except that there's a bass in measures 3 and 4 that leads well into the next section. So, you'll delete the first two measures.

4 Choose the Time Selection tool or press T.

5 If necessary, click the Snap button to enable snapping.

6 Click at measure 3:1 and drag left to select the first two measures. Zoom in far enough to ensure accurate snapping.

7 Choose Edit > Ripple Delete > Time Selection in All Tracks.

● **Note:** To edit a piece of music so that it's a particular length, you'll want to alternate the time display between Decimal—to see how edits to the music affect length—and then return to Bars and Beats—for editing the music so you can reference musical time.

● **Note:** Ripple Delete removes the selected section of a file; in addition, the section to the right of the selection moves left to where the selection started, thus closing the "hole" left by deletion.

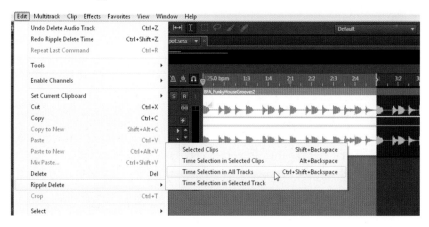

The section of the music that starts at measure 7 is similar to the section that starts at measure 11. So, let's eliminate measures 7–10.

8 Click at the beginning of measure 11:1, and drag left until measure 7:1.

9 Choose Edit > Ripple Delete > Time Selection in All Tracks.

10 Keep this project open for the next lesson.

## Editing individual clips in the Waveform Editor

Although the Multitrack Editor has many useful editing tools, for detailed or unusual edits, it's easy to flip a clip between Waveform and Multitrack Editors.

1 The bass slide starting at 6:3 is good, but the slide ends too soon. Shortening the bass slide and repeating it might sound more interesting, so start by trimming the bass note. Hover the cursor over the end of the first clip until the cursor turns into a red right bracket. Click and drag left to 6:4. This trims the last beat of the bass slide.

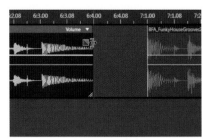

2 Choose the Razor Selected Clips tool or press R.

3 Position the Razor tool so that there's a line at the beginning of the bass slide at 6:3, and then click to split the bass note from the rest of the clip.

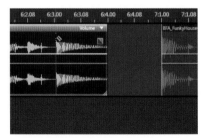

4 Choose the Move tool or press V.

5 Alt-click (Option-click) the name header at the top of the bass slide clip you just split, and drag right so that the copied clip starts at measure 6:4.

6 Place the playhead around the beginning of measure 6, and then click Play to hear the result of the two bass parts playing in a row.

That's more interesting, but let's make it even more interesting by processing the second slide independently from the first slide. However, a copied clip defaults to referencing the original clip, so any change you make to either clip changes both clips.

7 To convert the second slide into a unique clip, right-click (Control-click) the second slide and choose Convert To Unique Copy. Although the unique copy takes up additional disk space, you can edit it without affecting any other clips.

8   Click the Waveform Editor button to edit the second slide.

9   Choose Edit > Select > Select All or press Ctrl+A (Command+A).

10  Choose Effects > Reverse to play the bass slide backward, so it slides up instead of down.

11  Click the Multitrack Editor button to return to the Multitrack Session. The reversed section will default to being selected, so click anywhere in Track 1 other than the selected section to deselect it.

12  Position the playhead around the beginning of measure 6, and then click Play to hear how the two slides sound when played together. Keep the project open for the next lesson.

## Panning individual clips

Although Lesson 14, "Automation," covers clip automation in detail, now is an appropriate time to introduce the subject by altering the stereo position of the two bass clips. Let's take the bass processing one step further with panning, which is the process of altering a sound's position in the stereo field (left, right, center, or anywhere in between).

1   For each bass slide clip (forward and backward), click the right and left ends of the blue Pan line (just inside the clip edges) to create control points at the Pan line ends.

2   Click the first bass slide's left control point, and drag it all the way down. Then click the right control point and drag it all the way up. Click on the second bass slide's left control point and drag it all the way up, and then click on the right control point and drag it all the way down.

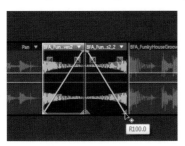

3   Position the playhead near the beginning of measure 6, and then click Play to hear how the two slides move in the stereo field.

## Combining Ripple Delete and crossfading

The file still needs one more ripple edit, but that would remove part of the audio that's worth keeping. However, it's possible to use crossfading to compensate for deletions caused by the effects of a ripple edit.

1. Change the Time Display to Decimal, and note that the file still needs to be a little shorter. Change the Time Display back to Bars and Beats for editing.

2. Position the playhead at measure 7 and click Play. The music gets a little quieter at measure 9, but then there's an interesting harmonic note at 10:3. So, using the Time Selection tool, select 8:3 to 10:3 and do a ripple delete, as in step 7 at the beginning of the "Editing for Length" section.

   Although a ripple delete removes audio, you can use crossfading to alter the clip length and reintroduce some of the audio that was deleted—yet still not add to the total length.

3. Position the playhead just before the previous transition, and then click Play.

   The transition sounds OK, but originally there was a nice little drum fill in the two beats before 10:3. Now the fill is gone because it was in the section that was subjected to the ripple delete. You can reintroduce them.

**Note:** When you trim a clip using the trim handles, you have not permanently altered the clip but merely changed how Audition plays back the clip in RAM. You can always re-trim to go back to the original length or a different length.

4. To restore the drum fill, trim the clip starting at 8:3 and make it longer by hovering the cursor over the left edge of the clip until it turns into a red left bracket. Click and drag left to 8:1. Now the section with the drum fill has been crossfaded with the end of the preceding clip.

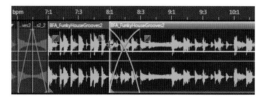

## Using global clip stretching to make fine length adjustments

Global clip stretching can stretch all clips proportionately to fine-tune their total, combined length. Although extreme amounts of stretching can sound unnatural, relatively small changes alter the sound quality imperceptibly, if at all.

1. Change the Time Display to Decimal; as luck would have it, the music is just a little over 30 seconds—very close to the goal. So, use global clip stretching to reduce the length slightly. Begin by pressing Ctrl+A (Command+A) to select all clips.

2. Click the Global Clip Stretching button (to the immediate left of the snap function's magnet icon).

3    Zoom in so you can see the difference clearly between where the music ends and the 30-second mark. Click on the white stretch triangle toward the upper right of the clip, just below the name heading, and drag left until the end of the audio snaps to exactly 30 seconds.

All clips have been stretched proportionately so that the audio track is now 30 seconds long.

4    Position the playhead at the beginning of the file, and then click Play to listen to the entire 30-second music bed.

## Clip edits: split, trim, volume

Digital audio editing allows for sound-warping options that would be difficult or even impossible to implement in any other way. Several of these involve isolating specific sections of a clip and processing them individually; the Split function is ideal for doing this. However, this lesson also employs other editing techniques to alter a clip.

1    With Audition open, navigate to the Lesson11 folder, and open the Multitrack Session StutterEdits.sesx from the StutterEdits folder.

2    Place the playhead at the beginning of the file, and click the Transport Play button to hear the BoringDrums clip.

3    Right-click (Control-click) on the timeline and choose Time Display > Bars and Beats.

4    Right-click (Control-click) on the timeline and choose Time Display > Edit Tempo. Enter **100** in the Tempo field, and then click OK.

5    Choose Edit > Snapping > Snap to Rule (Fine). Because you'll be zooming in quite a bit during this lesson, "fine" snapping will allow for snapping to finer resolutions, like eighth notes.

6    Click the Transport Loop Playback button.

7    Having two 16th note kick drum hits at the end would make a better lead-in back to the beginning. To isolate a kick drum, zoom in until you can see both 1:3.00 and 1:3.04 in the timeline.

8    Choose the Time Selection tool or press T.

9    Click at 1:3.00 and drag right to 1:3.04. Because Fine snapping was selected, the selection should snap to these times on the timeline. This selects the kick drum hit.

**10** Choose Clip > Split.

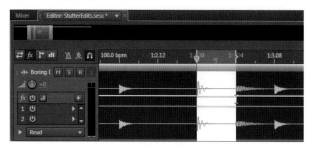

**11** Go to the end of the clip, and use the Trim tool to bring the end from 3:1.00 to 2:4.08.

**12** To make a copy of the clip, Alt-click (Option-click) on the isolated kick hit's name heading, and then drag right until the kick clip's left edge snaps to the end of the clip.

**13** Alt-click (Option-click) on the name heading of the kick hit you just moved, and then drag right until the newly copied kick clip's left edge snaps to the end of the previously copied kick hit. There should now be two kick hits between 2:4.08 and 3:1.00.

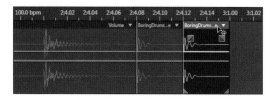

**14** If necessary, click outside of any selected area so it won't loop, and then click Play. You'll now hear the clip with the double kick lead-in at the end.

**15** Now add some dynamics by making the first copied kick hit a little softer. Click on the clip's yellow volume line, and then drag down to around -9dB. Click Play to hear how the two kicks have become more dynamic.

## Stutter edits

"Stutter" edits, which are commonly used in a variety of pop music, including dance music and hip-hop, slice and dice clips into pieces and then reassemble them in a different and usually rhythmic order. This lesson shows you how to "stutter edit" a hi-hat hit.

**1** Similarly to how you isolated the kick by splitting the clip, zoom in with the Time Selection tool still selected, click on 1:4.08, drag to 1:4.10, and then choose Clip > Split to isolate the hi-hat.

2　Trim the portion of the clip to the right of the hi-hat so that it starts at 2:1.00 instead of 1:4.10.

3　Alt-click (Option-click) and drag the isolated hi-hat four times so there are four hi-hat hits between 1:4.08 and 2:1.00 (starting at 1:4.10, 1:4.12, and 1:4.14).

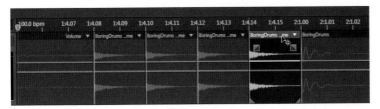

4　For a crazy stereo effect, click on the first of the four hi-hat hit's blue pan line, and drag all the way up to L100. Click on the second of the four hi-hat hit's blue pan line, and drag up to L32.2. Click on the third hi-hat hit's blue pan line, and drag up to R32.2. Click on the fourth hi-hat hit's blue pan line, and drag up to R100. Click Play to hear how this affects the loop.

## Adding effects to individual clips

Although adding effects to an entire track is convenient for making sweeping real-time changes, it's also possible to apply one or more effects to an individual clip, no matter how short it is.

1　To add an effect to individual clips, let's put a big reverb on the snare that hits at 1:4.00. To do this, isolate the snare; click at 1:4.0, drag to 1:4.08, and then choose Clip > Split.

2　Click the Effects Rack tab if needed, and then click the Clip Effects tab. With the isolated snare clip still selected, click the right arrow in the Clip Effects' Insert 1 slot, and choose Reverb > Studio Reverb.

3　In the Studio Reverb dialog box, select Drum Plate (large) from the Presets menu, and change the Wet slider to 50. Now when the drum loop plays, the snare will have reverb on it.

4　Suppose you like the reverb so much you wish all the snare hits had it. Simply copy it three times (Alt-click [Option-click] on the clip name, and then drag) so that the start of this clip snaps to 1:2.00, 2:2.00, and 2:4.00. Because the snare hit is "on top" of the clip below, it will play back instead of what's in the clip underneath.

5　If you're not sure whether you like having the reverb effect on all snare hits, there's an easy way to try different options. For example, if you want to hear what the loop sounds like without the reverb effect on the first and third snare hits, right-click (Control-click) on the first snare hit (the one that starts at 1:2.00) and choose Send Clip to Back. Next, right-click (Control-click) on the third snare hit (that starts at 2:2.00) and choose Send Clip to Back. Leave this as

▶ **Tip:** It's possible to play a clip on top and the clip underneath it simultaneously by choosing Edit > Preferences > Multitrack and selecting "Play overlapped portions of clips."

is for now, but if you want the snares to come back, you just need to right-click (Control-click) on the clip covering the snare, and choose Send Clip to Back. Remember that with layered clips, the upper layer on top has priority over the one underneath (unless you selected "Play overlapped portions of clips" after choosing Edit > Preferences > Multitrack).

**Note:** The Volume control for the track being bounced and the Master Output bus Volume control will affect the level of the bounced track. For example, if either control is set to -3dB, the bounced track will be 3dB lower in volume than the original track with the edits.

6   Bounce all these clips to a new track so that all these changes are consolidated into a single file. Right-click (Control-click) in the selected track, and choose Bounce to New Track > Selected Track. (If there was other material in this track you didn't want to bounce, you could select only these clips and choose Bounce to New Track > Selected Clips Only.) A new file appears in the track below that incorporates all your edits.

7   Keep the project open in preparation for the next lesson.

# Extending a clip via looping

Any clip can be turned into a loop and extended for as many iterations as desired using the following procedure.

1   To convert the bounced clip created in the previous lesson to a loop, first verify that the clip start and loop end points are snapped exactly on measure or beat boundaries. If a clip is slightly short or long, any errors will accumulate as you create more iterations of the loop.

2   Right-click (Control-click) anywhere in the clip (except for a fade control square, Volume automation line, or Pan automation line) and choose Loop. A small loop icon appears in the clip's lower left.

**Tip:** To extend a clip earlier compared to where it starts, you can click on the left edge and drag to the left.

3   Position the cursor over the clip's right edge. It turns into the Trim tool (red right bracket) but also shows a loop symbol. Drag right to extend the clip for the desired length. A vertical dashed line indicates the end of one iteration and the beginning of another.

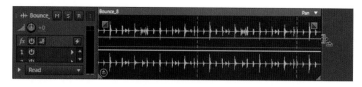

## Review questions

1   When crossfading clips to create a DJ mix, aside from having a common tempo, what else is extremely important?

2   What is a ripple delete?

3   How do you apply an effect to something like a single drum hit?

4   What's the solution if snapping doesn't seem to work?

5   How can all clips be stretched proportionately to shorten or lengthen a piece of music?

## Review answers

1   Make sure clips snap precisely to the beat. Otherwise, the clips can be out of sync with each other during the crossfaded section.

2   A ripple delete removes a selected section of a file; in addition, the section to the right of the selection moves left to where the selection started, which closes the "hole" left by the deletion.

3   Isolate the hit by splitting it into a separate clip, and then insert an effect for only that clip.

4   Zoom in further for higher resolution; you might also need to select "Fine" snapping.

5   Turn on Global Clip Stretching, click on the right edge of the last clip, and then drag it to the desired length.

# 12 CREATING MUSIC WITH SOUND LIBRARIES

## Lesson overview

In this lesson, you'll learn how to do the following:

- Create music without needing to know how to play an instrument

- Listen to clips in the Media Browser before bringing them into the Multitrack Session

- Modify clip lengths to add more variety to a composition

- Use files from a "music construction kit" to assemble music quickly

- Use pitch transposition and time-stretching to incorporate clips with a different native tempo or pitch than the current session

- Add effects processing to a track to complete the composition

This lesson takes about 60 minutes to complete. This assumes you've copied the Lesson12 folder that contains the audio examples into the Lessons folder that you created on your hard drive for these projects. Remember that you needn't be concerned about modifying these files, because you can always return to the original versions by copying them from the *Adobe Audition CS6 Classroom in a Book* CD-ROM.

Using commercially available sound libraries and
Audition's Multitrack Editor, you can create music
easily for commercials and audio for video, kiosks,
and other applications—even if you don't play a
musical instrument.

# About sound libraries

Before computers, *needledrop music* often provided music for commercials, radio station breaks, and even some TV shows and movies. Needledrop music got its name because various companies produced sets of vinyl records with different types of music, sometimes classified by mood, and you would "drop the needle" on a suitable track for your background music. These records were usually expensive, and you needed to pay for a new license every time you wanted to use the music—even if the same song was used twice in a single project.

► **Tip:** The Adobe Resource Central, with thousands of royalty-free loops, sound effects, music beds, and more, is a great source of content for Audition CS6 owners. You can access it by choosing Help > Download Sound Effects and More and then following the onscreen directions to download the content.

Today, many companies make sound libraries available on CD-ROM, DVD-ROM, or via download that consist of musical fragments, loops, and sound effects.

You can assemble these various sound clips to create professional-quality, custom music. Sound library licensing agreements vary; many are royalty-free, but read the fine print to avoid potential legal problems.

There are two main types of libraries: *Construction kits* typically include folders, each with compatible files at a consistent tempo and key, which makes it easy to mix and match the files within the folder to create a custom arrangement. *General-purpose* sound libraries consist of collections of loops that are often themed (e.g., dance music, jazz, rock, etc.) but whose key and tempo may vary.

The Lesson12 folder contains a construction kit created especially for this book called Moebius, which contains 13 loops and a loop called Moebius Mix that provides a representative mix of these loops. The construction kit loops are all at 120 bpm and in the key of F#. Although this lesson suggests assembling the various loops in a particular manner, music is all about creativity; feel free to depart from the suggestions and create your own piece of music once you know how the process works.

# Getting started

Before assembling a piece of music, you need to create a Multitrack Session and listen to the various available loops to become familiar with the construction kit elements.

1 Open Audition, and click the Multitrack tab.

**2** In the New Multitrack Session dialog box, enter **Moebius** as the Session Name. For Sample Rate, Bit Depth, and Master, choose 44100 Hz, 16 bits, and Stereo, respectively. Click OK.

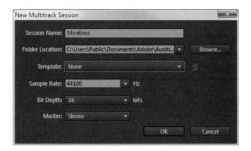

**3** Click the Media Browser tab, and then navigate to the Lesson12 folder. Click its disclosure triangle to expand it, and then expand the Moebius_120BPM_F# folder to show the files in the Moebius construction kit.

**4** Click the Media Browser's Auto-Play button.

**5** Click files in the Moebius_120BPM_F# folder to hear them play. Click the file _Moebius_Mix.wav to hear a representative mix of the various files playing together.

**6** Choose View > Zoom Out Full (All Axes) to see an overview of the tracks as you build the composition in subsequent steps.

**7** Right-click in the timeline, and choose Time Display > Bars and Beats.

▶ **Tip:** To reveal the complete filename in the Media Browser, you may need to click on the divider between Name and Duration and drag to the right.

**Note:** Snap helps align the start of an audio clip to a rhythmic value. The resolution depends on the zoom level; for example, when zoomed full out, audio clips will snap to the nearest measure. Zoom in further, and they'll snap to the nearest beat.

**Note:** Adding more tracks increases the output level. You'll probably need to scroll down to the Master track and reduce the volume to avoid the Output meters going "into the red."

**Note:** If you move the mouse after a clip has snapped to a rhythmic division, the clip may move off the rhythm. To make sure it has snapped properly, after dropping the clip, click on the clip's name and move the clip until it snaps into place.

8 Right-click again on the Time Display, and choose Time Display > Edit Tempo. Confirm that the Tempo is 120 beats/minute with a Time Signature of 4/4 and a Subdivisions setting of 16. If any of these values differ, enter the specified values. Click OK.

9 Click the Snap button (the magnet icon to the Time Display's immediate left) or type **S**.

# Building a rhythm track

Although there are no "rules" about creating a piece of music, it's common to start with a rhythm track consisting of drums and bass, and then add other melodic elements.

1 From the Media Browser, drag the file Drums_F#L into Track 1 so its left edge is flush with the beginning of the session.

2 Hold down the Alt (Option) key and click the clip's name (Drums_F#L). Drag right to copy the audio clip, and release the mouse when the clip's start is at the beginning of measure 5.

3 Similarly, create another copy so that the new clip copy starts at measure 9.

4 Create another copy so that the new clip copy starts at measure 13. There should now be four successive Drums_F#L clips in a row, lasting a total of 16 measures (e.g., the right edge of the last Drums_F#L clip is at the start of measure 17).

5 Enable the Transport Loop button, return the playhead to the beginning, and click Play. The music should play through to the end and then jump back to the beginning and repeat. Click Stop after verifying this.

6 From the browser, drag the file Bass_Sub_F#H into Track 2 so the clip's left edge starts at measure 5.

7 Similarly to how you copied the drum file, copy two more iterations of the Bass_Sub_F#H so that the second copy starts at measure 9 and the third copy starts at measure 13.

8 Because a constant bass part can get monotonous, you can trim some of the file so it drops out and let the drums carry the beat. To do this, hover the cursor over the right edge of the bass clip that begins at measure 5—in the part of the waveform just below the name—until the cursor turns into the Trim tool, as signified by a red right bracket.

9 Click and drag left until the clip ends at the beginning of measure 8.

**10** Similarly, drag the right edge of the third copy left so that it ends at measure 16.

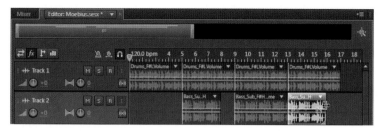

**11** Add some variety to the drum track as well. Similar to how you shortened the bass clip, hover the cursor over the right edge of the last drum clip until it turns into a red right bracket, click, and then drag to the left to trim the clip so that it ends at measure 16.

**12** From the Media Browser, drag the file Drums_F#H into Track 1 so the clip's left edge starts at measure 16. Hover the cursor over the right edge of this drum clip until it turns into a red right bracket, click, and then drag to the left so that this clip ends at the beginning of measure 17.

**13** Return the playhead to the beginning, and click Play to listen to the drum and bass tracks.

**14** The transition between the fourth and fifth drum clips seems a little abrupt. To smooth this, zoom in for a detailed view of the transition between the two clips at measure 16. Click on the fourth drum clip (the one that ends at measure 16) to select it.

**15** Hover the cursor over the right edge of the fourth drum clip until it turns into a red right bracket, click, and then drag right so that the clip now ends at measure 16, beat 2 (shown as 16:2 on the Time Display if you're zoomed in far enough). This will auto-crossfade the end of the fourth clip with the beginning of the fifth clip. Play that transition; it will sound much smoother.

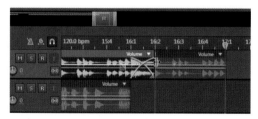

# Adding percussion

Before moving on to additional melodic elements, let's add a little light percussion to augment the rhythmic feel.

1 From the browser, drag the file Seq_TunedNoiseSeq into Track 3 so its left edge snaps to the beginning of measure 5.

**Note:** The file Seq_TunedNoiseSeq.wav doesn't include a key because it's an unpitched percussion sound.

2 Hover the cursor over the right edge of this clip until the cursor turns into a red right bracket, click, and then drag left so that the clip ends at the beginning of measure 7.

3 Hold down the Alt (Option) key, click the clip's name, and drag right to copy the audio clip. Release the mouse button when the clip starts at the beginning of measure 9.

4 Hold down the Alt (Option) key, click the clip's name, and drag right to copy the audio clip. Release the mouse button when the clip starts at the beginning of measure 13.

5 Hover the cursor over the right edge of this clip until the cursor turns into a red right bracket, click, and then drag right so that the clip ends at the beginning of measure 16.

6 Return the playhead to the beginning, and click Play to hear the music so far. After playing through the music, click Stop.

# Adding melodic elements

With drums, bass, and percussion covered, you'll now add some melodic elements. Because you're already familiar with the process of dragging from the Media Browser, aligning clips to rhythmic divisions via snapping, and shortening clips, this process will go expeditiously.

1  Drag the file Pad_DreamyBrass_F#L into Track 4 so it starts at measure 7.

2  Drag the file Pad_DreamyBrass_F#H into Track 4 so it starts at measure 13.

3  Drag the file Organ_Church_F#L into Track 5 so it starts at measure 9.

4  Drag the file String_Harp_F#H into Track 6 so it starts at measure 11.

5  Drag the file Seq_Bouncy_F#L into Track 7 so it starts at measure 13.

6  Return the playhead to the beginning, and click Play to hear what you've assembled so far.

▶ **Tip:** If you minimize the track heights and choose View > Zoom Out Full (All Axes), you'll see all the tracks and their associated clips.

**Note:** If you need to create additional tracks, right-click (Control-click) in a blank space in the Multitrack Editor and choose Track > Add Stereo Audio Track.

# Using loops with different pitch and tempo

The advantage of the construction kit approach is that files within the kit will have a common pitch and tempo. However, it's also possible to use files with different pitches and tempos if they're not too different from the current session—extreme changes can lead to an unnatural sound.

In this lesson, you'll use a file in the key of E instead of F# with a tempo of 125 bpm instead of 120 bpm. It even has a different file format—AIF instead of WAV.

1 If you need to create a new track for another loop, right-click (Control-click) within the Multitrack Editor and choose Track > Add Stereo Audio Track.

2 Drag the file BeatFilter_E_125.aif from the Lesson12 folder into Track 8 or any empty track. It should start at the beginning of the track.

3 Return the playhead to the beginning and click Play. You'll hear that this new clip is out of time and out of tune with the rest of the music.

4 To match the clip tempo to the Session tempo, activate the Toggle Global Clip stretching button (a clock with a double arrow underneath located to the left of the timeline). Then click on the white stretch triangle toward the right of the clip (just underneath the clip's name header), and drag right until the end of the clip reaches the beginning of measure 5 (shown as 5:1 on the timeline).

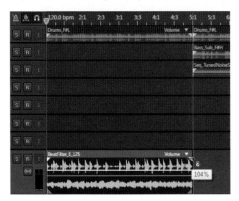

5 With the BeatFilter_E_125.aif clip selected, click the Waveform tab (pitch edits need to be made in the Waveform Editor).

6 In the Waveform Editor, press Ctrl+A (Control+A) to select the entire waveform. Choose Effects > Time and Pitch > Stretch and Pitch (process).

7 In the Stretch and Pitch dialog box, choose Default from the Presets drop-down menu.

8 Click the Advanced disclosure triangle. If necessary, select Solo Instrument or Voice, and deselect Preserve Speech Characteristics.

**9** The BeatFilter_E_125.aif needs to transpose up two semitones so that its key is F# instead of E (E-F-F#). Click on the Semitones field and type **2**. Click OK.

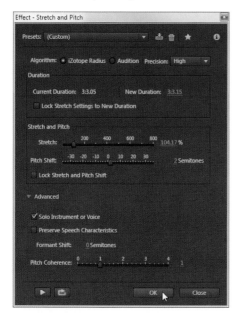

**10** A dialog box warns you that this file is used in a Multitrack Session and will modify that session. This is what you want, so click OK.

**11** When the file is finished processing, click the Multitrack tab to return to the Multitrack Session.

**12** Click Play. BeatFilter_E_125 is now in time and in pitch with the rest of the music.

## Adding processing

The basics of the music are in place. You can now use some of the techniques described in Lessons 10 and 11 to modify the music further, such as change clip levels, add processing, alter panning, and so on. In this section, you'll make the brass pad even dreamier with some echo.

**1** Click and drag on the divider between Track 4 and Track 5, and drag down until you can see Track 4's Effects Rack. Remember that the fx button in the Multitrack Editor's toolbar must be enabled.

**2** In Track 4's Effects Rack, click insert 1's right arrow and choose Delay and Echo > Echo. This turns the master fx button on automatically.

**3** If necessary, choose the Echo's Default preset from the Presets drop-down menu, and then choose beats from the Delay Time Units drop-down menu.

**4** Set the Echo parameters as follows: Left Channel Delay Time to 2, Right Channel Delay Time to 3, and for both channels, Feedback and Echo Level to 80. Set all Successive Echo Equalization sliders to 0. Select Echo Bounce so the echo creates a wider stereo image.

**5** Click Play to hear how the echo affects the overall sound.

**6** The second clip in Track 4 seems a bit loud. To reduce its level so it sits more in the background, click on the clip's yellow volume line, and drag it down to around -5.5dB.

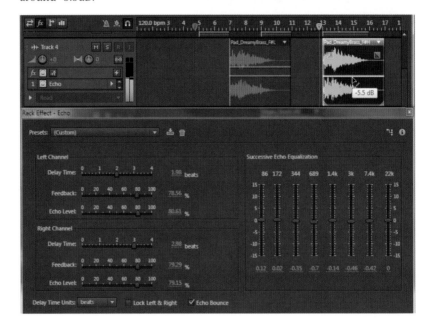

# Review questions

1 What are the important characteristics of a sound library's construction kit?

2 Can you use files from sound libraries in commercials or video soundtracks?

3 Where can you find royalty-free content for use in your projects?

4 Can files be used if they have a different pitch or tempo than the Multitrack Session?

5 Are there any limitations to stretching or changing pitch?

# Review answers

1 The files are matched with respect to tempo and pitch.

2 The legal agreements for sound libraries vary; be sure to read them to avoid getting into possible copyright infringement issues.

3 Adobe's Resource Central is available for Audition CS6 users and contains thousands of files.

4 Yes, you can process pitch with the Waveform Editor's stretch and pitch processing function, and stretch a clip to a different tempo simply by clicking and dragging in the Multitrack Editor.

5 The greater the amount of stretching or pitch transposition, the less natural the sound.

# 13 RECORDING IN THE MULTITRACK EDITOR

## Lesson overview

In this lesson, you'll learn how to do the following:

- Assign a track to your audio interface's input or your computer's default sound inputs so you can record into a Multitrack Editor track

- Monitor the interface input while you record

- Set up the metronome for different patterns and sounds

- Record an overdub (additional part)

- "Punch in" over a mistake to correct it

- Record multiple takes and choose the best parts to create a composite track

 This lesson takes about 50 minutes to complete. This assumes you've copied the Lesson13 folder that contains the audio examples into the Lessons folder that you created on your hard drive for these projects. Remember that you needn't be concerned about modifying these files, because you can always return to the original versions by copying them from the *Adobe Audition CS6 Classroom in a Book* CD-ROM.

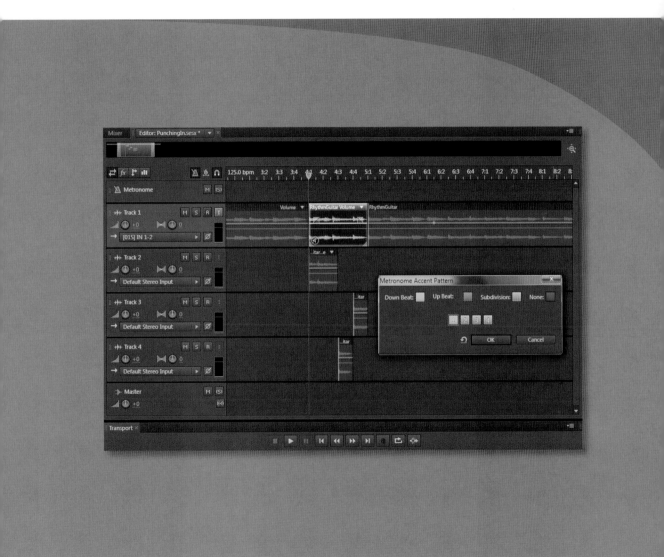

In addition to simply recording into a track in the Multitrack Editor, you can also "punch" over mistakes and assemble multiple takes into an idealized, composite take.

# Getting ready to record a track

You can record directly into the Multitrack Editor. For the purposes of this lesson, use any audio source that's compatible with your audio interface—a microphone, a USB microphone that plugs directly into your computer, a musical instrument like a guitar or drum machine, CD or MP3 player output, and so on. Start with a new Multitrack Session.

1  With Audition open, choose File > New > Multitrack Session or press Ctrl+N (Command+N), name the Session **Recording**, and choose the template Empty Stereo Session. Click OK.

2  Choose Multitrack > Track > Add [Mono or Stereo, depending on the source]. For example, if you're recording a voice, that would require a Mono track. However, most drum machines have stereo outputs, so if you were recording a drum machine to lay down a rhythm part, you'd choose a Stereo audio track.

**Note:** The Input field arrow points inward toward the Multitrack Editor; the Output field arrow points outward, away from the Multitrack Editor.

3  From the Multitrack Editor four-button main toolbar, choose the Inputs/Outputs area for the newly created track, and extend the track height so you can see the Input and Output fields.

**Note:** If you add a Mono track, the input will nonetheless show Default Stereo Input. However, the default input will actually be the left channel, or lower-numbered input, of a stereo pair. For example, if your default stereo input is called 1+2, with a Mono track the default input will be 1.

4  The input defaults to the Default Stereo Input, as described in Lesson 1, "Audio Interfacing." Verify that your signal source is plugged into the correct default hardware input. If it is plugged into an input that is not the default input, you can change the default using the Input field drop-down menu (also described in Lesson 1).

**Note:** Because the track's output is assigned to the Master track output bus, you should also see signal level in the Master bus meter.

5  The output will default to the Master track output bus. If for any reason you want to bypass the Master track output and send the input directly to an audio interface hardware output, choose the appropriate Mono or Stereo output from the Output field drop-down menu.

6  Click the track's Arm for Record (R) button and play your audio source. The track meter should indicate signal level. Like most recording software, you'll need to adjust levels at the audio source or with your interface; there is no internal input level adjustment within Audition. Make sure that with the loudest anticipated signal, the meter does not go into the red.

**7**  Click the Monitor Input button. The input signal will pass through Audition and to the default output. With slower computers, this may result in *latency*— an audible delay between what you're hearing compared to the input. For information on minimizing latency, refer to Lesson 1.

**8**  Keep this project open in preparation for the next lesson.

## Setting up the metronome

The metronome helps you record by providing a rhythmic reference during the recording process. The metronome signal is not recorded into any track but is routed directly to the Master track output bus so you can hear it.

**1**  Click the Toggle Metronome button to the left of the timeline. The metronome track appears above any audio tracks, but it can be moved within a project, like any other track.

**2**  Click Play and you'll hear the metronome signal.

**3**  You can modify which sounds play on which beats. Right-click (Control-click) on the Toggle Metronome button and choose Edit Pattern to define a rhythmic pattern.

**4** The metronome plays four "clicks." The default is a downbeat using one sound and three "subdivision" beats using a different sound (e.g., TICK - tock - tock - tock). However, clicking on any beat square (labeled 1–4) cycles through four options for what that beat can play: Down Beat, Upbeat, Subdivision, or None. Click once on beat 3 to select None, and then click OK.

**5** Click Play, and you'll notice that the third beat is missing.

**6** Right-click (Control-click) on the Toggle Metronome button again, and then choose Edit Pattern. This time click twice on beat 3 to select Up Beat (it will turn orange); click OK. Click Play, and you'll hear a different accent for the third beat.

**7** Return the metronome to the standard setting. Right-click (Control-click) on the Toggle Metronome button, choose Edit Pattern, and then click the Reset Accent Pattern button to the immediate left of the OK button. Click OK.

**8** You can also change the metronome sound. Right-click (Control-click) on the Toggle Metronome button and choose Change Sound Type > [*desired sound*]. Sticks is the most conventional, followed by Cymbals, Kit, and Beeps; other options are available for more unusual sounds. Click Play after choosing an option to audition it.

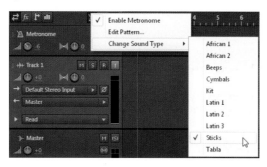

**9** After choosing a sound, adjust the Metronome Volume and Pan controls, which work identically to other tracks.

**10** Keep this project open in preparation for the next lesson.

## Recording a part in a track

Now that the levels have been set and the metronome is set up, you can record a part.

▶ **Tip:** If you can't enable Arm for Record, it means no input is selected.

**1** If necessary, return the playhead to the file start and make sure the track's Arm for Record button is on.

**2** Click the Transport Record button or press Shift+spacebar to begin recording. Several events occur:

- The playhead starts moving to the right and the metronome plays.

- The Transport Record button glows red.
- The Arm for Record button remains off until the transport is stopped.
- A red-tinted clip (the color indicates the clip is currently recording) shows the waveform being recorded.

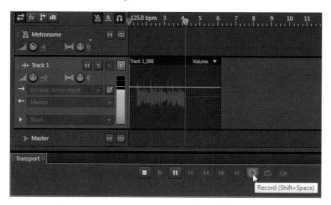

3  When you're finished recording, click the Transport Stop button.

4  Keep this project open in preparation for the next lesson.

# Recording an additional part (overdub)

Recording an additional part is equally simple. This process is called *overdubbing* and is a mainstay of modern recording techniques. For example, a vocalist will often over-dub an additional vocal part to create a thicker sound, or a drummer might overdub hand percussion parts (like tambourine) over a standard acoustic drum part.

1  Create a new track, select an input, enable Arm for Record and Monitor Input, and set levels as described previously.

2  Turn off the Arm for Record button on the previously recorded track.

3  Click the Transport Record button, and then click Stop when you're done.

4  Close Audition; you'll be opening a new project for the next lesson.

**Tip:** If you forget to turn off a previously recorded track's Arm for Record button and accidentally record on that track, a new clip records on top of any existing clip. When you're finished recording, simply click the accidentally recorded track to select it, and then press Delete.

# "Punching in" over a mistake

If you make a recording mistake, you may be able to edit it, for example, by finding someplace else in the song where you play the same part and then copying that part and pasting it over the mistake. But sometimes it's easier and more natural just to play the part again. However, you don't have to play the entire part; you can select only the section of the part with a mistake and record over that.

As mentioned previously, although you'll be punching in on a guitar part for the purposes of this lesson, use any audio source that's compatible with your audio interface—a microphone, a USB microphone that plugs directly into your computer, a musical instrument like a guitar or drum machine, CD or MP3 player output, and so on. The object is to demonstrate the process of punching more than to fix the guitar part.

1  With Audition open, navigate to the Lesson13 folder, and open the Multitrack Session PunchingIn.sesx.

2  Click Play. Note the mistake between measures 4:1 and 5:1.

3  Enable Snap. Choose the Time Selection tool, and then click at 4:1 and drag to 5:1.

4  In the timeline, place the playhead before measure 4:1—for example, at the beginning or at measure 2:1.

▶ **Tip:** Because recording won't start until the playhead reaches the beginning of a selection, you can start listening well before the punch-in point to get warmed up and play along with the track. Then when punching occurs, you're already "in the groove."

5  Click the Track 1 Arm for Record button and Monitor Input, because you'll want to hear yourself play the part you're punching in.

6  Click the Transport Record button. Several events occur:

• You can hear the previously recorded clip along with what you're playing into the interface input.

• Recording ("punch-in") begins only when the playhead reaches the selection's beginning.

• While recording within the selection, the previously recorded clip mutes.

• When the playhead reaches the selection end, recording stops ("punch-out"); you can again hear the previously recorded clip, and playback continues. The section that was punched in is tinted red until you click Stop.

7  Click Play. The punched part, being on top of the previously recorded clip, will play back and "cover over" the mistake. You can just leave it there or temporarily move it so you can remove the part with the mistake and replace it with the new clip.

8  Close Audition to start fresh with the next lesson.

# Composite recording

Some recording software allows looping a selection while in record mode so you can record take after take without stopping, and then choose the version you like best after you stop. Although Audition doesn't have that exact function, it provides a similar option. The process is called *composite recording* because you composite several takes into a single, perfected take.

This lesson explains how to create several alternate takes and then choose the best one (or assemble parts of the best ones).

1 With Audition open, navigate to the Lesson13 folder, and open the Multitrack Session PunchingIn.sesx.

2 As in the previous lesson, enable Snap, choose the Time Selection tool, and then click at 4:1 and drag to 5:1.

3 In the timeline, place the playhead somewhere before measure 4:1 (e.g., measure 2:1).

4 Click the Track 1 Arm for Record button and Monitor Input.

5 Right-click (Control-click) on the Play button and choose Return Playhead to Start Position on Stop.

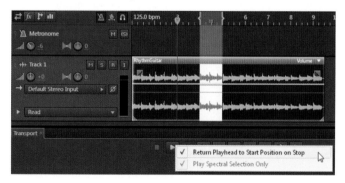

6 Click the Transport Record button, and record something during the selection. This will be your first take.

7 After the playhead passes the selection, click Stop. The playhead returns to where it started.

8 Click the Transport Record button again, and record something during the selection. This will be your second take.

9 Click Stop. The playhead returns to where it started.

10 Repeat the previous procedure to create one more take (for a total of three).

11 Click Stop, and then disable the Record and Monitor Input buttons.

**12** Click the header in the clip on top of the original clip (take 3 in the selection area), and drag straight down to create a new track with only this take.

**13** Click on the next clip (take 2) in the selection area and drag down into another track, and then click on the next clip (take 1) in the selection area and drag down into another track. Now each take is in its own track.

**14** With the selection you made back in step 2 still active, click on the original clip's header (the clip with the mistake in it) to select it.

**15** Choose Clip > Split to delete the section with the mistake.

**16** Click the section you just split to select it, and then press Delete, or right-click (Control-click) on it and choose Mute.

▶ **Tip:** If you can't solo more than one track at a time, Ctrl-click (Command-click) on a Solo button to enable it in addition to other Solo buttons.

**17** Solo the original track, solo the track with the first take, and listen to how they sound together.

**18** Un-solo the track with the first take, solo the track with the second take, and listen to how they sound together. Similarly, listen to the track with the third take.

**19** If you like one take best, drag it into place in the original track, and then delete the tracks with the unused takes.

▶ **Tip:** To delete a track, right-click (Control-click) on an empty space in the track to be deleted, and then choose Track > Delete Selected Track.

**20** If you like different parts of different takes, use the Trim tool to isolate the sections you like, and then drag them into place on the original track. Remember that if a clip is on top of another clip, the uppermost clip is what you'll hear.

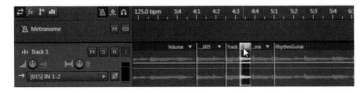

## Review questions

1   What is the disadvantage of monitoring the input signal through Audition?

2   Is clicking the Transport Record button sufficient to initiate the recording process?

3   What is the purpose of the metronome?

4   What is "punching in" and "punching out"?

5   What is "composite recording"?

## Review answers

1   With slower computers, you may experience latency, where the signal you hear coming out of Audition is delayed slightly compared to the input.

2   No; you also need to arm at least one track for recording.

3   The metronome provides a rhythmic reference while you record.

4   Punching in initiates recording at a designated start point; recording stops at the designated punch-out point.

5   Composite recording involves recording multiple takes of the same part and then assembling the best sections into a final, composite take.

# 14 AUTOMATION

## Lesson overview

In this lesson, you'll learn how to do the following:

- Automate volume, pan, and effect changes within clips by using automation envelopes

- Use keyframes to edit automation envelopes with a high degree of precision

- Use spline curves to smooth automation envelopes

- Show/hide clip envelopes

- Automate Mixer fader and Pan control moves

- Create and edit envelopes in the Multitrack Editor track Lanes

- Protect envelopes from accidental overwriting

 This lesson takes about 60 minutes to complete. This assumes you've copied the Lesson14 folder that contains the project examples into the Lessons folder that you created on your hard drive for these projects. Remember that you needn't be concerned about modifying these files, because you can always return to the original versions by copying them from the *Adobe Audition CS6 Classroom in a Book* CD-ROM.

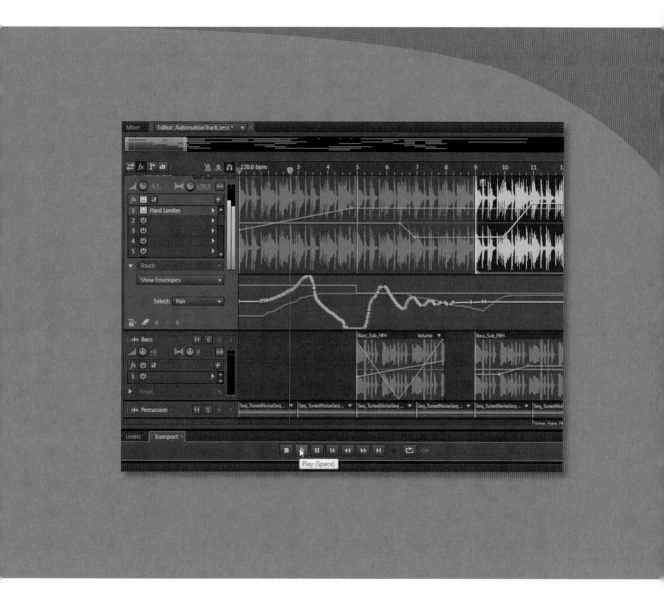

Audition can remember parameter changes you make in a Multitrack Session and store those changes as part of the Session file—whether those changes are performed in real time as control movements or created/edited in non-real time. These automation processes can apply to individual clips or complete tracks.

# About automation

Automation records the control changes you make while mixing, including track parameters and effects. Before automation existed, if during mixdown you forgot to mute one channel at the right time or alter a mixer channel's volume when needed, you usually needed to start the mix from scratch. With automation, not only can you record your mixing "moves," you can edit them. For example, if a mix is perfect except that you didn't mute a track in time, simply add the mute where needed.

Audition offers two types of automation in the Multitrack Editor: clip automation and track automation. The Waveform Editor does not support automation.

Automation can be recorded during recording or during playback; it is not necessary to put a track into record mode to record automation moves. These moves are recorded as envelopes, which are lines—superimposed on a clip or track—that graphically indicate the value of the parameter being automated over time. There are multiple ways to create and edit envelopes, as you'll see in this lesson.

# Clip automation

Every clip includes two default envelopes—one for controlling volume, the other for pan. You can manipulate these envelopes to create automation within a clip. Later in this lesson you'll learn how to automate clip effect envelopes as well.

**Note:** If you want to remove a keyframe, click on it to select it and press Delete, or right-click (Control-click) on it and choose Delete Selected Keyframes. If multiple keyframes were selected via Ctrl-click (Command-click) or by selecting a string of keyframes by clicking at one end of the string and Shift-clicking at the other end of the string, deleting one keyframe will delete all selected keyframes.

1 With Audition open, navigate to the Lesson14 folder, and open the Multitrack Session AutomationClip.sesx.

2 You'll add a volume fade-in to the first clip in the Main Drums track. For easy viewing of the envelope, extend the track height and zoom in so the clip fills much of the window.

3 Note the yellow Volume envelope (currently a straight line) in the clip's upper half and the blue Pan envelope that marks the clip's middle. Click on the Volume envelope and while holding down the mouse button, drag down. The tooltip shows how much the gain is being reduced; this acts like a Volume control, because you're changing volume for the entire clip. Because the object is to create a fade-in, drag back up so the tooltip shows a level of +0.0dB.

4 You can add control points called *keyframes* along the envelope to change the line's shape. Click once on the Volume envelope around 3:1. This places a keyframe on the envelope. Click on the envelope again around 1:3 to create a second keyframe.

**5** Click on the second keyframe you made at 1:3 and drag it down and to the left so it's at the clip's beginning and shows a volume of around -14dB.

▶ **Tip:** Hover the cursor over a keyframe to see a tooltip with the keyframe's parameter value.

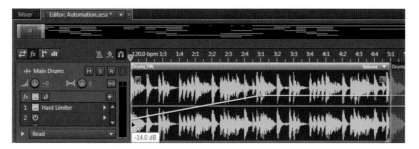

**6** Start playback from the beginning of the song, and you'll hear the drums fade in.

**7** Suppose you want the music to fade in a little faster but not reach full volume until 3:1. Click on the line between the first and second keyframes, and then drag to around -3.6dB at 1:4. Click Play, and you'll hear that the fade-in is a little faster at first and then fades in at a slower rate.

**8** Now pan this clip so it starts in the left channel, moves to the right channel, and then ends up centered. Click on the blue Pan envelope at 4:2 to add a keyframe. This will be where the panning returns to center.

**9** Click on the Pan envelope around 2:4, and drag all the way down so the tooltip shows R100.0.

**10** Click toward the beginning of the Pan envelope, and drag all the way up and to the left until the tooltip shows L100.0.

**11** Click Play, and you'll hear the sound pan.

**12** Make the pan a little more complex: Click on the Pan envelope around 3:3, and drag this new keyframe all the way up. Click Play, and you'll hear the sound move from left to right, back to left, and then end up in the center.

**13** The panning transitions seem a little abrupt because the lines change angles sharply at each keyframe. To change these angles into smooth curves, right-click (Control-click) anywhere on the envelope and choose Spline Curves. Now the envelope becomes similar to a "rubber band," which allows you to click and drag to create any kind of curved shape you want.

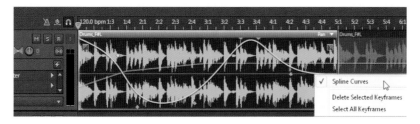

**14** Keep this project open for the next lesson.

## Move parts of an envelope or an entire envelope

You've already learned that you can click on a single keyframe and move it around. However, you can select multiple keyframes and move them around as a group. For example, suppose you like the shape of the fade-in you created for the drums but want to raise the level of the entire envelope so that it makes for a slightly louder introduction before more clips start playing. Here's how to do it.

**Tip:** If you click on a Volume or Pan envelope to select it, you'll place a keyframe on the envelope. To select the envelope without adding a keyframe, right-click (Control-click) on it.

1 Right-click (Control-click) on the Volume envelope you created in the first Main Drums clip to select it for editing.

2 Right-click (Control-click) on the envelope or an envelope keyframe and choose Select All Keyframes.

3 Click on any keyframe, and drag up so the tooltip shows around +4dB. All the other keyframes move simultaneously.

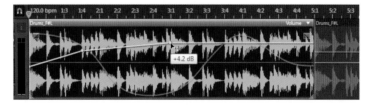

**Tip:** To select a string of keyframes, click on the leftmost one, and then Shift-click on the rightmost one. Those keyframes and all keyframes in between are selected.

4 You can also select particular keyframes and have those move together as a group. Click the clip outside of the Volume envelope to deselect all keyframes.

5 Click on the leftmost keyframe (the one at the beginning of the clip) to select it, and then Ctrl-click (Command-click) the second keyframe from the left (the one at 2:1).

6 Click on the first selected keyframe, and drag up until the second selected keyframe reaches the top of the clip (you could click on either keyframe, but choosing the first one allows you to learn an additional characteristic of moving keyframe groups). The line defined by the two keyframes will move, and the nonselected keyframe to the right will remain "anchored."

**Note:** When you move a keyframe up or down within a clip, you cannot move it any farther than the clip's upper and lower limits. When moving a group of keyframes left or right, you can't move the group farther than the leftmost keyframe allows or farther than the rightmost keyframe allows.

7 Keep moving the first keyframe up. Note that the second keyframe remains "stuck" at the top; however, it "remembers" its original position. Drag the first keyframe back down again to where it started (around -7.5dB), and the second keyframe will return to its original position.

8 Leave this project open for the next lesson.

## Keyframe hold

The Hold Keyframe option keeps an envelope at the current value set by the key-frame until the next keyframe, at which point the envelope jumps instantly to the next value. Here's how to use this effect to create abrupt panning changes.

1 Locate the first clip in the second track (Bass) and zoom in so you can easily see the clip and its automation envelopes.

2 Click on the Pan envelope just before the note that starts after 6:4 to create a keyframe.

3 Click on the Pan envelope just before the note that starts after 5:4 to create a keyframe. Drag this all the way down.

4 Click on the Pan envelope toward the left of the envelope, and then drag the keyframe to the upper-left corner.

5 Hover the cursor over the leftmost keyframe until you see the tooltip, which means you're hovering directly over the keyframe. Right-click (Control-click) and choose Hold Keyframe.

6 Similarly, hover over the next keyframe to the right, right-click (Control-click) on it, and choose Hold Keyframe. The envelope now makes sharp, right-angle turns as the envelope jumps to the next value.

7 Leave this project open for the next lesson.

● **Note:** A Hold Keyframe has a square shape, whereas a standard keyframe has a diamond shape.

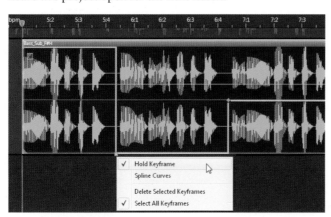

## Clip effects automation

In addition to volume and pan, you can automate the parameters of clip effects within the clip (see Lesson 11 for more information about clip effects).

1 Rather than working with the clip you just used to learn about Volume and Pan envelopes, you'll use a different clip to learn about clip effects automation. Locate the clip in the Main Drums track that begins around 9:2 and select it.

**2**  In the Effects Rack, click the Clip Effects tab. You'll add a wah effect.

**3**  In the first insert, click the right arrow and choose Filter and EQ > Parametric Equalizer. Choose Default from the Presets menu.

**4**  Turn off all bands except band 2. Set its gain to around 20dB and Q to around 12.

**5**  Click the triangle in the clip's upper right, and choose Parametric Equalizer > EQ Band 2 Center Frequency. This specifies the automation envelope that will be added to the clip.

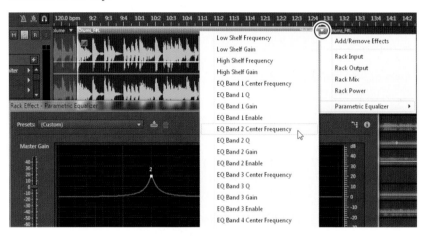

**6**  An envelope appears and a small fx icon. Click on each end of the envelope to add two keyframes.

**7**  Drag the left keyframe to the lower left until the tooltip indicates a frequency of around 100Hz. You may need to extend the track height to obtain the necessary resolution.

**8**  Drag the right keyframe to the upper right until the tooltip indicates a frequency of around 4000Hz.

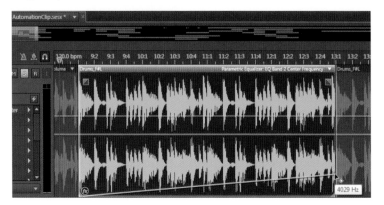

**9** Place the playhead before the clip starts, and then click Play. You'll hear a filtering effect that goes from low to high over the course of the clip. You may want to click the track's Solo button so you can focus in on hearing the effect; keep the effect's window open if you want to see the parameter change in real time.

**10** Leave this project open for the next lesson.

● **Note:** When you select an automation envelope in a clip, the upper right of the clip header displays the name of the parameter it controls.

## Show/hide clip envelopes

If you have lots of envelopes in a clip, the view can become cluttered. However, you can show and hide particular envelope types. Note that this changes the view for all clips in the project, not just a selected clip.

**1** Choose the View menu.

**2** Select the envelopes you want to see—Volume, Pan, or Effect.

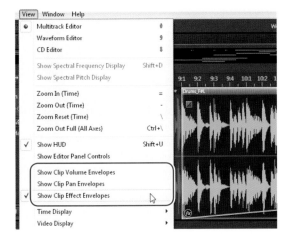

# Track automation

Track automation has some similarities to clip automation but is more flexible and applies to an entire track. You can work with track automation from either the Multitrack Editor or Mixer view.

For individual tracks, you can automate:

- Volume

- Mute

- Pan

- Track EQ (including all EQ parameters—frequency, gain, Q, and so on)

- Rack Input level

- Rack Output level

- Rack Mix (crossfades between the dry sound and the sound processed by the Effects Rack)

- Rack Power

- Most plug-in parameters, including VST and AU-format plug-ins. For example, you could automate delay so that the delay feedback increases over a certain number of measures and then decreases.

There are three main ways to work with track automation:

- Move onscreen controls in real time and record the control motions as envelopes.

- Create an envelope, and then add keyframes to create an envelope shape.

- Combine the two—create the envelope with control motion, and then edit it by adding, moving, or deleting keyframes.

## Clip vs. track automation

Given that you can automate volume changes with clip automation or track automation, sometimes you need to decide which to choose. The most important consideration is that you can create complex volume, pan, or effect changes within a clip, but then subject that to overall level changes using track automation. For example, you could apply clip automation to boost individual snare drum hits in a drum clip, and then use track automation to fade the overall clip in or out.

Another major difference is that clip automation is part of the clip, so if you move the clip, the automation moves with it. If you move a clip that's being automated by track automation, the automation will remain stationary. However, you can select multiple automation keyframes and move the envelope so it matches up with the clip you moved. In this case, it's a good idea to put a keyframe where the clip starts or ends *before* you move the clip, so you have a reference point when you move the envelope.

Additionally, you can create track automation either by drawing and modifying envelopes or by moving onscreen controls. With clip automation, you can work only with envelopes.

What makes both clip and track automation so useful goes beyond being able to capture mixing moves like levels and panning, because automation can add nuanced expressiveness to electronically oriented music by automating signal processing plug-ins. Also, note that you can edit automation data so you can tweak one parameter to perfection, then another, and so on.

## Automating fader mixes

In addition to automating using keyframes, you can take a more "hands-on" approach by automating mixing moves you make with the Mixer faders.

1   With Audition open, navigate to the Lesson14 folder, and open the Multitrack Session AutomationTrack.sesx.

    You'll want to start the file from the beginning after stopping playback in most of this lesson.

2   To start file playback from the beginning, position the playhead at the beginning of the file, and then right-click (Control-click) on the Transport Play button and choose Return Playhead to Start Position on Stop.

3   With Audition open, click the Mixer tab.

4   Click the Main Drums track's fader automation drop-down menu and choose Write.

5   Start with the fader for Track 1 (Main Drums) at around -18dB, because you'll fade the level up.

6   Start playback from the file beginning. As the file plays, bring up the fader to around 0. Let the file play for several seconds, and then fade the drums out all the way.

7   Stop playback. Note that the Main Drums automation drop-down menu option changes automatically from Write to Touch. As you'll see, this makes it convenient to fine-tune your fader moves.

8   Start playback, and the fader re-creates the fader moves you made. After the fader fades out, stop playback.

● **Note:** In Touch mode, any existing automation remains as is until you "touch" the fader (i.e., click on it) and move it. Then the new fader moves take over for as long as you hold down the mouse button. When you release the mouse button, the automation returns to any previous automation data.

9 Suppose you decide that fading out all the way wasn't a great idea, and once the level starts fading out, you want the drums to fade back in again. You can always write new automation, but it's easier just to "punch in" with the new automation move by using Touch mode. Start playback, grab the fader partway through the fadeout, and then fade back up to 0. Let the file play for a seconds, and then release the mouse and stop playback. The fader returns to 0, because that was the automation data prior to adding the new automation moves.

10 You can also automate panning. With the automation drop-down menu set to either Touch or Write, start playback and move the Pan control. Panning back and forth rhythmically will provide plenty of data to work with. When you've done at least several measures of panning moves, stop playback.

11 Now automate an effect. Expand the fx section by clicking its disclosure triangle.

12 In the Percussion channel's automation drop-down menu, choose Write.

13 In the Percussion track's fx area, double-click on the Echo insert to bring up its interface so you can modify its controls. Locate the 1.4k slider in the Echo effect's Successive Echo Equalization area; that's the one you'll be altering.

14 Start playback from the file beginning, and move the 1.4k fader up to around 5dB.

15 The echo sound will start feeding back after a few seconds. Before it gets too out of control, pull the fader down to around -5dB to reduce the amount of echo feedback. Stop playback.

16 Start playback, and you'll see the 1.4k slider re-create your mixing moves. When the mixing moves end, stop playback.

17 When you're finished making automation moves, change the automation drop-down menus for the Main Drums and Percussion channels to Read. This will prevent accidental erasures or edits (Off ignores any automation data).

18 Keep this project open in preparation for the next lesson.

## Editing envelopes

Although you can edit automation by using the Touch, Latch, and Write modes to make real-time edits, these automation moves also create envelopes that you can access and edit in the Multitrack Editor, similarly to how you edit clip envelopes.

1 Click the Editor tab.

2 Expand the Main Drums track height until you see the automation drop-down menu (which should show Read).

**3**  Click the disclosure arrow to the left of the automation drop-down menu to view the automation envelope Lane.

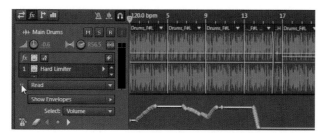

**4**  If you use lots of envelopes, showing them all simultaneously can clutter up a Lane. As a result, Audition lets you specify which envelopes you want to see in the automation envelope Lane. Click the Show Envelopes drop-down menu, and select the automation envelopes you want shown. Because you recorded both Volume and Pan automation, select those.

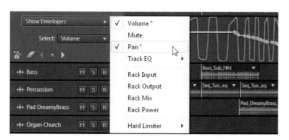

▶ **Tip:** If you're interested in editing automation only for a particular parameter, usually it's best to show only that envelope. However, sometimes two parameters are interrelated, and you'll want to edit one envelope while referencing changes in another envelope. In these situations, being able to show multiple envelopes is ideal.

**5**  If multiple envelopes are visible, seeing all those keyframes in multiple envelopes can sometimes be confusing. Therefore, Audition lets you choose which envelope to edit (you can still see the other envelopes you've chosen to show, but you can't edit them). Choose the envelope you want to edit in the Select drop-down menu. The chosen envelope will be highlighted, and the other envelopes will be dimmed.

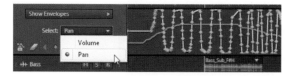

Keyframes in track envelopes work exactly as they do in clip envelopes. For example, suppose your panning envelope doesn't look smooth enough but more like an on-off switch. You can fix this with spline curves.

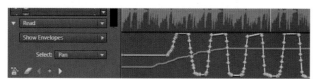

**6** Choose Spline Curves, and curves will form between the keyframes instead of straight lines. You can also delete selected keyframes to "thin out" the curve, either by clicking on them and pressing Delete or by right-clicking (Control-clicking) on a keyframe or selected number of keyframes and choosing Delete Selected Keyframes.

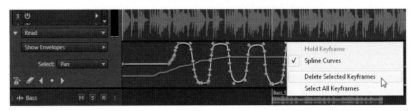

## Creating envelopes in the automation Lane

In addition to editing existing envelopes, you can create and edit track envelopes, as you did with clip envelopes. In this lesson you'll create a precise, hard-limiting change to make the drums beefier when they first start playing, and then dial back on the beefiness when the bass starts.

**1** Click on the Main Drums track's Show Envelopes drop-down menu and choose Hard Limiter > Input Boost. As soon as you choose a new envelope, it's automatically selected (you don't have to use the Select drop-down menu), highlighted in the automation Lane, and set to whatever its current value is in the effect. The default Input Boost for the Hard Limiter is 0.0dB (no boost).

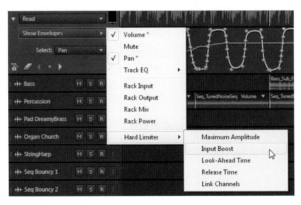

**2** Because you don't want any boost when the bass starts playing (at measure 5:1), click on the Input Boost envelope at 5:1. This places an envelope keyframe at 0.0dB.

**3** Click on the envelope to the left of the keyframe you just added. Drag it up to around 20dB, and position it just before the keyframe that reduces the Input Boost.

**4** Start playback from the beginning, and listen to how this affects the sound.

**5** Keep this project open for the next lesson.

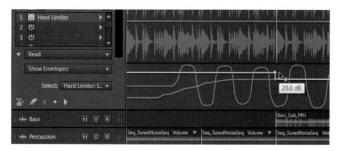

## Precision keyframe editing

In some cases, you might want to do precise keyframe editing. Selecting and deleting can become tedious, so Audition includes four keyframe editing tools.

**1** Select the Pan envelope, which presumably has multiple keyframes.

**2** Click the Next Keyframe button, and the playhead will move right from its current position to the next keyframe.

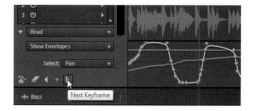

**3** Click the Add/Remove Keyframe button (the diamond icon to the immediate left of the Next Keyframe button) to delete the keyframe. If the playhead was not on a keyframe, clicking this button would add a keyframe.

**4** The Previous Keyframe button (left arrow icon) to the immediate left of the Add/Remove Keyframe button steps through keyframes from right to left. Click this button a few times to see how the playhead moves.

**5** Click the Clear All Keyframes button (the eraser icon) to delete all keyframes for the selected envelope.

**6** Keep this project open for the next lesson.

## Protecting automation envelopes

When you're doing lots of complex automation, you want to avoid accidentally writing new automation where it's not intended or overwriting existing automation (it can happen!). You can protect an envelope from these kinds of unintentional mistakes with a "write-protect"-like feature.

**1** Click the Protection button (the lock icon). The envelope dims to show it's protected, even if it's selected. Note that you can still edit it via the automation Lane when it's protected.

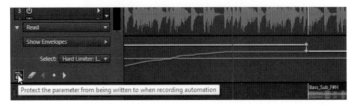

**2** In the Main Drums track, with the Hard Limiter Input Boost envelope still selected, choose Write from the automation drop-down menu.

**3** Double-click on the Effects Rack's Hard Limiter insert to open its user interface window.

**4** Make sure the playhead is at the beginning of the file, and then start playback.

**5** Move the Hard Limiter's Input Boost control back and forth. Stop playback; note that no change has been made to the envelope.

**6** Turn off the Protection button, start playback, and then vary the Hard Limiter Input Boost control again.

**7** Stop playback. Note that the Hard Limiter Input Boost envelope has been overwritten.

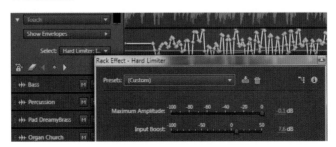

# Review questions

**1** Is there any parameter you can automate in tracks that you can't automate in clips?

**2** What is a keyframe?

**3** What is an automation Lane?

**4** What is the difference between Touch and Latch mode for writing automation?

**5** How does Audition prevent accidental editing of the wrong envelope?

# Review answers

**1** Clips cannot do mute automation.

**2** A keyframe is a point on an automation envelope that represents a particular parameter value.

**3** A Lane is part of the Multitrack Editor where you can create and edit envelopes for a track. Every track has a corresponding Lane.

**4** After releasing a control in Touch mode, from that point on the automation returns to any previously written automation. After releasing a control in Latch mode, the automation envelope retains the last control value prior to releasing it.

**5** Only the selected envelope can be edited, even though other envelopes are visible. You can also use the Protection button to prevent overwriting automation moves when recording automation.

# 15 MIXING

## Lesson overview

In this lesson, you'll learn how to do the following:

- Use Audition to help test your room acoustics and determine its suitability for creating accurate mixes

- Review tracks for glitches or other issues prior to mixing

- Change a song's arrangement through mixing and remixing techniques

- Optimize tracks to mesh well together using effects

- Take into account artistic considerations in mixing

- Set up the mixing environment for an efficient workflow

- Use automation in the Mixer view to record and edit your fader, panning, and other moves as you perfect each component of a mix

- Create clip groups

- Add a fade-out using the Master Track

- Export the completed song in a variety of formats

- Burn an audio CD of the completed song

 This lesson takes about 90 minutes to complete. This assumes you've copied the Lesson15 folder that contains the project examples into the Lessons folder that you created on your hard drive for these projects. Remember that you needn't be concerned about modifying these files, because you can always return to the original versions by copying them from the *Adobe Audition CS6 Classroom in a Book* CD-ROM.

Creating a mix is an art and a science. Audition's
Mixer view combined with automation, long-throw
faders, the ability to detach the mixer and "float" it on
another monitor, and various other crucial tools help
create the mix. You can then save it in a variety of file
formats (including MP3 for uploading to the web),
as well as burn an audio CD of the final stereo mix.

# About mixing

After recording your parts and doing any overdubs, you're ready for the next step: mixing and ultimately, mastering and publishing/distributing your project. Reduced to its basics, mixing simply means adjusting the levels, tonal balance, stereo or surround placement, and adding effects as needed to create a wonderful sonic experience.

However, part of mixing is making numerous value judgments. Which instrument should be most prominent at any given time? Do you want to mute some sections that seem redundant? Which is more appropriate—a raw, in-your-face sound or a smooth, well-produced sound? Do you want a massive guitar timbre or something that shares its space with other instruments? Who is your target audience?

How successfully you answer these types of questions determines the success of your mix. Mixing is a combination of art—being able to judge what sounds good—and science, knowing what technologies and processes will produce the sounds you want. This lesson covers both aspects.

Note that there are as many ways to approach mixing as there are people who mix, so consider the information in this lesson as guidelines, not rules.

# Testing your acoustics

Any effort you put into mixing means nothing if your monitoring system—which includes your hearing, the room's acoustics , the amp and cables that drive your monitors, and the speakers—aren't accurate. If you've ever done a mix that sounded great on your system but sounded wrong when played elsewhere, you've experienced what can go wrong with the monitoring process. A good mix should be able to "translate" over a wide variety of systems.

Fortunately, Audition provides tools you can use to do some basic diagnostic tests on your listening environment prior to mixing.

1  With Audition open, navigate to the Lesson15 folder, open the TestTones folder, and then open the file 100Hz_SineWave.wav.

2  Start with your monitoring system's volume control full off, and then click the Transport Play button.

3  Slowly turn up the monitoring system's volume to a comfortable listening level.

4  Walk around the room and listen. In an untreated acoustical space, there will be places where the sound gets louder and others where it gets softer. This is because the sound waves are reflecting around the room and interact with each other to cause peaks and cancellations.

▶ **Tip:** Placing large, acoustically treated tubes called *bass traps* in the corners of a room can help even out the bass response.

5   Now navigate to the Test Tones folder and open the file 1000Hz_SineWave.wav.

6   Again, walk around the room and listen. You'll probably note that in some places the sound will become very quiet if you reach a "null point" in the room where the sound waves cancel.

7   Navigate to the Test Tones folder and open the file 10000Hz_SineWave.wav.

8   If you can't hear this tone, consult an audiologist. Otherwise, walk around the room and listen. Because high-frequency wavelengths are so short, there will be even more peaks and cancellations than with the other frequencies.

## Acoustics and hearing

The ear's frequency response changes depending on the level. If you mix at too low a level, you might boost the bass and treble too much because the ear doesn't respond as well as those frequencies. Mix at a comfortable listening level (which also reduces listening fatigue), and then check at both high and low levels to find a good average setting. Also, avoid mixing within 24 hours of taking a plane flight.

The room and speakers work as a team. Because the walls, floors, and ceilings all interact with speakers, it's important that you place your speakers symmetrically within a room. Otherwise, if (for example) one speaker is three feet from a wall and another ten feet from a wall, any reflections from the walls will be wildly different and affect the response.

Near-field monitor speakers can reduce (but not eliminate) the impact of room acoustics on the overall sounds if placed around 3–5 feet from your ears with your head and the speakers forming a triangle. The reason is that the speakers' direct sound exceeds the reflections coming off the room surfaces. As a side benefit, because of their proximity to your ears, near-field monitors do not have to produce a lot of power.

Headphones eliminate room acoustics but can give an unnatural sound when mixing, like exaggerated reverb effects. Many pros listen to mixes on speakers and headphones as a "reality check," as well as different sets of speakers to hear what the music will sound like in different listening environments.

The subject of acoustical treatment deserves a book in itself; hiring a professional consultant to "tune" your room with bass traps and similar mechanical devices could be the best investment you ever make in your music. Meanwhile, you can find lots of educational information about acoustics in the Acoustics 101 and Auralex University sections at www.auralex.com.

▶ **Tip:** Acoustical diffusion and absorption panels can improve high-frequency response and smooth out the midrange response to create a more accurate monitoring environment.

● **Note:** Even acoustically treated rooms will have some anomalies. The most important aspect to check is that you do not hear significant null points in these waveforms at your mixing position.

## Testing for phase

Before doing any mixing, it's good practice to make sure your system's audio is in phase. For example, if the wiring to one speaker is reversed compared to the other speaker, its cone will push while the other cone pulls. This causes cancellations.

1   With Audition open, navigate to the Lesson15 folder, open the TestTones folder, and then open the file 100Hz_OutOfPhase.wav. Also make sure the file 100Hz_SineWave.wav file is loaded in Audition.

2   Use the Waveform Editor's drop-down menu to select the 100Hz_SineWave.wav file. Click Play and listen for several seconds.

3   Use the Waveform Editor's drop-down menu to select the 100Hz_OutOfPhase.wav file. Click Play and listen for several seconds. If this test tone is quieter than the 100Hz_SineWave.wav file, your system's stereo channels are in phase.

## Creating your own test tones

The three test tones you listened to are fairly standard choices in terms of frequency. However, you might want to create your own test tones to test the low-frequency response of your speakers, the upper limit of your own hearing, how your room responds to frequencies other than the frequencies you just tested, and so on.

1   With Audition open to the Waveform Editor, choose File > New > Audio File.

2   Name the file **20Hz_LowsTest**, choose the sample rate and bit depth (leave Channels set to Stereo), and click OK.

3   Choose Effects > Generate Tones.

4   Specify the test tone's characteristics. The crucial ones are Shape (Sine), Modulation Depth (0), and Base Frequency (the frequency you want to create). Amplitude will typically be -6 to -10dB. Duration doesn't really matter if you toggle the Loop button on.

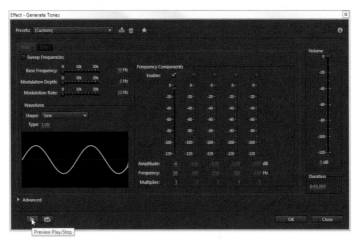

5  Click the dialog box Play button to hear the tone.

6  Close Audition without saving anything in preparation for the next lesson.

# The mixing process

Mixing involves several distinct stages, which is what we'll cover next. Again this is subjective view of mixing, but you'll find most mixes proceed along the same general trajectory.

The project you'll be mixing is intended to create background music for a 60-second, narrationless kiosk video that will fade out at the end. You'll be working with very basic tracks that you will arrange ("remix") as well as do more traditional mixing. Digital audio editors facilitate remixing where the mix engineer makes decisions about not just the mix, but the arrangement as well. In addition to pop music remixes, this can happen with audio for video where, for example, a single piece of music is arranged for 15-second, 30-second, and 60-second spots.

## Preparation

Before mixing, it's important to do a little "mix environment housekeeping."

1  With Audition open, navigate to the Lesson15 folder, open the Mixdown folder, and then open the file Mixdown.sesx.

2  Right-click (Control-click) in the timeline and choose Time Display > Bars and Beats.

3  Right-click (Control-click) in the timeline and choose Time Display > Edit Tempo. Enter a tempo of **128** beats/minute, with a Time Signature of **4/4** and a Subdivisions value of **16**. Click OK.

4  Right-click (Control-click) in the timeline and choose Snapping > Snap to Ruler (Coarse). Also make sure Snap to Markers and Enabled are selected, but deselect any other Snapping options for now.

5  Arrange your workspace for mixing. The most important panels are the Multitrack Editor, Mixer (in the same tabbed frame), Effects Rack, Markers, Selection/View, Time, and Levels meters.

6  If you come up with a particularly good workspace for mixing, consider creating a new workspace. Choose Window > Workspace > New Workspace; when the New Workspace dialog box appears, enter the name **Mixing** (or a similar name), and then click OK.

▶ **Tip:** Being able to change the Base Frequency and then click the dialog box Play button is helpful for testing. For example, to check out a speaker's low-frequency response, start with a Base Frequency of 50Hz, and then click Play. If you can hear that, enter 40Hz and click Play; continue lowering the Base Frequency until you find the frequency where the speaker can no longer reproduce the bass.

# The role of the producer, engineer, and musician

In professional situations, the musician is part of a team that includes a producer and engineer. In a project or postproduction studio environment, the musician often has to perform all three roles. It helps to be aware of the ideal role of each participant so you can assume these roles as needed while mixing.

The *producer* oversees the process, approves the arrangement, gauges the overall emotional impact, and makes artistic judgments about what does and does not work. To fulfill the function of a producer, you need to see each piece as part of a whole and each track as part of a final composition. If the producer knows the project's ultimate goal, it's a lot easier to create an appropriate mix. Don't just mix your music; produce it.

The *musician* participates in the mix on any one of several levels, from simply observing the producer to making sure the production remains true to the original intent of the music.

The *engineer* is responsible for translating the producer's needs into a technological solution. If the producer says the vocals need more "presence," it's up to the engineer to decide which tweaks will result in that particular effect. It can be helpful to adopt an engineer's attitude when mixing; forget about whether you could have done a better solo and simply work with what you have.

A common mistake among inexperienced recordists is to overproduce. Sometimes tracks are best left unprocessed, and sometimes parts should be removed to create space for other parts. Keep your focus on the final result, not individual parts; if there's a great guitar lick but it doesn't support the song, mute it.

The fact that one person can write, play, produce, record, master, and even duplicate music is unique to modern times. But just because we *can,* does not mean we *should.* Human interaction can really enhance the creative process and provide the reality check that comes from a trusted associate who can provide honest, objective feedback from a second set of ears.

## Reviewing the tracks

Before you start moving any faders, listen to each track in isolation in case there are any glitches, hum, noise, or other issues that need to be fixed prior to mixing. Using headphones for review can make it easier to hear subtle issues you might miss over big speakers.

1   Return the playhead to the beginning of the Session. Click the Solo button for the first track (Drums), and listen to it all the way through.

2   Because there aren't any issues that need attention prior to mixing, return the playhead to the beginning of the Session. Deselect this Drum track's Solo button, and click the Solo button for the second track (Bass). Listen to it all the way through.

**3**  There's a click at the beginning of measure 17 that needs to be eliminated. Drag the playhead to measure 17, and click Zoom In repeatedly until you can see the reason for the click. You'll also want to extend the Bass track's height.

**4**  There's an abrupt transition at measure 17; adding a short fade can fix that. Click the Bass clip to select it, and then choose the Razor Selected Clips Tool from the top toolbar. Place it just after the abrupt transition, and then click to split the clip.

**5**  Choose the Time Select tool and click the left Bass clip. Click the Fade Out handle, and then drag to the left until around the next zero-crossing (i.e., where the waveform crosses the red centerline), as well as slightly down to a Cosine value of -25.

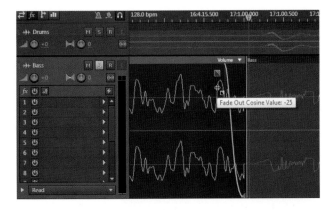

**Note:** If the Fade Out curve is set to Linear, hold down the Ctrl (Command) key while moving the Fade Out handle to toggle to the Cosine option. Either option will work in most situations requiring a fade, but Cosine can sound a tiny bit smoother.

**6**  Click the Zoom Out Full button, place the playhead before measure 17, click Play, and verify that the click is fixed.

**7**  Continue soloing and auditioning each track to look for more glitches (spoiler alert: there aren't any more) and also to become familiar with the tracks that make up the mix. Note that the tracks Wood Percussion, Bounce, Lead Synth, Lead Guitar, and Pad don't make any sound until measure 17; to save time, you don't need to listen to the first 16 measures.

**8**  Deselect the last Solo button you enabled. Keep Audition open in preparation for the next section.

## Making arrangement changes

The lead parts start at measure 17, so the song can logically be divided into two sections. The first 16 measures lead into the song and build, and set the music up for the "payoff"—the lead parts that carry the song to the end.

Currently, the Drums, Bass, 12-String Synth, and Rhythm Guitar tracks all play continuously for the first 16 measures, which doesn't build much. You can make the song more dramatic by modifying the arrangement so that the first 16 measures build over time. This involves value judgments about what would make the most effective beginning, so consider the following possible variation.

1  It's always dramatic to have drums come in after the song has already started. Click the Drums clip to select it, and then position the Time Selection tool over the clip's left edge so it becomes a Trimmer tool. Click and drag inward (right) to the beginning of measure 9.

2  The 12-String Synth part flows well and makes a good intro to the song. The bass seems sort of heavy, so you can delay its introduction for a more dramatic entrance. Click the left Bass clip (remember, we split it to fix a glitch) and use the Trimmer tool to drag the beginning of the Bass part to measure 5.

3  The rhythm guitar isn't necessary yet, so click the Rhythm Guitar track to select it, and then use the Trimmer tool to trim its beginning to measure 9. Now it will come in with the drums.

4  Return to the beginning of the song, and then click Play to hear the song so far.

5  The bass comes in a little suddenly; it might be preferable to have a short lead-in. Position the playhead at measure 5, and then zoom in to see the first few notes in the beginning of the clip. Use the Trimmer tool to extend the beginning of the Bass clip back to measure 4, beat 3 (4:3).

6  Position the playhead before 4:3 and start playback. You'll hear a slight click on the bass part at 4:3 because there's an abrupt transition from silence to the bass note. Click the Fade In handle, and add a very short fade-in (e.g., don't drag the Fade In handle any farther to the right than 4:3:01).

**7** Most drummers use a fill to lead in to their part; unfortunately, no lead-in was recorded prior to where the drum beginning was trimmed. However, if you recall from listening to the Drum track, there's a good fill starting at measure 16. Position the playhead just before measure 16, and then click Play to verify that there's a fill there.

**8** Let's steal that fill and use it at the beginning. With the Time Selection tool, click the Drums clip to select it, and then click at measure 16 and drag right to measure 17 to define measure 16 as a selection.

**9** Choose Clip > Split to isolate this selection, and then Alt-click (Option-click) on the Drum clip's header. Drag the copy left so it starts on measure 8.

**10** To emphasize the last beat of the drum fill, use the Time Selection tool to create a selection from 8:4:0 to 9:1:0 (you'll probably need to zoom in so that snap can be active for this). Select the 12-String Synth clip, and then choose Clip > Split. Click the header of the 12-String Synth note you just clicked, and press Delete. Now the 12-String Synth part is silent for the beat just before measure 9.

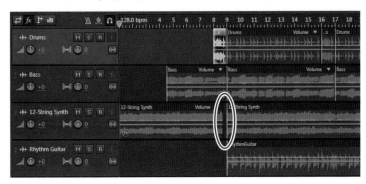

**11** Position the playhead back at the beginning of the song, click Play, and listen up to measure 17 or so. This arrangement is far better than just playing the four tracks at the same time—and nothing else (levels, panning, effects, etc.) has been adjusted yet.

**12** Note that the Master Track Output is overloading. Now would be a good time to lower all the track levels before the mixing process actually starts, because doing a major level change while mixing might unbalance the mix. Click the Mixer tab in the Multitrack Editor frame, and set all the track faders to -9.5dB. Don't adjust the Master Track Output Volume to compensate for the reduced level: If you want it louder, turn up your monitoring system's level. You want to keep the Master Track Volume as close to 0 as practical and use it only at the end to make any final output adjustments (if necessary).

**13** Click the Multitrack Editor tab to continue working on the arrangement.

**14** Listen to the first 16 measures. Aside from the drum fill at measure 16, the parts are pretty constant from measures 9 through 17. This would be a good space to bring in short pieces of some of the later parts as "teasers."

**15** With the Time Selection tool, or by dragging the selection In and Out point handles, select all of measure 17.

**16** Click the Wood Percussion clip to select it, and choose Clip > Split to isolate measure 17.

**17** Alt-click (Option-click) this isolated clip's header, and drag the copy left so it starts at measure 11.

**18** Create two more copies. Start one at measure 13 and the other at measure 15.

**19** Start playback from before measure 11. You probably won't hear the wood percussion part very distinctly, because the other parts are louder. These will become more prominent during the level-setting process.

**20** Keep Audition open in preparation for the next lesson. If you want to hear what this arrangement sounds like, listen to the file SongArrangement.wav in the Lesson15 folder.

## The brain and mixing

The brain is a dual-processing system. The left hemisphere is involved in more analytical tasks like setting levels and switching among various functions, whereas the right hemisphere handles creative tasks and emotional responses; it "feels" rather than "thinks" as it listens to the tracks. This relates to mixing because, in general, trying to straddle the two hemispheres is not easy. However, if working with Audition becomes second nature, it will be easier to stay in right-brain mode. Audition has two features that help considerably—keyboard shortcuts and workspaces—which are both covered in Lesson 2:

* Learn existing keyboard shortcuts, and create your own. After using them becomes ingrained, you'll find it saves time to type a few keys as opposed to "mousing around."

* Use workspaces to organize specific combinations of windows for certain tasks, like mixing, overdubbing, different types of editing, and so on. This requires less effort than opening windows and dragging them around.

## Optimizing tracks by using effects: drums and bass

The first part's basic arrangement is complete (notwithstanding any final tweaks you might make as the song develops further); you can change the second part's arrangement during the rest of the mixing process. Next, you'll turn your attention toward optimizing the sound of the various tracks with effects.

How you do this, as well as modify other aspects of the mix, will depend largely on the music's intended application. If there will be a voice-over, the music will probably need to be more subdued to provide a "bed" for the voice. On the other hand, to accompany a kiosk video with no narration, you might want a more attention-getting mix.

1 Solo the Drums track, and then select measures 9–17 because all instruments in the beginning play in that section. Click the Transport Loop Playback button or press Ctrl+L (Command+L), and then start playback. The drums sound a little muffled and could use more "punch."

2 Click the Multitrack Editor's fx area. Click the first insert's right arrow and choose Amplitude and Compression > Hard Limiter. From the Presets drop-down menu, choose Default.

3 Increase the Input Boost to 6.8dB. Toggle the Hard Limiter's power state button to hear how the processing gives the drums more presence and an "in-your-face" characteristic.

4 Set the Effects Rack's Mix slider to about 70%. This mixes in some of the more percussive peaks from the unprocessed sound with the hard limited sound. (If you can't see the Mix slider and Input/Output controls and meters, click the Toggle Input/Output Mix Controls button to the right of the Effects Rack's master power state button.)

5 The limiting brings out the cymbals a bit too much, and it would be good to have more "thud" with the kick. Click the Multitrack Editor's EQ area; extend the Drums track height if needed to see the EQ area.

6 Click the pencil icon to open the EQ's interface. From the EQ's Presets menu, choose Default.

7 Enable the LP band, and choose 24dB/octave. For Frequency, choose around 9200Hz. This tames the highs.

**8** For more kick, set Band 1's Frequency to 60Hz, Gain to 2dB, and Q to 2. The drums sound less thin and much beefier.

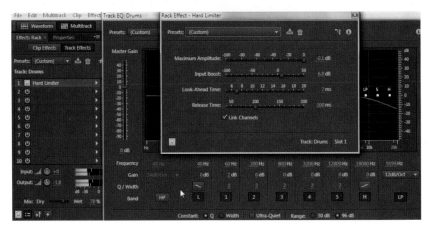

**9** Now turn off Solo for the drums, and solo the bass. This instrument has the opposite problem: The bass is too aggressive and present, so you'll make it smoother and rounder.

**10** With the EQ area still showing, open the Bass track's EQ section.

**11** Enable the LP section, set Gain to 12dB/octave, and Frequency to about 700Hz. This reduces the brightness. To make the bass "rounder," set Band 1's Frequency to 50Hz, Gain to 2.6dB, and Q to 0.6.

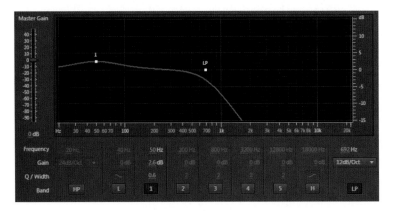

**12** Now solo the Drums so you hear the Bass and Drums tracks simultaneously. Turn off the Bass track EQ's power state, and you'll hear how the bass timbre gets in the way of the drums.

## Optimizing tracks by using effects: rhythm guitar

The Rhythm Guitar and 12-String Synth complement each other. The Rhythm Guitar is more percussive, and the 12-String Synth is more legato. They'll likely end up panned to opposite channels, but the guitar sound is too bland; it won't hold its own against the 12-String Synth. You'll use processing to fix that.

1 Solo the Rhythm Guitar track. It needs to sound more shimmering and bright but also less muddy—like the sound on the early Police albums.

2 Open the Rhythm Guitar's track EQ from the EQ area.

3 Set the L band around 450Hz, Gain to -6.3dB, and Q to the more shallow slope. Set the H band around 860Hz, Gain to 4.7dB, and again set the shallow slope for EQ.

4 The EQ took care of the lack of brightness and excess bass. To add a shimmering, animated quality to the sound, click the right arrow in the first insert of the Rhythm Guitar track's Effects Rack and choose Modulation > Chorus/Flanger. From the Presets drop-down menu, choose Default.

5 Change the Speed parameters to 0.1Hz, and Width to 30%.

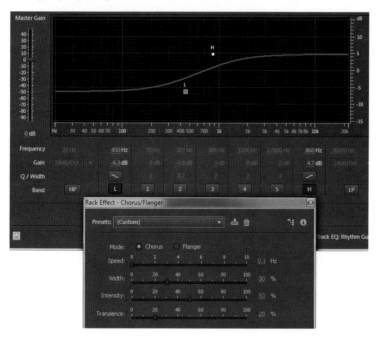

6 Now solo the 12-String Synth and Rhythm Guitar. Having both of them play at the same time is somewhat cluttered, but this can be addressed with levels and panning.

## Optimizing tracks by using effects: pads

A pad tends to be a fairly sustained, background sound designed to fill in some of the space in a piece of music and provide a "bed." Pads can be bright and thin, bassy, mostly midrange, or whatever is required to fulfill their function. The pad in this song needs to be tamed, which can be done with EQ.

1   There are three background tracks featured in the second half of the song—Wood Percussion, Bounce, and Pad. Solo those three tracks and nothing else.

2   Unsolo the Pad track, and note how Wood Percussion and Bounce sound much more percussive—the pad fills in the background too much.

3   Open the Pad track's EQ from the EQ area. Turn of all Bands except HP (set it to around 300Hz with 13dB/Octave gain) and LP (set it to around 1700Hz, also with 12dB/Octave gain). Note how this makes the pad subservient to the Wood Percussion and Bounce.

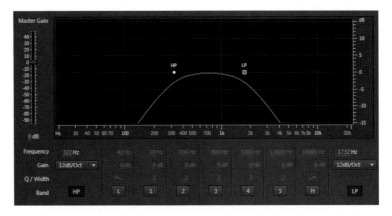

## Optimizing tracks by using effects: lead guitar

Two lead tracks remain, Lead Synth and Lead Guitar. Because they're essentially doubling each other, it's probably best for them to trade back and forth during the final mix. However, the Lead Guitar needs some serious processing in order to cut through the mix.

1   Unsolo all tracks and solo the Lead Guitar.

2   Click the right arrow in the first insert in the Lead Guitar track's Effects Rack and choose Special > Guitar Suite. From the Presets drop-down menu, choose Big and Dumb.

3   Deselect the Filter Bypass. Change Frequency to around 1700Hz and Resonance to around 50%.

4   Click the right arrow in the second insert in the Lead Guitar track's Effects Rack and choose Delay and Echo > Echo. From the Presets drop-down menu, choose Default.

5   Change Delay Time Units to Beats and select Echo Bounce. For the Left Channel Delay Time, type in **1.33** beats. For the Right Channel Delay time, type in **1.00** beats.

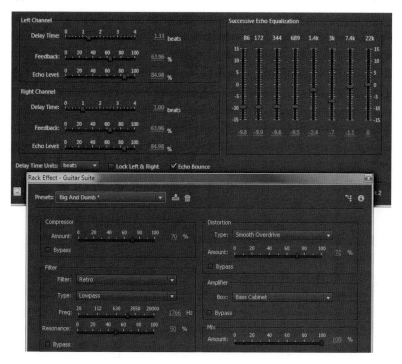

6   Toggle the Guitar Track Effects Rack's power state button to compare the sound before and after processing. That's quite a difference!

## Setting up the mixing environment

Now that the sounds are dialed in, it's time to set up levels and stereo imaging. Note that all of these edits are interactive: You might find while setting levels that you need to go back and tweak EQ on a track or delete a track altogether.

1   Let's create some markers so it's easy to get around in the song. If any part of the song is selected, click in the waveform (outside the selection) to deselect it.

2   Place the playhead at the beginning and press M. In the Markers panel name this marker **Start**.

3   Place the playhead at measure 16 and press M. In the Markers panel, name this marker **Solo Start**. It's set one measure before the solo starts on purpose, so you have a one-measure "count-in" before you reach the start of the solo.

**Note:** If you find it difficult to place the playhead exactly on the measure, you can type in the desired value in the Markers panel Start field—for example, 16:1.00.

▶ **Tip:** If you have a
two-monitor display,
you can float the Mixer
to one of the displays
while keeping the
Multitrack Editor open
in the other.

4 Place the playhead at measure 24 and press M. In the Markers panel, name this
marker **Solo Halfway**. Again, this is one measure before the actual halfway point.

5 Click the Mixer tab, because that environment is optimized for what you're
about to do next. Expand all the Mixer disclosure triangles, and if possible,
expand the Mixer panel so you can see all tracks and the Master Track at the
same time.

6 Choose Window > Transport to make it easy to get around while in the Mixer
environment. Docking it next to the Levels panel is one possible place to put it.
Check that all the track levels are at -9.5dB (or -9dB; it doesn't matter as long as
they're consistent) and the mixing environment is now ready.

## Setting levels and balance

Until now, all the tracks have been centered in the stereo field and all levels have been the same. Starting without stereo placement makes it apparent which tracks conflict with respect to frequency response; this might not be obvious when tracks are panned oppositely. In other words, if the music sounds "open" and distinct with all the parts centered, it will sound even more open and more distinct once you start working with the stereo placement. The reason for keeping levels the same is to establish a baseline level, which can then be altered during mixing.

You'll start by mixing the introduction, in other words, the section up to measure 17.

1 Double-click the Start marker, click the Transport Play button, and just listen to the introduction.

2 Pan the 12-String Synth to around L88, and pan the Rhythm Guitar to around R88. These will "bookend" the centered Drums and Bass tracks.

3 Listen again. It's good that the 12-String Synth starts off strong, because nothing else is playing. But it needs to come down a bit when the bass comes in and also because it will be too loud compared to the rhythm guitar when it enters. So, start playback, and when the bass comes in, move the 12-String Synth channel's fader down to around -11dB (check the yellow number just below the fader in Mixer view) so it hits that level before the drums come in. Practice this "move" a couple times to get a feel for how the fader responds.

4 When you have the move down, write it as automation. In the 12-String Synth Track, set the Automation drop-down menu to Latch. You can then write your move, and when you stop, the level will remain at -11dB (or wherever you left it).

5 Return the fader to -9 or so, and click Play. Make your fader change at the appropriate time, and click Stop when you've completed the move. Change the 12-String Synth automation drop-down menu to Read, so you don't write new automation by accident.

6 Now automate the drums. They seem a little soft overall, so they should end up around -7.6dB. But they should also come on strong during the opening fill. Practice starting with the Drums track at -6dB and then bringing it down to around -7.6dB when the rhythm guitar comes in. Bring it up to -6dB again during the fill that happens at measure 16. Then reduce it to -7.6dB or so when measure 17 starts. Practice this move a few times.

7 When you're ready, set the Drums track automation drop-down menu to Latch, and do your automation. Click Stop when you've completed the move, and change the Drums automation drop-down menu to Read.

8 Jump ahead to the two leads and let's automate them as well, because the plan is to trade off between the two leads. Double-click the marker Solo Start.

▶ **Tip:** Remember that you can right-click (Control-click) the Transport Play button and choose Return Playhead to Start Position on Stop. This can be helpful when you're mixing the introduction and want to return to the beginning.

**9** Pan the Lead Synth to R70 and the Lead Guitar to L70. The reason for this choice is so the Lead Guitar is in the opposite channel from the Rhythm Guitar, and the Lead Synth is in the opposite channel from the 12-String Synth. This helps differentiate the instruments.

**10** Automate the Lead Guitar first. Start with it at around -4.4dB (after all, it is the lead). Then just before measure 21 starts, click the Mute button. Leave Mute enabled until just before measure 25, and then turn off Mute to hear the Lead Guitar again. Leave Mute off, because both leads will play at the end.

**11** Practice this move until you have it down, and then set the Lead Guitar automation drop-down menu to Latch. Click Play and do your automation moves. When you're done, click Stop, and set the automation drop-down menu to Read.

**12** Now practice the Lead Synth automation moves. This time you can't use the Mute button because the lead plays continuously. So, start with the Lead Synth fader all the way off, and then fade it from 0 to -3.9dB during measure 20. Bring it back down again at measure 25. At measure 29, bring it up to about -7.5— loud enough to support the other lead but not compete with it.

**Note:** If you don't get your automation moves right or get them only partially right, set the track's automation drop-down menu to Touch. Any new moves you make will overwrite old ones as soon as you click on the fader and revert to the older moves when you release the mouse button.

**13** Once you have this move rehearsed, set the Lead Synth automation drop-down menu to Latch, click Play, and do your automation moves. When you're finished click Stop, and set the automation drop-down menu to Read.

**14** Now try some dynamic automation with the Wood Percussion track. Leave it parked around -15dB when the leads are playing notes, but in the spaces where the lead note just sustains, bring the Wood Percussion up to around -3dB to add an accent. Perform the same routine as before: Practice, choose Latch, click Play, make your moves, click Stop, and change the automation drop-down menu to Read.

**15** Bring in the Bounce track to support the Lead Synth track. Pan it opposite to the Lead Synth at L70. Leave it around -15dB, but bring it up to around 0 whenever the Lead Synth is playing.

**16** Double-click the Start marker, and listen to what you have so far.

**17** You need to complete two more tweaks: Some Wood Percussion bits existed before the solo started, but you couldn't really hear them. Set the Wood Percussion automation to Touch and the playhead back to the beginning of the song. Click Play, and then bring the Wood Percussion fader to -6. Leave it there until the solo starts, and then click Stop. Leave the automation on Touch.

**18** Pan the little Wood Percussion bits in the beginning. Click Play, and move the Wood Percussion track's Panner knob all the way to the left before measure 11. During measure 12, move the Panner knob all the way to the right. During measure 14, move it all the way to the left again. When the solo starts, keep moving it around to add some motion to the Wood Percussion part that plays in the spaces between solos.

**19** Click the Multitrack Editor tab, and extend the Track Height of a track where there's automation, like the Lead Synth part. The first time the volume was raised was a little too much, so in the Select field choose Volume (if it isn't already chosen), click the first keyframe of the section you want to change, Shift-click on the last keyframe in the section you want to change, and adjust the level as desired by dragging the envelope down a bit. In some cases, this is faster and/or a more precise method than trying to repeat the automation moves in Touch mode.

**20** After you've finished your mix, keep the project open because you're about to get a phone call.

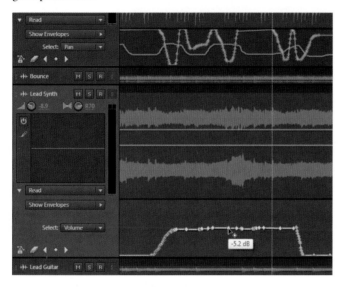

## Using Groups

You've finished your mix, automated your moves, and played the song over the phone to the clients who commissioned the soundtrack. Then the phone rings: They love it, but the video was extended to 1 minute 30 seconds, so they ask if there is any chance you could add the last part using the song's rhythm track, but without the leads, and have a long fade from 1:15 to 1:30?

In this situation you can separate just the section after the solo section begins with the Razor tool, group all the separated clips together except for the leads, and then copy the group to extend the song.

**1** Choose the Razor Selected Tracks tool (or press R).

**2** Zoom in on measure 17 where the solo begins, and extend the height of one of the clips so you can see the waveform. The Razor Selected Tracks tool must be inside a waveform in order to snap.

**3** Position the Razor Selected Tracks tool so you can see the line it creates at 17:1.00.

**4** Press Ctrl+A (Command+A) to select all tracks. The Razor Selected Tracks tool will split any tracks that are selected.

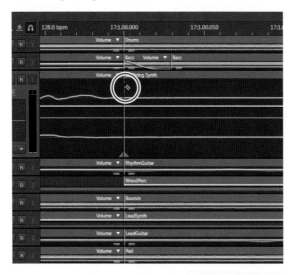

**Note:** Groups can be treated like an individual clip. You can move, copy, paste, or delete a group. Each copy of a group has a unique color. Groups also act like an individual clip in terms of mute, lock, loop, and other clip attributes: Applying an attribute applies it to the entire group. You can also choose Clip > Suspend Group if you want to make changes to an individual clip within a group, such as when you drag-copy a particular clip out of a group.

**5** Select the clips you want to group, either by drawing a marquee around them and/or Ctrl-clicking (Command-clicking) to add or subtract clips from the group.

**6** With the clips to be grouped still selected, choose Clip > Group Clips. The group turns a different color, and each clip shows a group symbol in the lower left.

**7** Alt-click (Option-click) on a clip header, and then drag-copy the group to the current end of the song. Now you have a piece of music that lasts 1 minute and 30 seconds.

## Adding a fade at the end

The easiest way to add a fade-out to the entire mix is to add Volume automation to the Master Track.

**1** Extend the height of the Master Track until you can see the automation lane.

**2** Click the automation disclosure triangle to expand the list.

**3** Click Show Envelopes and select Volume.

**4** Add a node to the envelope where you want the fade to begin, for example, around 15 seconds from the end.

**5** Add another node at the end of the song, and drag it down to 0.

**6** Add intermediate nodes or use spline curves to shape the fade further.

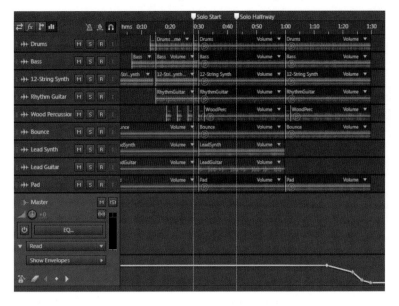

## Exporting a stereo mix of the song

Now that the song is mixed, you can export it as a stereo file in a variety of formats.

**1** Choose File > Export > Multitrack Mixdown, and then choose either Time Selection (if you've defined what should be exported as a time selection) or Entire Session (from the start of the first clip to the end of the last clip).

**2** The Export Multitrack Mixdown dialog box appears. Enter a filename, the location where you want to save it, and the format.

**Note:** Audition can export multiple file types, including WAV, AIF, MP3, MP2, FLAC, Ogg Vorbis, MOV (QuickTime, audio only), libsndifle, and APE (Monkey's Audio).

**3** Click the Change button for Sample Type to change the sample rate and bit depth (resolution). Click the dialog box's Advanced disclosure triangle to specify the type of dithering you want to use. Dithering can offset the effects of truncating bit resolution when converting from a higher resolution to a lower one, such as mixing audio recorded in 24-bit resolution down to the 16-bit resolution required by CDs. Enabling the default is the simplest option.

**4** Click OK, and the song will be exported as a stereo mix to the specified location.

# Burning an audio CD of the song

When you save a stereo mixdown, the file automatically becomes available from the Waveform Editor's drop-down menu. You can then master it or burn the mix to an audio CD.

**1** Choose the file using the Waveform Editor's drop-down menu.

**2** Choose File > Export > Burn Audio CD.

**3** Insert a blank recordable CD in your computer's CD/DVD writeable optical drive.

**4** Click OK.

**5** Choose the desired options from the Burn Audio dialog box.

**6** Click OK, and your CD will be ready shortly thereafter.

## Review questions

1   Why is it important to mix in an acoustically treated space?

2   What is a common signal processor that's used in mixing so tracks mesh well together?

3   Why is it a good idea to start a mix with all tracks centered in the stereo field?

4   What's the easiest way to add an overall fade-out to a song?

5   How does Audition make it easy to burn an audio CD?

## Review answers

1   You cannot produce a mix that will sound good over a variety of systems if the audio you're hearing is not accurate.

2   Equalization (EQ) can prevent tracks from interfering with each other by restricting them to particular frequency ranges.

3   If you can get the tracks to sound separate when they're all panned to center, they'll sound even more open and separate when placed in the stereo field.

4   Volume automation in the Master Track makes it easy to add a fade-out to all tracks simultaneously.

5   When you do a mixdown of a stereo file, it's automatically available in the Waveform Editor, from which you can then burn an audio CD.

# 16 SCORING AUDIO TO VIDEO

## Lesson overview

In this lesson, you'll learn how to do the following:

- Load a video preview file into Audition

- Analyze the video and alter Audition's tempo to create "hit points" so the music closely correlates to the video

- Create a soundtrack music bed

- Add musical or sonic "hits" in musically appropriate places to accent the visuals

- Synchronize ADR (dubbed) dialogue with original dialogue

- Evaluate which type of dialogue synchronization provides the best audio quality

 This lesson takes about 50 minutes to complete. This assumes you've copied the Lesson16 folder that contains the audio examples into the Lessons folder that you created on your hard drive for these projects. Remember that you needn't be concerned about modifying these files, because you can always return to the original versions by copying them from the *Adobe Audition CS6 Classroom in a Book* CD-ROM.

Audition can load video preview files; when composing soundtracks or adding dialogue, the video window provides a crucially important reference.

# Importing a video

**Note:** Audition recognizes the following video formats: AVI, DV, MOV, MPEG-1, MPEG-4, 3GPP, and 3GPP2. Audition is not a video editor and cannot edit the video preview; any video edits need to be done in a program like Adobe Premiere Pro prior to loading the file into Audition. However, its start point can be moved within the video track.

When working with video, Audition can create a separate video preview track at the top of the workspace. If you import video that also includes an audio track, the audio will likewise be imported into Audition and placed in the audio track immediately below the video track.

1   Open Audition and choose File > New > Multitrack Session.

2   Name the file **Audio for Video**. Choose None for Template, 44100Hz for Sample Rate, 16 for Bits, and Stereo for Master. Click OK.

3   From the Media Browser, click on the Lesson16 folder and then open the folder Audio for Video Files and drag the file Promo.mp4 into the beginning of Track 1. This creates a video track automatically, as well as opens a Video panel where you can see the video. You may want, or need, to resize the Video panel to see the entire video. (Note: The video file is provided courtesy of HarmonyCentral.com.)

**Tip:** You can right-click (Control-click) in the Video panel and choose five different scaling options and three different resolutions. Best Fit Scaling is usually the optimal choice, because the video size will conform to the size of the panel.

# Using markers to create hit points

The process of creating a soundtrack typically involves more than just throwing some library music into a couple of tracks and hoping that it matches the video. Sound libraries make it easy to create your own music; even if you consider yourself a "video" person instead of a musician, you might be surprised at how easily you can create a soundtrack, and with a little extra effort, customize the music to correlate to what's happening onscreen.

One way to create this correlation is to identify places in the video where there are important transitions or events and then try different tempos to see which one allows the music to match these "hit points" best.

1   Right-click (Control-click) in the timeline and choose Time Display > Decimal.

**2** Start playback from the beginning of the video. When there's a major transition in the video, press M to place a marker in the timeline and create a location point to aid you in placing musical effects (often called a "hit point"). For example, one point would be just before "the world's largest music show." Others would be just before "live updates from the show floor," "daily highlight videos," "dedicated discussion forum," "press release central," and just before "...and more."

**3** Now fine-tune the placement of the location points, because there will always be a slight lag between the time you view something onscreen and the time you press M. Fortunately, except at the first hit point area, the video has a white flash screen just before these important transitions. Drag the current time indicator (CTI, or playhead) to just before "the world's largest music show," and then drag Marker 01 to align with it.

**4** Drag the CTI until it lands on the white frames just before "live updates from the show flow." Drag Marker 02 to align with the CTI.

**5** Follow the same procedure to position the markers at the remaining white frames before the transition points.

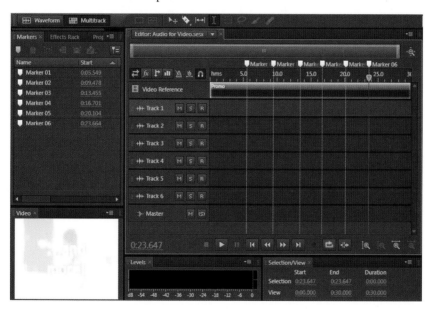

**6** Click on the Markers panel (choose Window > Markers if it's not visible). You should see markers at approximately 0:05.549, 0:09.478, 0:13.455, 0:16.701, 0:20.104, and 0:23.664. These values don't have to be exact as long as the last five markers are where the video shows a white flash. Double-click on each marker in the Markers panel to verify this.

**Note:** Conveniently, the video ends just after measure 17. Most pop music is constructed in groups of four measures, so the music used for this soundtrack can last for four groups of four measures and then fade out to the end of the video on something like a cymbal crash, sustained note, orchestral hit, or the like.

7 Right-click (Control-click) the timeline and choose Bars and Beats; then right-click (Control-click) the timeline and choose Edit Tempo. Enter **100BPM** to start, and then click OK.

8 Look at the extent to which the markers align with the tempo. Two fall on measure boundaries, but the rest fall in several places that have little to do with the tempo. You'll need to find a better match.

9 Change Edit Tempo to **130BPM**. This tempo works quite well—Markers 01, 04, and 05 are very close to a measure boundary. Markers 02 and 06 are quite close, too. The one that's still off a bit is Marker 03, but because the hit point occurs slightly after the measure boundary, you could add a sound that starts on the beat and builds slightly to the hit point. So, 130BPM is a good tempo for the video and fits the video's theme as well—it's upbeat and danceable. Note that finding hit points sometimes involves trial and error; you may need to try several different tempos before finding one that "fits."

10 Keep this project open in preparation for the next lesson.

## Don't forget video for audio

The term "audio for video" recognizes the reality that most of the time audio is added to existing video. However, if you have some degree of control over the audio *and* video process, sometimes it makes more sense to compose the music first and then lay video on top of the audio.

This is particularly true for videos that aren't critically dependent on timing. Kiosk videos, some ads, trailers, and promos are often fairly flexible in the way that video needs to be presented, and cutting it to the audio can simplify matters considerably.

But does the music matter that much? Some studies have indicated that people who were shown videos with identical video quality but differing audio quality judged those videos with better sound as having better *video* quality. If you can come up with a great piece of music, sometimes it's worth taking the "video-for-audio" route.

# Building the soundtrack

The basic strategy for this project is to lay down a rhythmic "bed" in the background that lasts the duration of the video and then overlay hits and additional sounds to emphasize the transitions.

**Note:** In this lesson it's very important that clips snap to precise measure beginnings. Zoom in to verify that the snapping is correct.

1 Right-click (Control-click) the timeline and choose Snapping. Disable all options except Snap to Ruler (Coarse).

2 Use the Media Browser to navigate to the Lesson16 folder, and open the folder Audio for Video Files. Drag Drums1.wav into Track 1, and snap its start to measure 4.

3 Alt-click (Option-click) the Drums1.wav clip's header to copy the file, and drag so that its start snaps to measure 6. Then make three more copies. Snap one clip's start to measure 8, one to measure 12, and the third to measure 14.

4 Drag Drums2.wav from the Audio for Video Files folder into Track 1, and snap its start to measure 10.

5 The last half of the Drums2.wav clip would make a good ending. Alt-click (Option-click) the header of the Drums2.wav clip that starts at measure 10, and drag it so that its start snaps to measure 15. To end up with only the second half, hover the cursor over the last Drums2.wav clip's left edge, and use the Trim tool to drag the clip's edge right so it snaps to the beginning of measure 16.

6 Play the file from the beginning to verify that the Drum track plays back correctly and that there aren't any gaps from not properly snapping to a measure beginning.

7 Drag the Pad.wav file into the session so it starts at the beginning of Track 2.

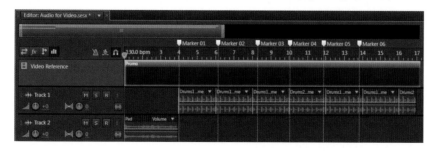

8 Drag the Bass.wav file into Track 3 and snap its start to measure 4. Copy it twice, and snap the beginning of one clip to measure 8 and the beginning of the other clip to measure 12.

9 Drag Rhythm1.wav from the Audio for Video Files folder into Track 4 and snap its beginning to measure 10; then drag Rhythm2.wav into Track 4 and snap its beginning to measure 13 so it crossfades with Rhythm1.wav over measure 13.

10 Click Rhythm2.wav's fade-out handle, and drag it to the left so the fade begins at measure 16. Also, drag down for a Cosine value of around 50.

11 The rhythm track is now complete. Play it from start to finish while looking at the video. You'll see that many of the musical transitions correlate to changes in the video, although some don't quite match up. You'll use the additional tracks to tighten up these transitions.

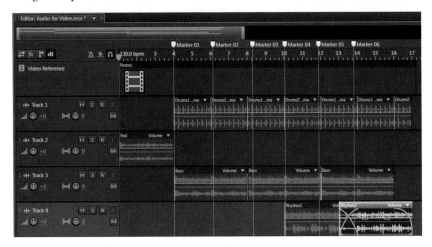

12 Keep the project open in preparation for the next lesson. Also note that you can open the Session file AudioForVideo to bring Audition to this point.

## Adding hits to the marker location points

Now you'll use short, usually percussive, sounds called *hits* to add audio accents to the video's highlights and transitions.

1 Drag RevCymbal2.wav into Track 5 so that the clip *ends* at the start of measure 4. This leads right into the "the world's largest music show" and makes a good transition from the opening pad to where the rhythmic bed starts. Play this transition.

2   You'll do the easiest transitions first, and then revisit the more difficult ones. Drag Hit.wav into Track 5, and position the clip's start at measure 10. Click the fade-in handle, and drag it right so it fades into Marker 04. The hit will then start in time with the music but only reach full volume at the video's transition point, so it will seem like the audio syncs up perfectly with the video. Play this transition to verify that the hit seems to happen at the same time as the white flash in the video.

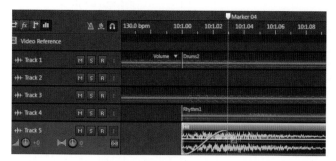

3   With the transition around measure 12, note that the white flash frames happen prior to the start of the measure. Drag CymbalElectro.wav into Track 5 so the clip starts at 11:4, and then click the fade-in handle and drag right to just a little before the start of measure 12. The cymbal fades into the flash and then fades out into the start of the measure. This is a "looser" transition (as opposed to a "tight" transition) that nonetheless bridges the visual flash and music. Play this transition.

4   The transition at measure 8 is a challenge. Drag Cymbal.wav into Track 6, and position its start at 8:1. Play this transition. It doesn't work; the cymbal hits too early compared to the flash.

5   Drag Cymbal.wav's start to Marker 03 to see if that works. Play this transition; it doesn't work either. However, note that Marker 03 is very close to 8:2, which at least falls on a beat. Snap Cymbal.wav's start to 8:2.

**6**  Drag CymbalHi.wav into Track 5, and snap its start to the start of measure 8. Having the two cymbals hit a beat apart works musically, and the second cymbal hit matches up perfectly with the white flash. A slight fade-in with the second cymbal improves the transition slightly, as does lowering its clip Volume envelope by around -3dB.

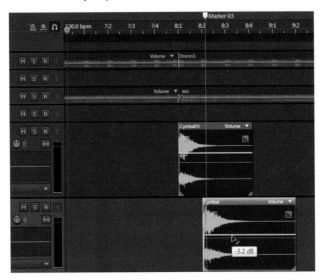

**7**  The transition around measure 6 (Marker 02) is also somewhat of a challenge, so you'll use a different strategy by adapting a clip to provide a slight flourish when the white flash hits in the video. Although it won't follow the beat of the music, by seeming more like an effect, it will still work well. You need to trim Rhythm2. wav to exactly one measure, drag it into the end of Track 5, and snap its *end* to a measure start. Next, hover the cursor over the clip's left side, and then drag it right so that the clip lasts exactly one measure.

**8**  Now drag this clip into its final position. Align the clip start with Marker 02, and then click the fade-out handle and drag it all the way to the left with a Cosine value of 0.

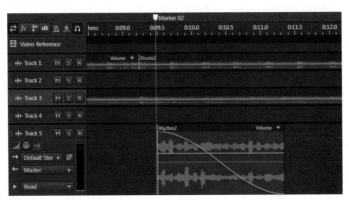

9   Place the playhead before Marker 06, and play through the transition at Marker 06. Note that this doesn't really need additional audio because it's a two-step transition—first there's the flash and then the video shows "...and more!" The background rhythm pattern changes more or less at the same time as this change in the video.

10  To wrap it up with a big finish, drag Hit.wav into Track 5 so the clip starts at measure 17. Now play the entire video through from start to finish to hear the soundtrack and hits, and how they relate to the video.

# Automatic Speech Alignment

Automatic speech alignment is very important when processing dialogue in movies. Dialogue that's recorded on location is often subject to noise, an inability to get actors close enough to the microphone without the mic appearing in the picture, and other issues. As a result, the actors will come in after the shoot and dub new parts. This process is also called *looping* or *ADR (Automated Dialogue Replacement)*.

Dubbing is not easy to do. The actor typically listens to the original part on headphones in a recording studio (as opposed to being on location) and tries to match the original speech as closely as possible. Sometimes actors do ADR even if it's not absolutely necessary, because they want to add a different emotional inflection than what they originally used while shooting the scene.

Audition's Automatic Speech Alignment feature automates this process. You load the original reference dialogue (which can even be relatively noisy) into an Audition track, and then record the new dialogue into a second track. Audition can then compare the new dialogue to the original and use a combination of stretching and alignment processes to match the new dialogue to the reference track.

1   With Audition open, navigate to the Lesson16 folder, and open the Multitrack Session Vocal Alignment that's located in the Vocal Alignment folder.

2   The Session has two tracks, OriginalVocal and ADRVocal. You can use the ADRVocal to experiment with the Automatic Speech Alignment feature, but it's instructive to record your own dialogue and try to match the OriginalVocal track. Mute the ADRVocal track and while listening to the OriginalVocal track on headphones, record a new vocal track where you try to match the OriginalVocal phrasing as closely as possible. If you decide to create your own ADR track, the B-movie-type dialogue is "Helen said she thought she'd found Tesla's lab notes on wireless power transmission, and if she did, that would explain her disappearance. She would instantly be targeted as one of the most wanted people on this planet."

**Note:** The ADRVocal supplied with this project is deliberately way out of sync with the original dialogue so you can hear how Automatic Speech Alignment affects the sound quality of the dialogue when it has to do lots of correction.

**3** You now have two tracks to align, using either the one supplied with the lesson or one you created. If you recorded a vocal, trim the new clip to the same length as the OriginalVocal track. Select the Move tool, and draw a marquee to select both tracks.

**4** Right-click (Control-click) the clip that will serve as the reference to which the other clip should be aligned, and choose Automatic Speech Alignment.

**5** A dialog box appears. For the Reference Clip, if needed, choose the clip to which you want the new dialogue aligned (in this project, OriginalVocal). There are three Alignment options; you'll try all three, so start with Tightest Alignment. Select the "Reference clip is noisy" check box because in this case, it is; also select the "Add aligned clip to new track" check box to allow for easy comparison. Click OK.

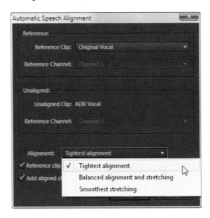

6   The aligned track appears below the reference track. Solo the OriginalVocal and ADRVocal tracks (or OriginalVocal and the ADR track you recorded), and then play them back together so you can hear the differences between the two.

7   Now solo the OriginalVocal track and the new, aligned track. You'll hear far fewer differences.

8   Click on the OriginalVocal clip, and then Ctrl-click (Command-click) on the ADRVocal track. Repeat steps 4 and 5, but this time select "Balanced alignment and stretching" in the Alignment drop-down menu. Click OK.

9   Repeat step 8, but this time select "Smoothest stretching" in the Alignment drop-down menu. Click OK.

10  You now have three clips with the suffix "Aligned." Solo each one to hear how the three different processes affect the sound quality.

● **Note:** The "Smoothest stretching" option usually provides the best audio quality, yet the alignment will still be very tight. Of course, the closer the ADR vocal is to the original, the less processing the Automatic Speech Alignment needs to do and therefore the higher the sound quality.

## Audition integration with Adobe Premiere Pro

Premiere Pro includes an Edit In Adobe Audition command. This makes it easy to send anything from individual clips to a selected work area (including reference video) to Audition for restoration, mastering, or processing ("sweetening"). With individual clips, any edits made in Audition will automatically update the clips in Adobe Premiere Pro. The same is true if you're editing clips from After Effects.

You can also link Audition Multitrack Sessions to exported mixdown files, so when you select the exported file in Premiere Pro, you can do editing and remixing in Audition. This makes it easy to modify a soundtrack when editing in Premiere Pro causes a video to change over time. However, if you don't need this level of flexibility, the two applications can simply share a mixed file from Audition's Multitrack Editor. Note that when you select a mixed file, you can choose to open either the Audition Multitrack Session that created it or open it in the Waveform Editor for simple sweetening.

The level of integration between Audition and Premiere Pro can smooth your workflow dramatically when you're combining audio and video projects. Although covering all aspects of this integration is beyond the scope of this book, there are many tutorials, blog posts, and additional information on the Adobe website.

## Review questions

1  Does Audition do video editing?

2  What is a "hit point"?

3  What is ADR or looping?

4  Why is it necessary to do automatic speech alignment in the Multitrack Editor instead of the Waveform Editor?

5  Are you limited to a single speech alignment process?


## Review answers

1  No. An imported video file is used as a preview, and Audition can add audio to the video.

2  A hit point is a transition or event in the video that you want to accent with some musical element.

3  ADR and looping are techniques that allow actors to replace low-quality dialogue in a movie with higher-quality dialogue, typically recorded in a studio instead of on location.

4  You must do automatic speech alignment in the Multitrack Editor because you need to have two tracks in the Session—the original dialogue and the replacement dialogue you want to align to the original dialogue.

5  No; there are three different ways to do alignment that trade off tighter alignment for smoother vocal quality.

# APPENDIX: PANEL REFERENCE

This appendix summarizes the functions of all panels included with Adobe Audition. Note that several panels can show a large amount of data, which practically speaking can be seen only if you undock or float the panel, and extend its length, height, or both.

## Amplitude Statistics

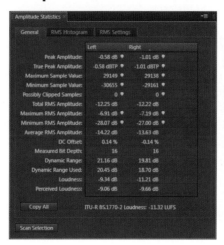 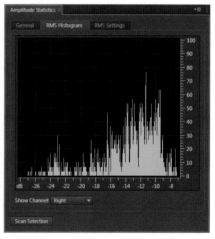

This panel applies to the Waveform Editor only, and provides detailed information about the waveform's amplitude, bit depth, dynamic range, the possibility that samples have been clipped, and more. Clicking Scan analyzes the entire waveform, unless only part of the waveform is selected; in that case, the button will say Scan Selection, and only that section will be analyzed. You can also click Copy to copy these statistics to the computer's clipboard, and paste the clipboard contents into a text document.

The RMS histogram tab shows how much energy (RMS amplitude; vertical axis) is present at various amplitude levels (horizontal axis). This can display the right or left channel, but not both.

# Batch Process

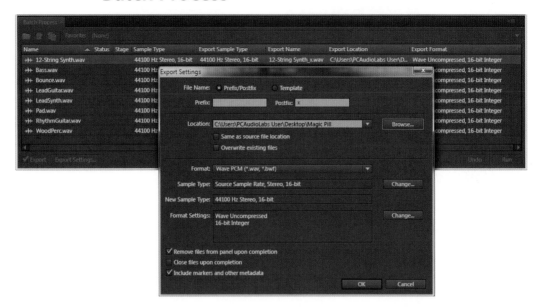

To convert and export files to a specific format, drag the files from the desktop, Media Browser, or Files panel into the Batch Process panel. The panel's Export Settings button opens a window that lets you choose the format to which the files will be converted, as well as add a distinctive prefix or suffix; click the Run button to initiate the conversion/export process.

# Diagnostics

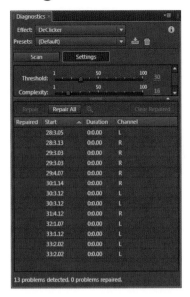

This panel is the same as the one that opens when you select part or all of a waveform in the Waveform Editor, then choose Effects > Diagnostics. It provides processing that can minimize clicks and clipping, as well as delete silence and show marked sections of a waveform.

# Editor

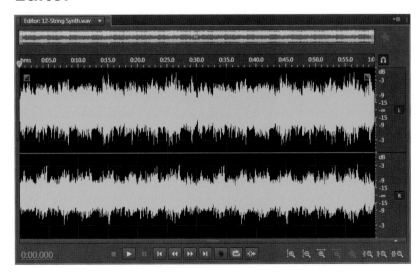

This panel shows the currently selected Editor (Waveform or Multitrack).

# Effects Rack

This panel shows the effects currently inserted into a selected track or clip in the Multitrack Editor, or waveform in the Waveform Editor. It can optionally display input/output and mix controls, as well as input/output metering.

# Files

This panel shows all files currently loaded into Audition (Waveform and Multitrack Editor), as well as several file attributes (duration, sample rate, channels, bit depth, file path, and so on). The file currently being displayed in either Editor is highlighted with tan text. A preview section along the bottom of the panel allows previewing files.

# Frequency Analysis

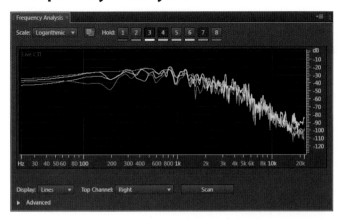

For a selected file (or portion of a file) in the Waveform Editor, this panel shows amplitude response (vertical axis) plotted against frequency (horizontal axis). The frequency range can be displayed linearly or logarithmically; you can store up to eight "snapshots" taken at particular points in the waveform, and for comparison, display each one using a separate color.

# History

This panel shows a history of operations that have been applied to the Waveform Editor or Multitrack Editor, depending on which is open. Clicking an entry returns you to the file status as of that operation, and is nondestructive. If you click an entry and then click the Trash icon, all history will be removed after (and including) that entry; this is destructive and cannot be undone.

# Levels

This panel displays a waveform's level in the Waveform Editor, or the Master Track output level in the Multitrack Editor. You can resize these meters to extend up to the entire width or length of your monitor screen to provide extremely high resolution.

# Markers

When markers are inserted in either the Waveform or Multitrack Editor, this panel shows information about them—name, start point, duration, type, and so on. You can also rename, delete, and change marker types in this panel. Note that it switches automatically to display the markers for the selected Editor.

# Match Volume

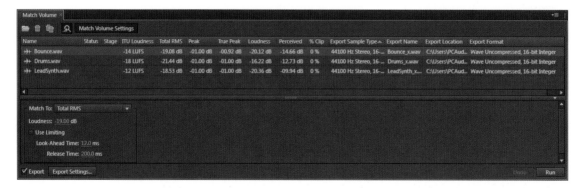

Intended primarily for mastering, this panel analyzes files dragged into the panel (from the desktop, Media Browser, or Files panel) for peak and average loudness levels. You can then choose to match these files to a reference. This panel also includes a batch processing function to export the matched files.

# Media Browser

This panel provides an Explorer- or Finder-like way to browse and display the drives, folders, and files on your computer. You can then drag files into either the Waveform or Multitrack Editor, as well as preview the file or auto-play files upon selecting them in the Media Browser. In addition to dragging files, you can drag folders into either Editor to load multiple files simultaneously.

# Metadata

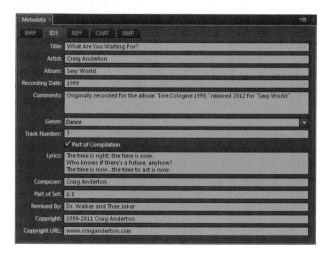

You can enter a variety of information that's saved with every file, whether audio from the Waveform Editor or a Session file from the Multitrack Editor. Types of Metadata include Broadcast Wave File data, ID3, Cart, etc.

# Mixer

This panel provides an alternate way to look at, and work with, the Multitrack Editor. The layout more closely resembles that of a traditional hardware mixer.

# Phase Meter

This panel displays the phase relationship between channels (stereo or surround) in the Waveform Editor, or the Master Track output in the Multitrack Editor. Readings toward the right indicate that the channels are more in-phase, while readings toward the left indicate the channels are out of phase to some degree. If the meter is all the way to the left, the two channels being compared are out of phase.

# Playlist

This panel works in conjunction with the Waveform Editor. You can place multiple selection markers within the waveform, then drag these markers from the Markers panel into the Playlist panel in any arbitrary order. This is an excellent way to test out different arrangements for a song; you can also choose to repeat (loop) the region defined by the selection marker an arbitrary number of times.

# Properties

This panel shows the properties for (depending on what's selected) a file in the Waveform Editor, a Multitrack Session if no clips are selected (as shown), or the properties for a selected clip within a Multitrack Session.

# Selection/View

The Selection line of this panel shows the start, end, and duration of the current selection. View shows the start, end, and duration of what you can see in the Waveform or Multitrack Editor, depending on which one is selected.

# Track Panner

This panel applies only to surround multitrack projects. It provides surround panning for whichever track is selected.

# Time

This panel displays the time at the Current Time Indicator (playhead), expressed in the same time units as the timeline calibration. You can also right-click this panel to change the time units, and resize it to a giant size so narrators and instrumentalists can see the time when at a distance from the computer screen.

# Tools

You can undock the toolbar that is normally located at the top of the Workspace. This not only includes the toolbar tools, but also, when undocked, it lets you choose a Workspace and provides a search box for Audition Help.

# Transport

This panel duplicates the transport functions normally located toward the bottom left of the Waveform and Multitrack Editors.

# Video

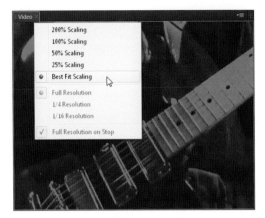

If a video file is loaded into the Multitrack Editor, you can see the video preview in the Video panel. Right-clicking (Control-clicking) the video panel allows choosing different levels of scaling, as well as resolution.

# Zoom

This panel duplicates the transport functions normally located toward the bottom right of the Waveform and Multitrack Editors.

# INDEX

## N

navigation, 34–42
    file and session, 38
    keyboard shortcuts for, 40
    markers used for, 40–41
    Media Browser, 36–38
    menu options, 34–35
    Transport, 41–42
    Zoom panel, 38–39
needledrop music, 198
noise print, 114
Noise Reduction/Restoration, 86, 110–115
    Automatic Click Remover, 112–113
    Hiss Reduction, 110–112
    Noise Reduction, 114–115
    *See also* audio restoration
nondestructive processing, 64
Normalize effect, 102
Notch Filter, 82

## O

Open Append option, 34–35
optimizing tracks, 245–249
overdubbing process, 156, 213

## P

pad optimization, 248
Pan control, 159
Pan envelope, 220–221
panels
    adding new, 30
    drop zones for, 28, 29, 30–31
    grouping within frames, 28–29
    reference guide to, 271–282
    sizing/resizing, 28
    undocking, 32–33
    *See also specific panels*
panning
    automating, 220–221, 228
    individual clips, 189
Parametric Equalizer, 78–80, 124–125, 137
pasting
    simultaneous mixing and, 53–54
    *See also* cutting/pasting
patch cable, 10
Pause button, 146
PCIe cards, 22
percussion track, 202
Phase Meter panel, 278

phase testing, 238
Phaser effect, 85
pitch
    correcting, 97–98, 104
    shifting, 135, 136
    stretching, 105
Play button, 42
playhead, 38
Playlist panel, 279
plug-ins, 99–100
pops
    fading p-pops, 55
    reducing clicks and, 112–113
Premiere Pro, 269
presets, effect, 106
producers, role of, 240
Properties panel, 279
protecting automation envelopes, 231–232
punch-in recording, 213–214

## R

rain sounds, 132–133
Razor Selected Clips tool, 188, 253–254
RCA phone jacks, 11
Record button, 146, 148, 212
recording
    composite, 215–216
    metronome setup for, 211–212
    mistake punch-ins, 213–214
    Multitrack Editor used for, 147–149, 208–217
    overdubbing process in, 213
    parts in a track, 212–213
    review questions/answers on, 217
    Waveform Editor used for, 144–146
regions
    cutting/pasting, 47–48
    deleting, 48
    fading, 55–56
    selecting, 46–47
    zero-crossings and, 49
renaming markers, 40
repeating parts of waveforms, 54–55
resizing panels, 28
resources, 5–6
restoring audio. *See* audio restoration
Reverb effects, 86–89
    Convolution Reverb, 86–87
    Full Reverb, 89
    Reverb, 88–89
    Studio Reverb, 87–88

## X

## Z

## Production Notes

The Adobe Audition Classroom in a Book was created electronically using Adobe InDesign CS5. Art was produced using Adobe Illustrator and Adobe Photoshop. The Myriad Pro and Warnock Pro OpenType families of typefaces were used throughout this book.

References to company names in the lessons are for demonstration purposes only and are not intended to refer to any actual organization or person.

### Images

Photographic images and illustrations are intended for use with the tutorials.

### Typefaces used

Adobe Myriad Pro and Adobe Warnock Pro are used throughout the lessons. For more information about OpenType and Adobe fonts, visit www.adobe.com/type/opentype/.

### Team credits

The following individuals contributed to the development of this edition of the Adobe Audition Classroom in a Book:

Writer: Craig Anderton
Project Editor: Valerie Witte
Developmental and Copy Editor: Anne Marie Walker
Production Editor: Becky Winter
Technical Editor: Sean Casella
Compositor: Danielle Foster
Proofreader: Liz Welch
Indexer: James Minkin
Cover designer: Eddie Yuen
Interior designer: Mimi Heft

# Contributor

Musician/author **Craig Anderton**, an internationally-recognized authority on musical electronics, has written more than twenty books and well over a thousand articles. He's also an award-winning recording artist who has played on, produced, or mixed fifteen major-label albums, mastered hundreds of tracks, and played Carnegie Hall; he's taken his solo act to Europe and the U. S., as well as guested with groups like Air Liquide and played in a "power duo" with former Public Enemy bandleader Brian Hardgroove. An accomplished analog circuit engineer, Anderton's designs have been used by bands such as Boston, the Motels, Sammy Hagar, and Van Halen, as well as solo artists from Larry Graham to Steve Cropper.

Because of his ability to demystify complex technology and present a practical, hands-on approach to getting a great sound, Craig is a popular lecturer who has given seminars in 38 states, 10 countries, and three languages. He also saw the potential of the net early on—his Sound, Studio, and Stage forum (started in 1995 on AOL) is the world's longest-running Internet forum for musicians. Anderton is currently Editor in Chief of www.harmonycentral.com, Executive Editor of *Electronic Musician* magazine (which he co-founded in the mid-'80s), Editor at Large for *Keyboard* magazine, and a monthly columnist for *Sound on Sound, Guitar Player,* and *Pro Sound News* magazines.

# LEARN BY VIDEO

Table of Contents never more than a click away

Up to 15 hours of high-quality video training

Lesson files are included on the DVD

The **Learn by Video** series from video2brain and Adobe Press is the only Adobe-approved video courseware for the Adobe Certified Associate Level certification, and has quickly established itself as one of the most critically acclaimed training products available on the fundamentals of Adobe software.

**Learn by Video** offers up to 15 hours of high-quality HD video training presented by experienced trainers, as well as lesson files, assessment quizzes, and review materials. The DVD is bundled with a full-color printed booklet that provides supplemental information as well as a guide to the video topics.

For more information go to
**www.adobepress.com/learnbyvideo**

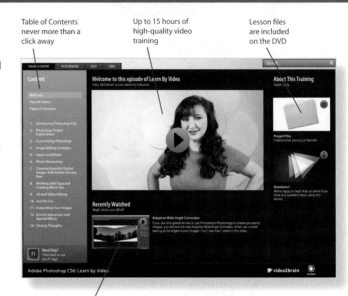

Video player remembers which movie you watched last

Watch-and-Work mode shrinks the video into a small window while you work in the software

## Titles

**Adobe Photoshop CS6: Learn by Video: Core Training in Visual Communication**
ISBN: 9780321840714

**Adobe Illustrator CS6: Learn by Video**
ISBN: 9780321840684

**Adobe InDesign CS6: Learn by Video**
ISBN: 9780321840691

**Adobe Flash Professional CS6: Learn by Video: Core Training in Rich Media Communication**
ISBN: 9780321840707

**Adobe Dreamweaver CS6: Learn by Video: Core Training in Web Communication**
ISBN: 9780321840370

**Adobe Premiere Pro CS6: Learn by Video: Core Training in Video Communication**
ISBN: 9780321840721

**Adobe After Effects CS6: Learn by Video**
ISBN: 9780321840387

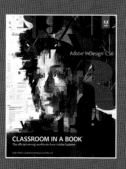